CASEBOOK SERIES

GENERAL EDITOR: A. E. Dyson

PUBLISHED

Jane Austen: *Emma* DAVID LODGE
William Blake: *Songs of Innocence and Experience* MARGARET BOTTRALL
Charlotte Brontë: *'Jane Eyre' and 'Villette'* MIRIAM ALLOTT
Emily Brontë: *Wuthering Heights* MIRIAM ALLOTT
Byron: *'Childe Harold's Pilgrimage' and 'Don Juan'* JOHN JUMP
Chaucer: *The Canterbury Tales* J. J. ANDERSON
Coleridge: *'The Ancient Mariner' and Other Poems* ALUN R. JONES
    AND WILLIAM TYDEMAN
Conrad: *The Secret Agent* IAN WATT
Dickens: *Bleak House* A. E. DYSON
Donne: *Songs and Sonets* JULIAN LOVELOCK
George Eliot: *Middlemarch* PATRICK SWINDEN
T. S. Eliot: *Four Quartets* BERNARD BERGONZI
T. S. Eliot: *The Waste Land* C. B. COX AND ARNOLD P. HINCHLIFFE
Henry Fielding: *Tom Jones* NEIL COMPTON
E. M. Forster: *A Passage to India* MALCOLM BRADBURY
Jonson: *Volpone* JONAS A. BARISH
James Joyce: *'Dubliners' and 'A Portrait of the Artist as a Young Man'*
    MORRIS BEJA
John Keats: *Odes* G. S. FRASER
D. H. Lawrence: *Sons and Lovers* GĀMINI SALGĀDO
D. H. Lawrence: *'The Rainbow' and 'Women in Love'* COLIN CLARKE
Marlowe: *Doctor Faustus* JOHN JUMP
Milton: *Paradise Lost* A. E. DYSON AND JULIAN LOVELOCK
John Osborne: *Look Back in Anger* JOHN RUSSELL TAYLOR
Pope: *The Rape of the Lock* JOHN DIXON HUNT
Shakespeare: *Antony and Cleopatra* JOHN RUSSELL BROWN
Shakespeare: *Hamlet* JOHN JUMP
Shakespeare: *Henry IV Parts I and II* G. K. HUNTER
Shakespeare: *Henry V* MICHAEL QUINN
Shakespeare: *Julius Caesar* PETER URE
Shakespeare: *King Lear* FRANK KERMODE
Shakespeare: *Macbeth* JOHN WAIN
Shakespeare: *Measure for Measure* C. K. STEAD
Shakespeare: *The Merchant of Venice* JOHN WILDERS
Shakespeare: *Othello* JOHN WAIN
Shakespeare: *Richard II* NICHOLAS BROOKE
Shakespeare: *The Tempest* D. J. PALMER
Shakespeare: *Twelfth Night* D. J. PALMER
Shakespeare: *The Winter's Tale* KENNETH MUIR
Swift: *Gulliver's Travels* RICHARD GRAVIL
Tennyson: *In Memoriam* JOHN DIXON HUNT
Virginia Woolf: *To the Lighthouse* MORRIS BEJA
Wordsworth: *Lyrical Ballads* ALUN R. JONES AND WILLIAM TYDEMAN
Wordsworth: *The Prelude* W. J. HARVEY AND RICHARD GRAVIL
Yeats: *Last Poems* JON STALLWORTHY

Chaucer

The Canterbury Tales

A CASEBOOK

EDITED BY

J. J. ANDERSON

MACMILLAN

1.

Selection and editorial matter © J. J. Anderson 1974

First published 1974 by
THE MACMILLAN PRESS LTD
London and Basingstoke
Associated companies in New York Dublin
Melbourne Johannesburg and Madras

SBN 333 14523 2 (hard cover)
     333 14524 0 (paper cover)

Printed in Great Britain by
THE ANCHOR PRESS LTD
Tiptree, Essex

CONTENTS

ACKNOWLEDGEMENTS

Ian Bishop, 'The Narrative Art of The Pardoner's Tale' from *Medium Ævum* XXXVI (1967) by permission of Basil Blackwell & Mott Ltd; Robert B. Burlin, 'The Art of Chaucer's Franklin' from *Neophilologus* LI (1967) pp. 55–73; John Burrow, 'Irony in The Merchant's Tale' from *Anglia* LXXV (1957) by permission of Max Niemeyer Verlag; E. T. Donaldson, 'Idiom of Popular Poetry in the Miller's Tale' from *Speaking of Chaucer* (London, Athlone Press, 1970) and *English Institute Essays* (1950) by permission of Columbia University Press; E. T. Donaldson, 'Chaucer the Pilgrim', *PMLA* 69 (1954) reprinted by permission of the Modern Language Association of America; William Frost, 'An Interpretation of Chaucer's Knight's Tale' from the *Review of English Studies* vol. 25 (1949) by permission of The Clarendon Press, Oxford; A. W. Hoffman, 'Chaucer's Prologue to Pilgrimage: The Two Voices', *English Literary History* vol. XXI (1954) pp. 1–16, © The Johns Hopkins University Press; G. L. Kittredge, 'Chaucer's Discussion of Marriage' from *Modern Philology* IX (1911–12) by permission of The University of Chicago Press; Charles Muscatine, extract from *Chaucer and the French Tradition*, originally published by the University of California Press, reprinted by permission of the Regents of the University of California; Paul G. Ruggiers, *The Art of the Canterbury Tales* (Madison: The University of Wisconsin Press; © 1965 by the Regents of the University of Wisconsin) pp. 184–96; Tony Slade, 'Irony in The Wife of Bath's Tale', *Modern Language Review* LXIV (1969).

GENERAL EDITOR'S PREFACE

Each of this series of Casebooks concerns either one well-known and influential work of literature or two or three closely linked works. The main section consists of critical readings, mostly modern, brought together from journals and books. A selection of reviews and comments by the author's contemporaries is also included, and sometimes comments from the author himself. The Editor's Introduction charts the reputation of the work from its first appearance until the present time.

The critical forum is a place of vigorous conflict and disagreement, but there is nothing in this to cause dismay. What is attested is the complexity of human experience and the richness of literature, not any chaos or relativity of taste. A critic is better seen, no doubt, as an explorer than as an 'authority', but explorers ought to be, and usually are, well equipped. The effect of good criticism is to convince us of what C. S. Lewis called 'the enormous extension of our being which we owe to authors'. A Casebook will be justified only if it helps to promote the same end.

A single volume can represent no more than a small selection of critical opinions. Some critics have been excluded for reasons of space, and it is hoped that readers will follow up the further suggestions in the Select Bibliography. Other contributions have been severed from their original context, to which some readers may wish to return. Indeed, if they take a hint from the critics represented here, they certainly will.

A. E. DYSON

INTRODUCTION

Geoffrey Chaucer was born in the early 1340s and he died in 1400. He was a successful public servant as well as a successful writer, at the centre of the political and literary life of the London of his day. His first major work, *The Book of the Duchess*, commemorating the death of Blanche, Duchess of Lancaster and the first wife of John of Gaunt, must have been written soon after her death in 1369, when Chaucer was still in his twenties. From this time until his death in 1400, Chaucer maintained a fairly steady output of literary work, culminating in the *Canterbury Tales*, begun about 1387 and unfinished at the time of his death.

The evidence shows that, from the first, no other English writer of the later fourteenth century equalled Chaucer in prestige. Today, there exist some eighty-four fifteenth-century manuscripts of the *Canterbury Tales* (of which fifty-eight are relatively complete) – more than for any other poem of the period. In the few contemporary references to Chaucer that we have (by Deschamps, Gower and Usk), he is praised highly, and many poets who come after him (such as Hoccleve, Lydgate, James I of Scotland, Douglas, Henryson and Dunbar) not only refer admiringly to Chaucer but consciously set out to follow him in their own poetry. It is true that, as the fifteenth century goes on, Chaucer's name is frequently coupled with those of Gower and Lydgate, but his primacy is rarely in question. He is revered chiefly as a 'high philosophical' poet (especially as a poet of *fin amour*), and as one who transformed 'our rude language' with 'the gold dew-drops of rhetoric' (Lydgate, *The History, Siege, and Destruction of Troy*, 1412–20). The same points are made again and again by writers of the fifteenth and earlier sixteenth centuries (cf. Caxton, p. 19); Chaucer was regarded as the first English poet with the learning and skill of his continental counterparts, and above all the first poet to demonstrate that the English language was capable of poetic expression as elevated as anything in French or Latin. Fifteenth-century writers are, on the whole, more interested in *Troilus and Criseyde* than in the

Canterbury Tales, but the latter poem is certainly not neglected.
Thus Lydgate refers appreciatively to the variety of the tales, and
pays the poem the compliment of imitating its opening, in *The
Siege of Thebes* (1420–2); and almost a century later, Skelton,
in *Philip Sparrow* (before 1509), alludes to the 'delectable,
solacious, and commendable' matter of the *Tales*. But in the
course of the sixteenth century the poem seems to fall from
favour to the extent that the phrase 'a Canterbury tale' is used
as a term of abuse; there is a marked decline in the appreciation
of Chaucer's writing generally, although *Troilus and Criseyde*
retains something of its former reputation. Conventional praise
of Chaucer (and of Gower and Lydgate) continues, but
becomes ever more mechanical. Reformation writers, seizing
on Chaucer's criticism of medieval clerics, make him out to be a
moralist and reformer, at the same time as others condemn his
coarseness – a feature of his writings which has persistently worried Chaucer's readers through the centuries (cf. for example
Dryden, p. 27). Towards the middle of the century, one begins
to come upon complaints that Chaucer's language, far from ex-
hibiting 'gold dew-drops of rhetoric', is obselete and rough, as is
his versification; already, in *Philip Sparrow*, Skelton notes that
there are those who wish to 'amend' Chaucer's language. Of the
great writers of the later sixteenth and earlier seventeenth centuries, some never allude to Chaucer, others allude to him fleet-
ingly, with respect or at least affection, but only Spenser calls him
'master' and sees himself as following in his footsteps. For most,
Chaucer has become a remote figure. Perhaps the famous comment of Sir Philip Sidney, in *An Apology for Poetry* (written *c.*
1581), best sums up the informed opinion of the day : 'Chaucer,
undoubtedly, did excellently in his *Troilus and Criseyde*; of
whom, truly, I know not whether to marvel more, either that he
in that misty time could see so clearly, or that we in this clear age
walk so stumblingly after him. Yet had he great wants, fit to be
forgiven in so reverend antiquity.'

In the seventeenth century, as the language problem becomes
more acute, Chaucer's reputation reaches its nadir, though there
are always a few who value him highly. Chaucer is not only rough
and difficult to understand, but he is to be blamed for corrupting
the language with French – a view the very opposite of that held

two centuries earlier. By the end of the century, Chaucer's language and versification are given up for lost, and he is generally felt to be a once-great poet now antiquated and superseded; if anything survives of him, it is his 'sense'. Thus Samuel Cobb writes in *Poetae Britannici* (*c.* 1700):

> A joking bard, whose antiquated muse
> In mouldy words could solid sense produce.
> Our English Ennius he, who claim'd his part
> In wealthy Nature, though unskill'd in Art.

The desire to do away with the 'mouldy words' so that the sense could shine led to several translations of Chaucer into contemporary English, the most important of which was Dryden's translation of some of the *Canterbury Tales* in *Fables Ancient and Modern* (1700) – a work which greatly boosted the popularity of the *Canterbury Tales* as compared to *Troilus*. Part of Dryden's long preface to his translations stands as undoubtedly the most significant landmark in the history of Chaucer criticism. It shares in many of the attitudes of the day, but it also contains sane, humane appreciation of various aspects of Chaucer's work, founded on a necessarily attentive reading of the original. Dryden perceptively discusses, amongst other matters, Chaucer's poetic decorum, his truth to nature, his skill in characterising the pilgrims, and the many-sided quality of his genius, summing up his author, as it seems, for all time: 'He is a perpetual fountain of good sense'; 'a man of a most wonderful comprehensive nature'; 'here is God's plenty'. There is adverse criticism, too, which goes beyond the commonplaces of Dryden's contemporaries; Chaucer 'sometimes mingles trivial things, with those of greater moment', and 'sometimes . . . knows not when he has said enough' (p. 28). With the Preface Chaucer criticism proper may be said to begin. To a modern reader, the translations themselves do not do Chaucer any service, but they were hailed at the time as comparable to Vergil's transformation of Ennius: 'He found him rubbish, and he left him gold' (Jabez Hughes, *c.* 1707). Dryden himself does not have quite so high an opinion of his function; nevertheless, he subscribes to the general low estimate of Chaucer's language and versification, and clearly regards him-

self as improver as well as translator : 'What beauties I lose in
some places, I give to others which had them not originally'
(p. 30).

Translation activity continued through the eighteenth century
into the nineteenth, but in the latter half of the eighteenth century the view that Chaucer was nothing unless in translation
began to be seriously challenged, notably by Warton, who found
that the original possessed 'what later and more refin'd ages could
hardly equal in true humour, pathos, or sublimity' (*Observations on the Faerie Queene*, 1754), and Gray, who defended
Chaucer's metre. In the nineteenth century the Romantics and
Victorians read Chaucer in the original, most with approval
(though Byron, at the age of nineteen, calls him 'obscene and
contemptible'), and several have left us interesting criticism, most
of it influenced by Dryden. I have selected from Blake's 'guide'
to his splendid painting of the Canterbury pilgrims (1809), in
which he explains the pilgrims as representatives of eternity;
from a lecture by Hazlitt (1818), who emphasises Chaucer's
sincerity and simplicity; and from a lecture by Arnold (1880),
who endorses Dryden's approbation of Chaucer's 'truly human
point of view' (p. 55), though he regards Chaucer as not being
in the first rank of poets because of his lack of 'high seriousness'.

This kind of criticism, by men interested in writers and writing in general, often outstanding creative writers themselves, is,
at its best, impressively large-minded, and it has given us some
memorable perceptions. But, towards the end of the nineteenth
century, a more 'professional' criticism begins to emerge, founded
on the work of the great scholars of the last half of the century,
when Chaucer scholarship comes into its own. Of course there
had always been those with a scholarly interest in Chaucer, men
who were concerned with establishing good texts and understanding Chaucer's work in a form as close to the original as
possible. In the early days of printing there was a succession of
editions – by Caxton (who published the *Canterbury Tales, c.*
1483), Pynson (1526), Thynne (the first 'complete' Chaucer,
1532), and Speght (1598). There was then a long gap, with
little evidence of any scholarly activity (but see Dryden's reference to 'some old Saxon friends' who think it 'little less than profanation and sacrilege' to alter Chaucer's language, p. 29) until

Urry's well-intentioned but very unsatisfactory edition of 1721. But now a number of good scholars became involved in Chaucer studies, and eventually, in 1775, a fine edition of the *Canterbury Tales* was brought out by Thomas Tyrwhitt, an edition which helped confirm the eighteenth- and nineteenth-century view of the *Canterbury Tales* as Chaucer's masterpiece. During the nineteenth century there was a growth of scholarly interest in the language and literature of medieval England generally, and an increasing awareness of the complexity of the problems, particularly textual problems, facing the student of Chaucer. In 1868 the Chaucer Society was founded to make a concentrated attack on these problems. Its work culminated in Skeat's great six-volume edition of 1894–7, the first truly critical edition of Chaucer, still by no means entirely superseded, although the edition by Robinson (1933, revised 1957) has become the standard edition for most purposes, and the *Canterbury Tales* has been edited on the basis of all the known manuscripts by Manly and Rickert (1940).

The work of the scholars is one reason for the fact that twentieth-century Chaucer criticism is better informed than that of preceding centuries. Another reason is that twentieth-century critics are almost always academics (even the reading of Chaucer, as of other poets, is now confined largely to academic institutions), and so have a more professional concern and are better able to specialise. Their output is vast and varied, and therefore difficult to summarise, but it may be helpful to offer a distinction (not always easy to apply) between a 'central' kind of criticism, which works primarily from the text, and which, however refined it may have become, goes back ultimately to Dryden; and another kind, which works primarily from a more or less specialised point of view, by means of which it seeks to interpret the text – this latter being a distinctively twentieth-century kind of criticism. Representative of the first kind are G. L. Kittredge, in his famous article (reprinted here) 'Chaucer's Discussion of Marriage' (1912), and his book *Chaucer and his Poetry* (Cambridge, Mass., 1915), who concentrates on the drama of Chaucer's 'human comedy'; J. L. Lowes (*Geoffrey Chaucer and the Development of His Genius*, Boston, 1934), who explains Chaucer's 'realism' in terms of contemporary life and ideas; Charles Muscatine (*Chaucer and the French Tradition*, California, 1957), who examines the interplay in Chaucer's work of two complementary styles, the 'realistic' and 'conventional'; E. T. Donaldson, who in a number of essays (two of which are reprinted here) explores Chaucer's ironies and ambiguities (Donaldson has collected several of these essays in his *Speaking of Chaucer*, London, 1970), and P. M. Kean (*Chaucer and the Making of English Poetry*, London, 1972), who considers the manner in which Chaucer uses traditional styles, themes, and structures. Specialist approaches through, for example, medieval science, philosophy, rhetoric, art, and specific sources and analogues, have all made important contributions to our understanding of Chaucer, though there is always the danger, with this type of approach, of a partial or distorted reading of the text. Successful examples of this kind of criticism are W. C. Curry's much-quoted *Chaucer and the Medieval Sciences* (Oxford, 1926); Robert O. Payne, *The Key of Remembrance: A Study of Chaucer's Poetics* (Yale, 1963), a sensitive study of rhetorical traditions as they apply to Chaucer; and Robert M. Jordan, *Chaucer and the Shape of Creation* (Cambridge, Mass., 1967), a study of medieval aesthetic theory and its relation to Chaucer's 'Gothic' structures. The most important of these specialist approaches, the 'exegetical', which holds that behind Chaucer's text is a body of theological meaning to which the text is allegorically related, has attracted a number of critics. The theory is set forth most fully, if not most clearly, in D. W. Robertson, *A Preface to Chaucer* (Princeton, 1963), a book which is a rich mine of ideas and information, admirably directing attention to the potential relevance of theological and aesthetic traditions to Chaucer's work, though the thesis *in toto* is unconvincing. At the other extreme from critics such as Robertson are attempts at a more evaluative criticism, orientated towards the present, in the Leavis mould; examples are John Speirs, *Chaucer the Maker* (London, 1951) and Ian Robinson, *Chaucer and the English Tradition* (Cambridge, 1972). But the approach strikes one as basically unsuited to medieval authors, and it has produced some eccentric judgements.

It is not difficult to discern broad shifts of emphasis in Chaucer criticism through the twentieth century, often reflecting changes in critical attitudes generally. Thus criticism has become steadily more detailed, closer and closer in focus. The view of Chaucer as 'realistic' and 'dramatic', inherited from the nineteenth century, has been sharply modified by a growing awareness of the conventional aspects of his work. The view (again inherited from the nineteenth century) that Chaucer's reputation rests on the *Canterbury Tales* rather than *Troilus and Criseyde* has given way to the recognition that both are great poems in their different ways. Above all, as is obvious from my selection of essays, there is an acute contemporary awareness of the ironic dimension in Chaucer's writing, which has produced, and is producing, much fruitful criticism.

In criticism specifically of the *Canterbury Tales*, the old dramatic view of the poem still has life in it (as shown, for example, by the continuing interest in the psychological appropriateness or otherwise of tale to teller, evinced in R. M. Lumiansky, *Of Sondry Folk; The Dramatic Principle in the Canterbury Tales*, Austin, 1955, and in the articles by Slade and Burlin reprinted in this book). There has been an increasing concern to find an artistic unity in the poem as a whole. Thus Ralph Baldwin (*The Unity of the Canterbury Tales*, Copenhagen, 1955) sees an organising principle in the concept of the spiritual pilgrimage, whereby the pilgrims are journeying not only to Canterbury but also to the Heavenly City, the poem's fundamental values being set out in the Parson's concluding sermon. Baldwin in his monograph deals mainly with the beginning and end of the poem, but his view is filled out, with due attention to the tales in between, by P. G. Ruggiers in his *The Art of the Canterbury Tales* (Madison, 1965). On the other hand, Jordan in *Shape of Creation* sees the poem's unity as dependent on 'the Gothic principle of juxtaposition', a unity in diversity. But whilst interest in larger issues continues, the characteristic critical publication today is an article on a single tale, considered largely as a separate entity. Of those tales which are old favourites, the Knight's Tale continues to generate an astonishing amount of good criticism, the Nun's Priest's Tale surprisingly little. The *fabliaux* tales (Miller's Tale, Reeve's Tale, Merchant's Tale, and so on) have lately received appreciative attention, which has demonstrated that they are much more than the simple bawdy

stories they were once thought to be. Other tales which have
recently risen in critical esteem are the Franklin's Tale and the
Canon's Yeoman's Tale; with respect to the latter, Charles
Muscatine notes 'the virtual absence of previous literary
criticism' (p. 237) in 1957, but there is a plethora of articles
today. Only the Parson's Tale and 'Melibee' and one or two
others still languish; were Dryden writing now, he would no
doubt apply his phrase 'Here is God's plenty' to the critics instead
of the pilgrims.

My selection of twentieth-century criticism is necessarily a very
limited one. It has seemed a fair reflection of contemporary
critical practice to concentrate on essays on individual tales, and
I have tried to cover the range of the better-known tales. I have
further limited myself to essays which deal in text-centred criticism,
and my aim has been to select from the best of these, regardless
of whether they are already well known or not; several have
classic status. The selection is only secondarily intended to
chronicle changing critical emphases, and I have not concerned
myself at all with specialist approaches to criticism, though it is
hoped that some of the essays, at least, will lead readers out into
specialist areas.

In the *Early Appreciations* section, all the selections are
extracts from longer pieces, though the extracts contain most of
what their authors have to say about Chaucer. I have modernised
Caxton's punctuation, capitalisation, and word-division, and have
abbreviated Hazlitt's extensive quotation of Chaucer. In the
Twentieth-century Criticism section, articles and chapters are
complete as in the indicated sources, apart from Burlin's article,
which is reprinted with minor revisions by the author, the notes to
Kittredge's article, which I have omitted as being peripheral to
his argument, occasional abbreviation of other notes, and some
regularisation of conventions.

In writing the Introduction, I have made extensive use of Caro-
line Spurgeon, *Five Hundred Years of Chaucer Criticism and
Allusion, 1357–1900* (Cambridge, 1925).

J. J. ANDERSON

PART ONE

Early Appreciations

William Caxton

Grete thankes, laude, and honour ought to be gyuen vnto the clerkes, poetes, and historiographs that haue wreton many noble bokes of wysedom, of the lyues, passions, and myracles of holy sayntes, of hystoryes of noble and famous actes and faittes, and of the cronycles sith the begynnyng of the creacion of the world vnto thys present tyme, by whyche we ben dayly enformed and have knowleche of many thynges of whom we shold not have knowen yf they had not left to vs theyr monumentis wreton. Emong whom and in especial tofore alle other we ought to gyue a synguler laude vnto that noble and grete philosopher Gefferey Chaucer, the whiche for his ornate wrytyng in our tongue may wel haue the name of a laureate poete. For tofore that he by hys labour enbelysshyd, ornated, and made faire our Englisshe, in thys royame was had rude speche and incongrue, as yet it appiereth by olde bookes whyche at thys day ought not to haue place ne be compared emong ne to hys beauteuous volumes and aournate writynges; of whom he made many bokes and treatyces of many a noble historye, as wel in metre as in ryme and prose, and them so craftyly made that he comprehended hys maters in short, quyck, and hye sentences, eschewyng prolyxyte, castyng away the chaf of superfluyte, and shewyng the pyked grayn of sentence vtteryd by crafty and sugred eloquence; of whom emonge all other of hys bokes I purpose t'emprynte, by the grace of God, the *Book of the Tales of Cauntyrburye*, in whiche I fynde many a noble hystorye of every astate and degre, fyrst rehercyng the condicions and th'arraye of eche of them as properly as possyble is to be sayd, and after theyr tales, whyche ben of noblesse, wysedom, gentylesse, myrthe, and also of veray holynesse and vertue, wherin he fynysshyth thys sayd booke; whyche book I haue dylygently ouersen and duly examyned, to th'ende that it be made acordyng vnto his owen makyng. . . .

SOURCE: Proem to Caxton's Second Edition of *The Canterbury Tales* (1484).

John Dryden

... I proceed to *Ovid*, and *Chaucer*; considering the former only in relation to the latter. With *Ovid* ended the Golden Age of the *Roman* Tongue: From *Chaucer* the Purity of the *English* Tongue began. The Manners of the Poets were not unlike: Both of them were well-bred, well-natur'd, amorous, and Libertine, at least in their Writings, it may be also in their Lives. Their Studies were the same, Philosophy, and Philology. Both of them were knowing in Astronomy, of which *Ovid's* Books of the *Roman* Feasts, and *Chaucer's* Treatise of the *Astrolabe*, are sufficient Witnesses. But *Chaucer* was likewise an Astrologer, as were *Virgil*, *Horace*, *Persius*, and *Manilius*. Both writ with wonderful Facility and Clearness; neither were great Inventors: For *Ovid* only copied the *Grecian* Fables; and most of *Chaucer's* Stories were taken from his *Italian* Contemporaries, or their Predecessors: *Boccace* his *Decameron* was first publish'd; and from thence our *Englishman* has borrow'd many of his *Canterbury* Tales: Yet that of *Palamon* and *Arcite* was written in all probability by some *Italian* Wit, in a former Age; as I shall prove hereafter: The Tale of *Grizild* was the Invention of *Petrarch*; by him sent to *Boccace*; from whom it came to *Chaucer*: *Troilus* and *Cressida* was also written by a *Lombard* Author; but much amplified by our *English* Translatour, as well as beautified; the Genius of our Countrymen in general being rather to improve an Invention, than to invent themselves; as is evident not only in our Poetry, but in many of our Manufactures. I find I have anticipated already, and taken up from *Boccace* before I come to him: But there is so much less behind; and I am of the Temper of most Kings, *who love to be in Debt*, are all for present Money, no matter how they pay it afterwards: Besides, the Nature of a Preface is rambling; never wholly out of the Way, nor in it. This I have learn'd from the Practice of honest *Montaign*, and return at my pleasure to *Ovid* and *Chaucer*, of whom I have little more to say. Both of them built on the Inventions of other Men; yet since *Chaucer* had something of his own, as *The Wife of Baths*

Tale, The Cock and the Fox, which I have translated, and some others, I may justly give our Countryman the Precedence in that Part; since I can remember nothing of *Ovid* which was wholly his. Both of them understood the Manners; under which Name I comprehend the Passions, and, in a larger Sense, the Descriptions of Persons, and their very Habits: For an Example, I see *Baucis* and *Philemon* as perfectly before me, as if some ancient Painter had drawn them; and all the Pilgrims in the *Canterbury* Tales, their Humours, their Features, and the very Dress, as distinctly as if I had supp'd with them at the *Tabard* in *Southwark*: Yet even there too the Figures of *Chaucer* are much more lively, and set in a better Light: Which though I have not time to prove; yet I appeal to the Reader, and am sure he will clear me from Partiality. The Thoughts and Words remain to be consider'd, in the Comparison of the two Poets; and I have sav'd my self one half of that Labour, by owning that *Ovid* liv'd when the *Roman* Tongue was in its Meridian; *Chaucer*, in the Dawning of our Language: Therefore that Part of the Comparison stands not on an equal Foot, any more than the Diction of *Ennius* and *Ovid*; or of *Chaucer*, and our present *English*. The Words are given up as a Post not to be defended in our Poet, because he wanted the Modern Art of Fortifying. The Thoughts remain to be consider'd: And they are to be measur'd only by their Propriety; that is, as they flow more or less naturally from the Persons describ'd, on such and such Occasions. The Vulgar Judges, which are Nine Parts in Ten of all Nations, who call Conceits and Jingles Wit, who see *Ovid* full of them, and *Chaucer* altogether without them, will think me little less than mad, for preferring the *Englishman* to the *Roman*: Yet, with their leave, I must presume to say, that the Things they admire are only glittering Trifles, and so far from being Witty, that in a serious Poem they are nauseous, because they are unnatural. Wou'd any Man who is ready to die for Love, describe his Passion like *Narcissus*? Wou'd he think of *inopem me copia fecit*, and a Dozen more of such Expressions, pour'd on the Neck of one another, and signifying all the same Thing? If this were Wit, was this a Time to be witty, when the poor Wretch was in the Agony of Death? This is just *John Littlewit* in *Bartholomew Fair*, who had a Conceit (as he tells you) left him in his Misery; a miserable Conceit. On these Occasions the Poet shou'd endeavour to raise Pity : But instead of this, *Ovid* is tickling you to laugh. *Virgil* never made use of such Machines, when he was moving you to commiserate the Death of *Dido* : He would not destroy what he was building. *Chaucer* makes *Arcite* violent in his Love, and unjust in the Pursuit of it : Yet when he came to die, he made him think more reasonably : He repents not of his Love, for that had alter'd his Character; but acknowledges the Injustice of his Proceedings, and resigns *Emilia* to *Palamon.* What would *Ovid* have done on this Occasion? He would certainly have made *Arcite* witty on his Death-bed. He had complain'd he was farther off from Possession, by being so near, and a thousand such Boyisms, which *Chaucer* rejected as below the Dignity of the Subject. They who think otherwise, would by the same reason prefer *Lucan* and *Ovid* to *Homer* and *Virgil*, and *Martial* to all four of them. As for the Turn of Words, in which *Ovid* particularly excels all Poets; they are sometimes a Fault, and sometimes a Beauty, as they are us'd properly or improperly; but in strong Passions always to be shunn'd, because Passions are serious, and will admit no Playing. The *French* have a high Value for them; and I confess, they are often what they call Delicate, when they are introduc'd with Judgment; but *Chaucer* writ with more Simplicity, and follow'd Nature more closely, than to use them. I have thus far, to the best of my Knowledge, been an upright Judge betwixt the Parties in Competition, not medling with the Design nor the Disposition of it; because the Design was not their own; and in the disposing of it they were equal. It remains that I say somewhat of *Chaucer* in particular.

In the first place, As he is the Father of *English* Poetry, so I hold him in the same Degree of Veneration as the *Grecians* held *Homer*, or the *Romans Virgil* : He is a perpetual Fountain of good Sense; learn'd in all Sciences; and therefore speaks properly on all Subjects : As he knew what to say, so he knows also when to leave off; a Continence which is practis'd by few Writers, and scarcely by any of the Ancients, excepting *Virgil* and *Horace*. One of our late great Poets is sunk in his Reputation, because he cou'd never forgive any Conceit which came in his way; but swept like a Drag-net, great and small. There was plenty enough, but the Dishes were ill sorted; whole Pyramids of

Sweet-meats, for Boys and Women; but little of solid Meat, for Men : All this proceeded not from any want of Knowledge, but of Judgment; neither did he want that in discerning the Beauties and Faults of other Poets; but only indulg'd himself in the Luxury of Writing; and perhaps knew it was a Fault, but hop'd the Reader would not find it. For this Reason, though he must always be thought a great Poet, he is no longer esteem'd a good Writer : And for Ten Impressions, which his Works have had in so many successive Years, yet at present a hundred Books are scarcely purchas'd once a Twelvemonth : For, as my last Lord *Rochester* said, though somewhat profanely, *Not being of God, he could not stand.*

Chaucer follow'd Nature every where; but was never so bold to go beyond her : And there is a great Difference of being *Poeta* and *nimis Poeta*, if we may believe *Catullus*, as much as betwixt a modest Behaviour and Affectation. The Verse of *Chaucer*, I confess, is not Harmonious to us; but 'tis like the Eloquence of one whom *Tacitus* commends, it was *auribus istius temporis accommodata* : They who liv'd with him, and some time after him, thought it Musical; and it continues so even in our Judgment, if compar'd with the Numbers of *Lidgate* and *Gower* his Contemporaries : There is the rude Sweetness of a *Scotch* Tune in it, which is natural and pleasing, though not perfect. 'Tis true, I cannot go so far as he who publish'd the last Edition of him; for he would make us believe the Fault is in our Ears, and that there were really Ten Syllables in a Verse where we find but Nine : But this Opinion is not worth confuting; 'tis so gross and obvious an Errour, that common Sense (which is a Rule in every thing but Matters of Faith and Revelation) must convince the Reader, that Equality of Numbers in every Verse which we call *Heroick*, was either not known, or not always practis'd in *Chaucer*'s Age. It were an easie Matter to produce some thousands of his Verses, which are lame for want of half a Foot, and sometimes a whole one, and which no Pronunciation can make otherwise. We can only say, that he liv'd in the Infancy of our Poetry, and that nothing is brought to Perfection at the first. We must be Children before we grow Men. There was an *Ennius*, and in process of Time a *Lucilius*, and a *Lucretius*, before *Virgil* and *Horace*; even after *Chaucer* there was a

Spencer, a *Harrington*, a *Fairfax*, before *Waller* and *Denham*
were in being : And our Numbers were in their Nonage till these
last appear'd. I need say little of his Parentage, Life, and Fortunes : They are to be found at large in all the Editions of his
Works. He was employ'd abroad, and favour'd by *Edward* the
Third, *Richard* the Second, and *Henry* the Fourth, and was
Poet, as I suppose, to all Three of them. In *Richard*'s Time, I
doubt, he was a little dipt in the Rebellion of the Commons;
and being Brother-in-Law to *John of Ghant*, it was no wonder
if he follow'd the Fortunes of that Family; and was well with
Henry the Fourth when he had depos'd his Predecessor. Neither
is it to be admir'd, that *Henry*, who was a wise as well as a valiant
Prince, who claim'd by Succession, and was sensible that his Title
was not sound, but was rightfully in *Mortimer*, who had married
the Heir of *York*; it was not to be admir'd, I say, if that great
Politician should be pleas'd to have the greatest Wit of those
Times in his Interests, and to be the Trumpet of his Praises.
Augustus had given him the Example, by the Advice of
Mæcenas who recommended *Virgil* and *Horace* to him; whose
Praises help'd to make him Popular while he was alive, and after
his Death have made him Precious to Posterity. As for the
Religion of our Poet, he seems to have some little Byas towards
the Opinions of *Wickliff*, after *John of Ghant* his Patron; some-
what of which appears in the Tale of *Piers Plowman* : Yet I can-
not blame him for inveighing so sharply against the Vices of the
Clergy of his Age : Their Pride, their Ambition, their Pomp, their
Avarice, their Worldly Interest, deserv'd the Lashes which he
gave them, both in that, and in most of his *Canterbury Tales* :
Neither has his Contemporary *Boccace*, spar'd them. Yet both
those Poets liv'd in much esteem, with good and holy Men in
Orders : For the Scandal which is given by particular Priests,
reflects not on the Sacred Function. *Chaucer*'s *Monk*, his
Chanon, and his *Fryar*, took not from the Character of his *Good
Parson*. A Satyrical Poet is the Check of the Laymen, on bad
Priests. We are only to take care, that we involve not the
Innocent with the Guilty in the same Condemnation. The Good
cannot be too much honour'd, nor the Bad too coursly us'd : For
the Corruption of the Best, becomes the Worst. When a Clergy-
man is whipp'd, his Gown is first taken off, by which the Dignity

of his Order is secur'd : If he be wrongfully accus'd, he has his
Action of Slander; and 'tis at the Poet's Peril, if he transgress
the Law. But they will tell us, that all kind of Satire, though
never so well deserv'd by particular Priests, yet brings the whole
Order into Contempt. Is then the Peerage of *England* any thing
dishonour'd, when a Peer suffers for his Treason? If he be libell'd,
or any way defam'd, he has his *Scandalum Magnatum* to
punish the Offendor. They who use this kind of Argument, seem
to be conscious to themselves of somewhat which has deserv'd
the Poet's Lash; and are less concern'd for their Publick Capacity,
than for their Private : At least, there is Pride at the bottom of
their Reasoning. If the Faults of Men in Orders are only to be
judg'd among themselves, they are all in some sort Parties : For,
since they say the Honour of their Order is concern'd in every
Member of it, how can we be sure, that they will be impartial
Judges? How far I may be allow'd to speak my Opinion in this
Case, I know not : But I am sure a Dispute of this Nature caus'd
Mischief in abundance betwixt a King of *England* and an
Archbishop of *Canterbury*; one standing up for the Laws of his
Land, and the other for the Honour (as he call'd it) of God's
Church; which ended in the Murther of the Prelate, and in the
whipping of his Majesty from Post to Pillar for his Penance. The
Learn'd and Ingenious Dr. *Drake* has sav'd me the Labour of
inquiring into the Esteem and Reverence which the Priests have
had of old; and I would rather extend than diminish any part
of it : Yet I must needs say, that when a Priest provokes me without any Occasion given him, I have no Reason, unless it be the
Charity of a *Christian*, to forgive him : *Prior læsit* is Justification
sufficient in the Civil Law. If I answer him in his own Language,
Self-defence, I am sure, must be allow'd me; and if I carry it
farther, even to a sharp Recrimination, somewhat may be indulg'd to Humane Frailty. Yet my Resentment has not wrought
so far, but that I have follow'd *Chaucer* in his Character of a
Holy Man, and have enlarg'd on that Subject with some
Pleasure, reserving to my self the Right, if I shall think fit hereafter, to describe another sort of Priests, such as are more easily
to be found than the Good Parson; such as have given the last
Blow to Christianity in this Age, by a Practice so contrary to their
Doctrine. But this will keep cold till another time. In the mean

while, I take up *Chaucer* where I left him. He must have been a Man of a most wonderful comprehensive Nature, because, as it has been truly observ'd of him, he has taken into the Compass of his *Canterbury Tales* the various Manners and Humours (as we now call them) of the whole *English* Nation, in his Age. Not a single Character has escap'd him. All his Pilgrims are severally distinguish'd from each other; and not only in their Inclinations, but in their very Phisiognomies and Persons. *Baptista Porta* could not have describ'd their Natures better, than by the Marks which the Poet gives them. The Matter and Manner of their Tales, and of their Telling, are so suited to their different Educations, Humours, and Callings, that each of them would be improper in any other Mouth. Even the grave and serious Characters are distinguish'd by their several sorts of Gravity: Their Discourses are such as belong to their Age, their Calling, and their Breeding; such as are becoming of them, and of them only. Some of his Persons are Vicious, and some Vertuous; some are unlearn'd, or (as *Chaucer* calls them) Lewd, and some are Learn'd. Even the Ribaldry of the Low Characters is different: The *Reeve*, the *Miller*, and the *Cook*, are several Men, and distinguish'd from each other, as much as the mincing Lady Prioress, and the broad-speaking gap-tooth'd Wife of *Bathe*. But enough of this: There is such a Variety of Game springing up before me, that I am distracted in my Choice, and know not which to follow. 'Tis sufficient to say according to the Proverb, that here is God's Plenty. We have our Fore-fathers and Great Grand-dames all before us, as they were in *Chaucer*'s Days; their general Characters are still remaining in Mankind, and even in *England*, though they are call'd by other Names than those of *Moncks*, and *Fryars*, and *Chanons*, and *Lady Abbesses*, and *Nuns*: For Mankind is ever the same, and nothing lost out of Nature, though every thing is alter'd. May I have leave to do my self the Justice, (since my Enemies will do me none, and are so far from granting me to be a good Poet, that they will not allow me so much as to be a Christian, or a Moral Man) may I have leave, I say, to inform my Reader, that I have confin'd my Choice to such Tales of *Chaucer*, as savour nothing of Immodesty. If I had desir'd more to please than to instruct, the *Reve*, the *Miller*, the *Shipman*, the *Merchant*, the *Sumner*, and

above all, the *Wife of Bathe*, in the Prologue to her Tale, would
have procur'd me as many Friends and Readers, as there are
Beaux and Ladies of Pleasure in the Town. But I will no more
offend against Good Manners : I am sensible as I ought to be of
the Scandal I have given by my loose Writings; and make what
Reparation I am able, by this Publick Acknowledgment. If any
thing of this Nature, or of Profaneness, be crept into these Poems,
I am so far from defending it, that I disown it. *Totum
hoc indictum volo. Chaucer* makes another manner of Apologie
for his broad-speaking, and *Boccace* makes the like; but I will
follow neither of them. Our Country-man, in the end of his
Characters, before the *Canterbury Tales*, thus excuses the
Ribaldry, which is very gross, in many of his Novels.

> *But first, I pray you, of your courtesy,*
> *That ye ne arrete it nought my villany,*
> *Though that I plainly speak in this mattere*
> *To tellen you her words, and eke her chere:*
> *Ne though I speak her words properly,*
> *For this ye knowen as well as I,*
> *Who shall tellen a tale after a man*
> *He mote rehearse as nye, as ever He can:*
> *Everich word of it been in his charge,*
> All speke he, never so rudely, ne large.
> *Or else he mote tellen his tale untrue,*
> *Or feine things, or find words new:*
> *He may not spare, altho he were his brother,*
> *He mote as well say o word as another.*
> Christ *spake himself full broad in holy Writ,*
> *And well I wote no Villany is it.*
> Eke Plato *saith, who so can him rede,*
> *The words mote been Cousin to the dede.*

Yet if a Man should have enquir'd of *Boccace* or of *Chaucer*,
what need they had of introducing such Characters, where
obscene Words were proper in their Mouths, but very undecent
to be heard; I know not what Answer they could have made :
For that Reason, such Tales shall be left untold by me. You have
here a *Specimen of Chaucer*'s Language, which is so obsolete,
that his Sense is scarce to be understood; and you have like-

wise more than one Example of his unequal Numbers, which
were mention'd before. Yet many of his Verses consist of Ten
Syllables, and the Words not much behind our present *English*:
As for Example, these two Lines, in the Description of the
Carpenter's Young Wife:

> *Wincing she was, as is a jolly Colt,*
> *Long as a Mast, and upright as a Bolt.*

I have almost done with *Chaucer*, when I have answer'd some
Objections relating to my present Work. I find some People are
offended that I have turn'd these Tales into modern *English*; because they think them unworthy of my Pains, and look on *Chaucer*
as a dry, old-fashion'd Wit, not worth receiving. I have often
heard the late Earl of *Leicester* say, that Mr. *Cowley* himself was
of that opinion; who having read him over at my Lord's Request,
declar'd he had no Taste of him. I dare not advance my Opinion
against the Judgment of so great an Author: But I think it fair,
however, to leave the Decision to the Publick: Mr. *Cowley* was
too modest to set up for a Dictatour; and being shock'd perhaps
with his old Style, never examin'd into the depth of his good
Sense. *Chaucer*, I confess, is a rough Diamond, and must first be
polish'd e'er he shines. I deny not likewise, that living in our early
Days of Poetry, he writes not always of a piece; but sometimes
mingles trivial Things, with those of greater Moment. Sometimes also, though not often, he runs riot, like *Ovid*, and knows
not when he has said enough. But there are more great Wits,
beside *Chaucer*, whose Fault is their Excess of Conceits, and
those ill sorted. An Author is not to write all he can, but only all
he ought. Having observ'd this Redundancy in *Chaucer*, (as it
is an easie Matter for a Man of ordinary Parts to find a Fault in
one of greater) I have not ty'd my self to a Literal Translation;
but have often omitted what I judg'd unnecessary, or not of
Dignity enough to appear in the Company of better Thoughts.
I have presum'd farther in some Places, and added somewhat of
my own where I thought my Author was deficient, and had not
given his Thoughts their true Lustre, for want of Words in the
Beginning of our Language. And to this I was the more em-
bolden'd, because (if I may be permitted to say it of my self) I
found I had a Soul congenial to his, and that I had been con-

versant in the same Studies. Another Poet, in another Age, may take the same Liberty with my Writings; if at least they live long enough to deserve Correction. It was also necessary sometimes to restore the Sense of *Chaucer*, which was lost or mangled in the Errors of the Press : Let this Example suffice at present; in the Story of *Palamon* and *Arcite*, where the Temple of *Diana* is describ'd, you find these Verses, in all the Editions of our Author :

> *There saw I* Danè *turned unto a Tree,*
> *I mean not the Goddess* Diane,
> *But* Venus *Daughter, which that hight* Danè.

Which after a little Consideration I knew was to be reform'd into this Sense, that *Daphne* the Daughter of *Peneus* was turn'd into a Tree. I durst not make thus bold with *Ovid*, lest some future *Milbourn* should arise, and say, I varied from my Author, because I understood him not.

But there are other Judges who think I ought not to have translated *Chaucer* into *English*, out of a quite contrary Notion : They suppose there is a certain Veneration due to his old Language; and that it is little less than Profanation and Sacrilege to alter it. They are farther of opinion, that somewhat of his good Sense will suffer in this Transfusion, and much of the Beauty of his Thoughts will infallibly be lost, which appear with more Grace in their old Habit. Of this Opinion was that excellent Person, whom I mention'd, the late Earl of *Leicester*, who valu'd *Chaucer* as much as Mr. *Cowley* despis'd him. My Lord dissuaded me from this Attempt, (for I was thinking of it some Years before his Death) and his Authority prevail'd so far with me, as to defer my Undertaking while he liv'd, in deference to him : Yet my Reason was not convinc'd with what he urg'd against it. If the first End of a Writer be to be understood, then as his Language grows obsolete, his Thoughts must grow obscure, *multa renascentur quæ nunc cecidere; cadentque quæ nunc sunt in honore vocabula, si volet usus, quem penes arbitrum est et jus et norma loquendi*. When an ancient Word for its Sound and Significancy deserves to be reviv'd, I have that reasonable Veneration for Antiquity, to restore it. All beyond this is Superstition. Words are not like Landmarks, so sacred as never to be remov'd :

Customs are chang'd, and even Statutes are silently repeal'd, when the Reason ceases for which they were enacted. As for the other Part of the Argument, that his Thoughts will lose of their original Beauty, by the innovation of Words; in the first place, not only their Beauty, but their Being is lost, where they are no longer understood, which is the present Case. I grant, that something must be lost in all Transfusion, that is, in all Translations; but the Sense will remain, which would otherwise be lost, or at least be maim'd, when it is scarce intelligible; and that but to a few. How few are there who can read *Chaucer*, so as to understand him perfectly? And if imperfectly, then with less Profit, and no Pleasure. 'Tis not for the Use of some old *Saxon* Friends, that I have taken these Pains with him : Let them neglect my Version, because they have no need of it. I made it for their sakes who understand Sense and Poetry, as well as they; when that Poetry and Sense is put into Words which they understand. I will go farther, and dare to add, that what Beauties I lose in some Places, I give to others which had them not originally : But in this I may be partial to my self; let the Reader judge, and I submit to his Decision. Yet I think I have just Occasion to complain of them, who because they understand *Chaucer*, would deprive the greater part of their Countrymen of the same Advantage, and hoord him up, as Misers do their Grandam Gold, only to look on it themselves, and hinder others from making use of it. In sum, I seriously protest, that no Man ever had, or can have, a greater Veneration for *Chaucer*, than my self. I have translated some part of his Works, only that I might perpetrate his Memory, or at least refresh it, amongst my Countrymen. If I have alter'd him any where for the better, I must at the same time acknowledge, that I could have done nothing without him : *Facile est inventis addere*, is no great Commendation; and I am not so vain to think I have deserv'd a greater. I will conclude what I have to say of him singly, with this one Remark : A Lady of my Acquaintance, who keeps a kind of Correspondence with some Authors of the Fair Sex in *France*, has been inform'd by them, that *Mademoiselle de Scudery* who is as old as *Sibyl*, and inspir'd like her by the same God of Poetry, is at this time translating *Chaucer* into modern *French*. From which I gather, that he has been formerly translated into the old *Provencall*, (for,

how she should come to understand Old *English*, I know not.)
But the Matter of Fact being true, it makes me think, that there
is something in it like Fatality; that after certain Periods of Time,
the Fame and Memory of Great Wits should be renew'd, as
Chaucer is both in *France* and *England*. If this be wholly
Chance, 'tis extraordinary; and I dare not call it more, for fear
of being tax'd with Superstition.

Boccace comes last to be consider'd, who living in the same
Age with *Chaucer*, had the same Genius, and follow'd the same
Studies: Both writ Novels, and each of them cultivated his
Mother-Tongue: But the greatest Resemblance of our two
Modern Authors being in their familiar Style, and pleasing way
of relating Comical Adventures, I may pass it over, because I
have translated nothing from *Boccace* of that Nature. In the
serious Part of Poetry, the Advantage is wholly on *Chaucer*'s
Side; for though the *Englishman* has borrow'd many Tales
from the *Italian*, yet it appears, that those of *Boccace* were not
generally of his own making, but taken from Authors of former
Ages, and by him only modell'd: So that what there was of Invention in either of them, may be judg'd equal. But *Chaucer*
has refin'd on *Boccace*, and has mended the Stories which he
has borrow'd, in his way of telling; though Prose allows more
Liberty of Thought, and the Expression is more easie, when un-
confin'd by Numbers. Our Countryman carries Weight, and
yet wins the Race at disadvantage. I desire not the Reader should
take my Word; and therefore I will set two of their Discourses
on the same Subject, in the same Light, for every Man to judge
betwixt them. I translated *Chaucer* first, and amongst the rest,
pitch'd on the Wife of *Bath*'s Tale; not daring, as I have said,
to adventure on her Prologue; because 'tis too licentious: There
Chaucer introduces an old Woman of mean Parentage, whom
a youthful Knight of Noble Blood was forc'd to marry, and
consequently loath'd her: The Crone being in bed with him on
the wedding Night, and finding his Aversion, endeavours to win
his Affection by Reason, and speaks a good Word for her self,
(as who could blame her?) in hope to mollifie the sullen Bridegroom. She takes her Topiques from the Benefits of Poverty, the
Advantages of old Age and Ugliness, the Vanity of Youth, and
the silly Pride of Ancestry and Titles without inherent Vertue,

which is the true Nobility. When I had clos'd *Chaucer*, I return'd to *Ovid*, and translated some more of his Fables; and by this time had so far forgotten the Wife of *Bath*'s Tale, that when I took up *Boccace*, unawares I fell on the same Argument of preferring Virtue to Nobility of Blood, and Titles, in the Story of *Sigismonda*; which I had certainly avoided for the Resemblance of the two Discourses, if my Memory had not fail'd me. Let the Reader weigh them both; and if he thinks me partial to *Chaucer*, 'tis in him to right *Boccace*.

I prefer in our Countryman, far above all his other Stories, the Noble Poem of *Palamon* and *Arcite*, which is of the *Epique* kind, and perhaps not much inferiour to the *Ilias* or the *Æneis*: the Story is more pleasing than either of them, the Manners as perfect, the Diction as poetical, the Learning as deep and various; and the Disposition full as artful: only it includes a greater length of time; as taking up seven years at least; but *Aristotle* has left undecided the Duration of the Action; which yet is easily reduc'd into the Compass of a year, by a Narration of what preceded the Return of *Palamon* to *Athens*. I had thought for the Honour of our Nation, and more particularly for his, whose Laurel, tho' unworthy, I have worn after him, that this Story was of *English* Growth, and *Chaucer*'s own: But I was undeceiv'd by *Boccace*; for casually looking on the End of his seventh *Giornata*, I found *Dioneo* (under which name he shadows himself) and *Fiametta* (who represents his Mistress, the natural Daughter of *Robert* King of *Naples*) of whom these Words are spoken. *Dioneo e Fiametta gran pezza cantarono insieme d'Arcita, e di Palamone*: by which it appears that this Story was written before the time of *Boccace*; but the Name of its Author being wholly lost, *Chaucer* is now become an Original; and I question not but the Poem has receiv'd many Beauties by passing through his Noble Hands. Beside this Tale, there is another of his own Invention, after the manner of the *Provencalls*, call'd *The Flowers and the Leaf*; with which I was so particularly pleas'd, both for the Invention and the Moral; that I cannot hinder my self from recommending it to the Reader. . . .

S O U R C E : Preface to *Fables Ancient and Modern* (1700).

William Blake

. . . The characters of Chaucer's Pilgrims are the characters which compose all ages and nations: as one age falls, another rises, different to mortal sight, but to immortals only the same; for we see the same characters repeated again and again, in animals, vegetables, minerals, and in men; nothing new occurs in identical existence; Accident ever varies, Substance can never suffer change nor decay.

Of Chaucer's characters, as described in his Canterbury Tales, some of the names or titles are altered by time, but the characters themselves for ever remain unaltered, and consequently they are the physiognomies or lineaments of universal human life, beyond which Nature never steps. Names alter, things never alter. I have known multitudes of those who would have been monks in the age of monkery, who as this deistical age are deists. As Newton numbered the stars, and as Linneus numbered the plants, so Chaucer numbered the classes of men.

The Painter has consequently varied the heads and forms of his personages into all Nature's varieties; the Horses he has also varied to accord to their Riders; the costume is correct according to authentic monuments.

The Knight and Squire with the Squire's Yeoman lead the procession, as Chaucer has also placed them first in his prologue. The Knight is a true Hero, a good, great, and wise man; his whole length portrait on horseback, as written by Chaucer, cannot be surpassed. He has spent his life in the field; has ever been a conqueror, and is that species of character which in every age stands as the guardian of man against the oppressor. His son is like him with the germ of perhaps greater perfection still, as he blends literature and the arts with his warlike studies. Their dress and their horses are of the first rate, without ostentation, and with all the true grandeur that unaffected simplicity when in high rank always displays. The Squire's Yeoman is also a great character, a man perfectly knowing in his profession:

And in his hand he bare a mighty bow.

Chaucer describes here a mighty man; one who in war is the
worthy attendant on noble heroes.

The Prioress follows these with her female chaplain :

Another Nonne also with her had she,
That was her Chaplaine, and Priests three.

This Lady is described also as of the first rank, rich and
honoured. She has certain peculiarities and little delicate affecta-
tions, not unbecoming in her, being accompanied with what is
truly grand and really polite; her person and face Chaucer has
described with minuteness; it is very elegant, and was the beauty
of our ancestors, till after Elizabeth's time, when voluptuousness
and folly began to be accounted beautiful.

Her companion and her three priests were no doubt all perfectly delineated in those parts of Chaucer's work which are now
lost; we ought to suppose them suitable attendants on rank and
fashion.

The Monk follows these with the Friar. The Painter has also
grouped with these the Pardoner and the Sompnour and the
Manciple, and has here also introduced one of the rich citizens
of London : Characters likely to ride in company, all being above
the common rank in life or attendants on those who were so.

For the Monk is described by Chaucer as a man of the first
rank in society, noble, rich, and expensively attended; he is a
leader of the age, with certain humorous accompaniments in his
character, that do not degrade, but render him an object of dignified mirth, but also with other accompaniments not so respectable.

The Friar is a character also of a mixed kind :

A friar there was, a wanton and a merry.

but in his office he is said to be a 'full solemn man' : eloquent,
amorous, witty, and satyrical; young, handsome, and rich; he
is a complete rogue, with constitutional gaiety enough to make
him a master of all the pleasures of the world.

> His neck was white as the flour de lis,
> Thereto strong he was as a champioun.

It is necessary here to speak of Chaucer's own character, that I may set certain mistaken critics right in their conception of the humour and fun that occurs on the journey. Chaucer is himself the great poetical observer of men, who in every age is born to record and eternize its acts. This he does as a master, as a father, and superior, who looks down on their little follies from the Emperor to the Miller; sometimes with severity, oftener with joke and sport.

Accordingly Chaucer has made his Monk a great tragedian, one who studied poetical art. So much so, that the generous Knight is, in the compassionate dictates of his soul, compelled to cry out :

> 'Ho,' quoth the Knyght, – 'good Sir, no more of this;
> That ye have said is right ynough I wis;
> And mokell more, for little heaviness
> Is right enough for much folk, as I guesse.
> I say, for me, it is a great disease,
> Whereas men have been in wealth and ease,
> To heare of their sudden fall, alas,
> And the contrary is joy and solas.'

The Monk's definition of tragedy in the proem to his tale is worth repeating :

> Tragedie is to tell a certain story,
> As old books us maken memory,
> Of hem that stood in great prosperity,
> And be fallen out of high degree,
> Into miserie, and ended wretchedly.

Though a man of luxury, pride and pleasure, he is a master of art and learning, though affecting to despise it. Those who can think that the proud Huntsman and Noble Housekeeper, Chaucer's Monk, is intended for a buffoon or a burlesque character, know little of Chaucer.

For the Host who follows this group, and holds the center of the cavalcade, is a first rate character, and his jokes are no trifles; they are always, though uttered with audacity, and equally free with the Lord and the Peasant, they are always substantially and weightily expressive of knowledge and experience; Henry Baillie, the keeper of the greatest Inn of the greatest City, for such was the Tabarde Inn in Southwark, near London : our Host was also a leader of the age.

By way of illustration, I instance Shakspeare's Witches in Macbeth. Those who dress them for the stage, consider them as wretched old women, and not as Shakspeare intended, the Goddesses of Destiny; this shews how Chaucer has been misunderstood in his sublime work. Shakspeare's Fairies also are the rulers of the vegetable world, and so are Chaucer's; let them be so considered, and then the poet will be understood, and not else.

But I have omitted to speak of a very prominent character, the Pardoner, the Age's Knave, who always commands and domineers over the high and low vulgar. This man is sent in every age for a rod and scourge, and for a blight, for a trial of men, to divide the classes of men; he is in the most holy sanctuary, and he is suffered by Providence for wise ends, and has also his great use, and his grand leading destiny.

His companion, the Sompnour, is also a Devil of the first magnitude, grand, terrific, rich and honoured in the rank of which he holds the destiny. The uses to Society are perhaps equal of the Devil and of the Angel, their sublimity, who can dispute.

> In daunger had he at his own gise,
> The young girls of his diocese,
> And he knew well their counsel, &c.

The principal figure in the next groupe is the Good Parson; an Apostle, a real Messenger of Heaven, sent in every age for its light and its warmth. This man is beloved and venerated by all, and neglected by all; He serves all, and is served by none; he is, according to Christ's definition, the greatest of his age. Yet he is a Poor Parson of a town. Read Chaucer's description of the Good Parson, and bow the head and the knee to him, who, in every age, sends us such a burning and a shining light. Search, O ye rich and powerful, for these men and obey their counsel, then shall the golden age return: But alas! you will not easily distinguish him from the Friar or the Pardoner; they, also, are 'full solemn men', and their counsel you will continue to follow.

I have placed by his side the Sergeant at Lawe, who appears delighted to ride in his company, and between him and his brother, the Plowman; as I wish men of Law would always ride with them, and take their counsel, especially in all difficult points. Chaucer's Lawyer is a character of great venerableness, a Judge, and a real master of the jurisprudence of his age.

The Doctor of Physic is in this groupe, and the Franklin, the voluptuous country gentleman, contrasted with the Physician, and on his other hand, with two Citizens of London. Chaucer's characters live age after age. Every age is a Canterbury Pilgrimage; we all pass on, each sustaining one or other of these characters; nor can a child be born, who is not one of these characters of Chaucer. The Doctor of Physic is described as the first of his profession; perfect, learned, completely Master and Doctor in his art. Thus the reader will observe, that Chaucer makes every one of his characters perfect in his kind; every one is an Antique Statue; the image of a class, and not of an imperfect individual.

This groupe also would furnish substantial matter, on which volumes might be written. The Franklin is one who keeps open table, who is the genius of eating and drinking, the Bacchus; as the Doctor of Physic is the Esculapius, the Host is the Silenus, the Squire is the Apollo, the Miller is the Hercules, &c. Chaucer's characters are a description of the eternal Principles that exist in all ages. The Franklin is voluptuousness itself, most nobly pourtrayed:

It snewed in his house of meat and drink.

The Plowman is simplicity itself, with wisdom and strength for its stamina. Chaucer has divided the ancient character of Hercules between his Miller and his Plowman. Benevolence is the plowman's great characteristic; he is thin with excessive labour, and not with old age, as some have supposed:

> He would thresh, and thereto dike and delve
> For Christe's sake, for every poore wight,
> Withouten hire, if it lay in his might.

Visions of these eternal principles or characters of human life appear to poets, in all ages; the Grecian gods were the ancient Cherubim of Phoenicia; but the Greeks, and since them the Moderns, have neglected to subdue the gods of Priam. These gods are visions of the eternal attributes, or divine names, which, when erected into gods, become destructive to humanity. They ought to be the servants, and not the masters of man, or of society. They ought to be made to sacrifice to Man, and not man compelled to sacrifice to them; for when separated from man or humanity, who is Jesus the Saviour, the vine of eternity, they are thieves and rebels, they are destroyers.

The Plowman of Chaucer is Hercules in his supreme eternal state, divested of his spectrous shadow; which is the Miller, a terrible fellow, such as exists in all times and places for the trial of men, to astonish every neighbourhood with brutal strength and courage, to get rich and powerful to curb the pride of Man.

The Reeve and the Manciple are two characters of the most consummate worldly wisdom. The Shipman, or Sailor, is a similar genius of Ulyssean art; but with the highest courage superadded.

The Citizens and their Cook are each leaders of a class. Chaucer has been somehow made to number four citizens, which would make his whole company, himself included, thirty-one, But he says there was but nine and twenty in his company :

> Full nine and twenty in a company.

The Webbe, or Weaver, and the Tapiser, or Tapestry Weaver, appear to me to be the same person; but this is only an opinion, for full nine and twenty may signify one more or less. But I dare say that Chaucer wrote 'A Webbe Dyer', that is, a Cloth Dyer :

> A Webbe Dyer, and a Tapiser.

The Merchant cannot be one of the Three Citizens, as his dress is different, and his character is more marked, whereas Chaucer says of his rich citizens :

> All were yclothed in o liverie.

The characters of Women Chaucer has divided into two classes, the Lady Prioress and the Wife of Bath. Are not these leaders of the ages of men? The lady prioress, in some ages, predominates; and in some the wife of Bath, in whose character Chaucer has been equally minute and exact, because she is also a scourge and a blight. I shall say no more of her, nor expose what Chaucer has left hidden; let the young reader study what he has said of her : it is useful as a scare-crow. There are of such characters born too many for the peace of the world.

I come at length to the Clerk of Oxenford. This character varies from that of Chaucer, as the contemplative philosopher varies from the poetical genius. There are always these two classes of learned sages, the poetical and the philosophical. The painter has put them side by side, as if the youthful clerk had put himself under the tuition of the mature poet. Let the Philosopher always be the servant and scholar of inspiration and all will be happy . . .

S o u r c e : *A Descriptive Catalogue of Pictures, Poetical and Historical Inventions, Painted by William Blake* (1809).

William Hazlitt

. . . I shall take, as the subject of the present lecture, Chaucer and Spenser, two out of four of the greatest names in poetry, which this country has to boast. Both of them, however, were much indebted to the early poets of Italy, and may be considered as belonging, in a certain degree, to the same school. The freedom and copiousness with which our most original writers, in former periods, availed themselves of the productions of their predecessors, frequently transcribing whole passages, without scruple or acknowledgement, may appear contrary to the etiquette of modern literature, when the whole stock of poetical common-places has become public property, and no one is compelled to trade upon any particular author. But it is not so much a subject of wonder, at a time when to read and write was of itself an honorary distinction, when learning was almost as great a rarity as genius, and when in fact those who first transplanted the beauties of other languages into their own, might be considered as public benefactors, and the founders of a national literature. There are poets older than Chaucer, and in the interval between him and Spenser; but their genius was not such as to place them in any point of comparison with either of these celebrated men; and an inquiry into their particular merits or defects might seem rather to belong to the province of the antiquary, than be thought generally interesting to the lovers of poetry in the present day.

Chaucer (who has been very properly considered as the father of English poetry) preceded Spenser by two centuries. He is supposed to have been born in London, in the year 1328, during the reign of Edward III, and to have died in 1400, at the age of seventy-two. He received a learned education at one, or at both of the universities, and travelled early into Italy, where he became thoroughly imbued with the spirit and excellences of the great Italian poets and prose-writers, Dante, Petrarch, and Boccace; and is said to have had a personal interview with one of these, Petrarch. He was connected, by marriage, with the famous John

of Gaunt, through whose interest he was introduced into several
public employments. Chaucer was an active partisan, a religious
reformer, and from the share he took in some disturbances, on
one occasion, he was obliged to fly the country. On his return, he
was imprisoned, and made his peace with government, as it is
said, by a discovery of his associates. Fortitude does not appear,
at any time, to have been the distinguishing virtue of poets. There
is, however, an obvious similarity between the practical turn of
Chaucer's mind and restless impatience of his character, and the
tone of his writings. Yet it would be too much to attribute the
one to the other as cause and effect : for Spenser, whose poetical
temperament was as effeminate as Chaucer's was stern and
masculine, was equally engaged in public affairs, and had mixed
equally in the great world. So much does native disposition pre-
dominate over accidental circumstances, moulding them to its
previous bent and purposes! For while Chaucer's intercourse
with the busy world, and collision with the actual passions and
conflicting interests of others, seemed to brace the sinews of his
understanding, and gave to his writings the air of a man who
describes persons and things that he had known and been
intimately concerned in; the same opportunities, operating on a
differently constituted frame, only served to alienate Spenser's
mind the more from the 'close-pent up' scenes of ordinary life,
and to make him 'rive their concealing continents', to give himself up to the unrestrained indulgence of 'flowery tenderness'.

It is not possible for any two writers to be more opposite in
this respect. Spenser delighted in luxurious enjoyment; Chaucer,
in severe activity of mind. As Spenser was the most romantic and
visionary, Chaucer was the most practical of all the great poets,
the most a man of business and the world. His poetry reads like
history. Everything has a downright reality; at least in the re-
lator's mind. A simile, or a sentiment, is as if it were given in
upon evidence. Thus he describes Cressid's first avowal of her
love :

> And as the new abashed nightingale,
> That stinteth first when she beginneth sing,
> When that she heareth any herde's tale,
> Or in the hedges any wight stirring,
> And after, sicker, doth her voice outring;

> Right so Cresseide, when that her dread stent,
> Open'd her heart, and told him her intent.

This is so true and natural, and beautifully simple, that the two things seem identified with each other. Again, it is said in the Knight's Tale —

> Thus passeth yere by yere, and day by day,
> Till it felle ones in a morwe of May,
> That Emelie that fayrer was to sene
> Than is the lilie upon his stalke grene;
> And fresher than the May with floures newe,
> For with the rose-colour strof hire hewe:
> I n'ot which was the finer of hem two.

This scrupulousness about the literal preference, as if some question of matter of fact was at issue, is remarkable. I might mention that other, where he compares the meeting between Palamon and Arcite to a hunter waiting for a lion in a gap:

> That stondeth at a gap with a spere,
> Whan hunted is the lion or the bere,
> And hereth him come rushing in the greves,
> And breking bothe the boughes and the leves —

or that still finer one of Constance, when she is condemned to death:

> Have ye not seen somtime a pale face
> (Among a prees) of him that hath been lad
> Toward his deth, wheras he geteth no grace,
> And swiche a colour in his face hath had,
> Men mighten know him that was so bestad,
> Amonges all the faces in that route;
> So stant Custance, and loketh hire aboute.

The beauty, the pathos here does not seem to be of the poet's seeking, but a part of the necessary texture of the fable. He speaks of what he wishes to describe with the accuracy, the discrimination of one who relates what has happened to himself, or has had the best information from those who have been eye-witnesses of it. The strokes of his pencil always tell. He dwells only on the essential, on that which would be interesting to the persons really concerned : yet as he never omits any material circumstance, he is prolix from the number of points on which he touches, without being diffuse on any one; and is sometimes tedious from the fidelity with which he adheres to his subject, as other writers are from the frequency of their digressions from it. The chain of his story is composed of a number of fine links, closely connected together, and rivetted by a single blow. There is an instance of the minuteness which he introduces into his most serious descriptions in his account of Palamon when left alone in his cell :

> Swiche sorrow he maketh that the grete tour
> Resouned of his yelling and clamour :
> The pure fetters on his shinnes grete
> Were of his bitter salte teres wete.

The mention of this last circumstance looks like a part of the instructions he had to follow, which he had no discretionary power to leave out or introduce at pleasure. He is contented to find grace and beauty in truth. He exhibits for the most part the naked object, with little drapery thrown over it. His metaphors, which are few, are not for ornament, but use, and as like as possible to the things themselves. He does not affect to show his power over the reader's mind, but the power which his subject has over his own. The readers of Chaucer's poetry feel more nearly what the persons he describes must have felt, than perhaps those of any other poet. His sentiments are not voluntary effusions of the poet's fancy, but founded on the natural impulses and habitual prejudices of the characters he has to represent. There is an inveteracy of purpose, a sincerity of feeling, which never relaxes or grows vapid, in whatever they do or say. There is no artificial, pompous display, but a strict parsimony of the poet's materials, like the rude simplicity of the age in which he lived. His poetry resembles the root just springing from the ground, rather than the full-blown flower. His muse is no 'babbling gossip of the air', fluent and redundant; but, like a stammerer, or a dumb person, that has just found the use of speech, crowds many things together with eager haste, with anxious pauses, and fond repetitions to prevent mistake. His words point as an index to the objects, like the eye or finger. There were none of the commonplaces of poetic diction in our author's time, no reflected lights of fancy, no borrowed roseate tints; he was obliged to inspect things for himself, to look narrowly, and almost to handle the object, as in the obscurity of morning we partly see and partly grope our way; so that his descriptions have a sort of tangible character belonging to them, and produce the effect of sculpture on the mind. Chaucer had an equal eye for truth of nature and discrimination of character; and his interest in what he saw gave new distinctness and force to his power of observation. The picturesque and the dramatic are in him closely blended together, and hardly distinguishable; for he principally describes external appearances as indicating character, as symbols of internal sentiment. There is a meaning in what he sees; and it is this which catches his eye by sympathy. Thus the costume and dress of the Canterbury Pilgrims – of the Knight – the Squire – the Oxford Scholar – the Gap-toothed Wife of Bath, and the rest – speak for themselves . . .

The Serjeant at Law is the same identical individual as Lawyer Dowling in *Tom Jones*, who wished to divide himself into a hundred pieces, to be in a hundred places at once.

> No wher so besy a man as he ther n'as,
> And yet he semed besier than he was.

The Frankelein, in 'whose hous it snewed of mete and drinke'; the Shipman, 'who rode upon a rouncie, as he couthe'; the Doctour of Phisike, 'whose studie was but litel of the Bible'; the Wif of Bath, in

> All whose parish ther was non,
> That to the offring before hire shulde gon,
> And if ther did, certain so wroth was she,
> That she was out of alle charitee;

the poure Persone of a toun, 'whose parish was wide, and houses fer asonder'; the Miller, and the Reve, 'a slendre colerike man' –

are all of the same stamp. They are every one samples of a kind;
abstract definitions of a species. Chaucer, it has been said, numbered the classes of men, as Linnaeus numbered the plants. Most
of them remain to this day : others that are obsolete, and may
well be dispensed with, still live in his descriptions of them. Such
is the Sompnoure :

> A Sompnoure was ther with us in that place,
> That hadde a fire-red cherubinnes face,
> For sausefleme he was, with eyen narwe,
> As hote he was, and likerous as a sparwe,
> With scalled browes blake, and pilled berd :
> Of his visage children were sore aferd.
> Ther n'as quicksilver, litarge, ne brimston,
> Boras, ceruse, ne oile of tartre non,
> Ne oinement that wolde clense or bite,
> That him might helpen of his whelkes white,
> Ne of the knobbes sitting on his chekes.
> Wel loved he garlike, onions, and lekes,
> And for to drinke strong win as rede as blood.
> Than wolde he speke, and crie as he were wood.
> And whan that he wel dronken had the win,
> Than wold he speken no word but Latin.
> A fewe termes coude he, two or three,
> That he had lerned out of som decree;
> No wonder is, he heard it all the day. –
> In danger hadde he at his owen gise
> The yonge girles of the diocise,
> And knew hir conseil, and was of hir rede.
> A gerlond hadde he sette upon his hede
> As gret as it were for an alestake :
> A bokeler hadde he made him of a cake.
> With him ther rode a gentil Pardonere –
> That hadde a vois as smale as hath a gote.

It would be a curious speculation (at least for those who think
that the characters of men never change, though manners,
opinions, and institutions may) to know what has become of this
character of the Sompnoure in the present day; whether or not

it has any technical representative in existing professions; into
what channels and conduits it has withdrawn itself, where it
lurks unseen in cunning obscurity, or else shows its face boldly,
pampered into all the insolence of office, in some other shape, as it
it deterred or encouraged by circumstances. *Chaucer's characters
modernized*, upon this principle of historic derivation, would be
an useful addition to our knowledge of human nature. But who
is there to undertake it?

The descriptions of the equipage, and accoutrements of the
two kings of Thrace and Inde, in the Knight's Tale, are as
striking and grand, as the others are lively and natural:

> Ther maist thou se coming with Palamon
> Licurge himself, the grete king of Trace:
> Blake was his berd, and manly was his face.
> The cercles of his eyen in his hed
> They gloweden betwixen yelwe and red,
> And like a griffon loked he about . . .
>
>   With Arcita, in stories as men find,
> The grete Emetrius, the king of Inde,
> Upon a stede bay, trapped in stele,
> Covered with cloth of gold diapred wele,
> Came riding like the god of armes Mars . . .

What a deal of terrible beauty there is contained in this description! The imagination of a poet brings such objects before
us, as when we look at wild beasts in a menagerie; their claws
are pared, their eyes glitter like harmless lightning; but we gaze
at them with a pleasing awe, clothed in beauty, formidable in the
sense of abstract power.

Chaucer's descriptions of natural scenery possess the same sort
of characteristic excellence, or what might be termed *gusto*. They
have a local truth and freshness, which gives the very feeling of
the air, the coolness or moisture of the ground. Inanimate objects are thus made to have a fellow-feeling in the interest of the
story; and render back the sentiment of the speaker's mind. One
of the finest parts of Chaucer is of this mixed kind. It is the beginning of the *Flower and the Leaf*, where he describes the
delight of that young beauty, shrouded in her bower, and listen-

ing, in the morning of the year, to the singing of the nightingale;
while her joy rises with the rising song, and gushes out afresh at
every pause, and is borne along with the full tide of pleasure,
and still increases, and repeats, and prolongs itself, and knows
no ebb. The coolness of the arbour, its retirement, the early time
of the day, the sudden starting up of the birds in the neighbour-
ing bushes, the eager delight with which they devour and rend
the opening buds and flowers, are expressed with a truth and
feeling, which make the whole appear like the recollection of an
actual scene. . . . There is here no affected rapture, no flowery
sentiment: the whole is an ebullition of natural delight 'welling
out of the heart', like water from a crystal spring. Nature is the
soul of art: there is a strength as well as a simplicity in the imagination that reposes entirely on nature, that nothing else can
supply. It was the same trust in nature, and reliance on his subject, which enabled Chaucer to describe the grief and patience of
Griselda; the faith of Constance; and the heroic perseverance
of the little child, who, going to school through the streets of
Jewry,

Oh *Alma Redemptoris mater*, loudly sung,

and who after his death still triumphed in his song. Chaucer has
more of this deep, internal, sustained sentiment, than any other
writer, except Boccaccio. In depth of simple pathos, and intensity of conception, never swerving from his subject, I think no
other writer comes near him, not even the Greek tragedians. I
wish to be allowed to give one or two instances of what I mean. I
will take the following from the Knight's Tale. The distress of
Arcite, in consequence of his banishment from his love, is thus
described:

> Whan that Arcite to Thebes comen was,
> Ful oft a day he swelt and said Alas,
> For sene his lady shall he never mo.
> And shortly to concluden all his wo,
> So mochel sorwe hadde never creature,
> That is or shall be, while the world may dure.
> His slepe, his mete, his drinke is him byraft.

That lene he wex, and drie as is a shaft.
His eyen holwe, and grisly to behold,
His hewe salwe, and pale as ashen cold,
And solitary he was, and ever alone,
And wailing all the night, making his mone.
And if he herde song or instrument,
Than wold he wepe, he mighte not be stent.
So feble were his spirites, and so low,
And changed so, that no man coude know
His speche ne his vois, though men it herd.

This picture of the sinking of the heart, of the wasting away
of the body and mind, of the gradual failure of all the faculties
under the contagion of a rankling sorrow, cannot be surpassed.
Of the same kind is his farewell to his mistress, after he has
gained her hand and lost his life in the combat :

'Alas the wo ! alas the peines stronge,
That I for you have suffered, and so longe !
Alas the deth ! alas min Emilie !
Alas departing of our compagnie;
Alas min hertes quene ! alas my wif !
Min hertes ladie, ender of my lif !
What is this world? what axen men to have?
Now with his love, now in his colde grave
Alone withouten any compagnie.'

The death of Arcite is the more affecting, as it comes after
triumph and victory, after the pomp of sacrifice, the solemnities
of prayer, the celebration of the gorgeous rites of chivalry. The
descriptions of the three temples of Mars, of Venus, and Diana,
of the ornaments and ceremonies used in each, with the recep-
tion given to the offerings of the lovers, have a beauty and
grandeur, much of which is lost in Dryden's version. For instance,
such lines as the following are not rendered with their true feeling :

Why shulde I not as well eke tell you all
The purtreiture that was upon the wall

> Within the temple of mighty Mars the rede –
> That highte the gret temple of Mars in Trace
> In thilke colde and frosty region,
> Ther as Mars hath his sovereine mansion.
> First on the wall was peinted a forest,
> In which ther wonneth neyther man ne best,
> With knotty knarry barrein trees old
> Of stubbes sharpe and hidous to behold;
> In which ther ran a romble and a swough,
> As though a storme shuld bresten every bough.

And again, among innumerable terrific images of death and slaughter painted on the wall, is this one :.

> The statue of Mars upon a carte stood
> Armed, and looked grim as he were wood.
> A wolf ther stood beforne him at his fete
> With eyen red, and of a man he ete.

The story of Griselda is in Boccaccio; but the Clerk of Oxenforde, who tells it, professes to have learned it from Petrarch. This story has gone all over Europe, and has passed into a proverb. In spite of the barbarity of the circumstances, which are abominable, the sentiment remains unimpaired and unalterable. It is of that kind, 'that heaves no sigh, that sheds no tear'; but it hangs upon the beatings of the heart; it is a part of the very being; it is as inseparable from it as the breath we draw. It is still and calm as the face of death. Nothing can touch it in its ethereal purity : tender as the yielding flower, it is fixed as the marble firmament. The only remonstrance she makes, the only complaint she utters against all the ill-treatment she receives, is that single line where, when turned back naked to her father's house, she says,

> Let me not like a worm go by the way.

The story of the little child slain in Jewry (which is told by the Prioress, and worthy to be told by her who was 'all conscience and tender heart') is not less touching than that of Griselda. It is simple and heroic to the last degree. The poetry of Chaucer has a religious sanctity about it, connected with the manners and superstitions of the age. It has all the spirit of martyrdom.

It has also all the extravagance and the utmost licentiousness of comic humour, equally arising out of the manners of the time. In this too Chaucer resembled Boccaccio that he excelled in both styles, and could pass at will 'from grave to gay, from lively to severe'; but he never confounded the two styles together (except from that involuntary and unconscious mixture of the pathetic and humorous, which is almost always to be found in nature), and was exclusively taken up with what he set about, whether it was jest or earnest. The Wife of Bath's Prologue (which Pope has very admirably modernized) is, perhaps, unequalled as a comic story. The *Cock and the Fox* is also excellent for lively strokes of character and satire. *January and May* is not so good as some of the others. Chaucer's versification, considering the time at which he wrote, and that versification is a thing in a great degree mechanical, is not one of his least merits. It has considerable strength and harmony, and its apparent deficiency in the latter respect arises chiefly from the alterations which have since taken place in the pronunciation or mode of accenting the words of the language. The best general rule for reading him is to pronounce the final *e*, as in reading Italian.

It was observed in the last Lecture that painting describes what the object is in itself, poetry what it implies or suggests. Chaucer's poetry is not, in general, the best confirmation of the truth of this distinction, for his poetry is more picturesque and historical than almost any other. But there is one instance in point which I cannot help giving in this place. It is the story of the three thieves who go in search of Death to kill him, and who meeting with him, are entangled in their fate by his words, without knowing him. In the printed catalogue to Mr. West's (in some respects very admirable) picture of Death on the Pale Horse, it is observed, that 'In poetry the same effect is produced by a few abrupt and rapid gleams of description, touching, as it were with fire, the features and edges of a general mass of awful obscurity; but in painting, such indistinctness would be a defect, and imply that the artist wanted the power to portray the conceptions of his fancy. Mr. West was of opinion that to delineate a physical form, which in its moral impression would approximate to that of the visionary Death of Milton, it was necessary to endow it, if possible, with the appearance of super-human strength and energy. He has therefore exerted the utmost force and perspicuity of his pencil on the central figure.' – One might suppose from this, that the way to represent a shadow was to make it as substantial as possible. Oh, no! Painting has its prerogatives (and high ones they are), but they lie in representing the visible, not the invisible. The moral attributes of Death are powers and effects of an infinitely wide and general description, which no individual or physical form can possibly represent, but by a courtesy of speech, or by a distant analogy. The moral impression of Death is essentially visionary; its reality is in the mind's eye. Words are here the only *things*; and things, physical forms, the mere mockeries of the understanding. The less definite, the less bodily the conception, the more vast, unformed, and unsubstantial, the nearer does it approach to some resemblance of that omnipresent, lasting, universal, irresistible principle, which everywhere, and at some time or other, exerts its power over all things. Death is a mighty abstraction, like Night, or Space, or Time. He is an ugly customer, who will not be invited to supper, or to sit for his picture. He is with us and about us, but we do not see him. He stalks on before us, and we do not mind him: he follows us close behind, and we do not turn to look back at him. We do not see him making faces at us in our life-time, nor perceive him afterwards sitting in mock-majesty, a twin-skeleton, beside us, tickling our bare ribs, and staring into our hollow eye-balls! Chaucer knew this. He makes three riotous companions go in search of Death to kill him, they meet with an old man whom they reproach with his age, and ask why he does not die, to which he answers thus:

> Ne Deth, alas! ne will not han my lif.
> Thus walke I like a restless caitiff,
> And on the ground, which is my modres gate,
> I knocke with my staf, erlich and late,
> And say to hire, 'Leve mother, let me in.
> Lo, how I vanish, flesh and blood and skin,
> Alas! when shall my bones ben at reste?
> Mother, with you wolde I changen my cheste,

That in my chambre longe time hath be,
Ye, for an heren cloute to wrap in me.'
But yet to me she will not don that grace,
For which ful pale and welked is my face.

They then ask the old man where they shall find out Death
to kill him, and he sends them on an errand which ends in the
death of all three. We hear no more of him, but it is Death that
they have encountered! ...

SOURCE: 'On Chaucer and Spenser', Lecture 2 in *Lectures
on the English Poets* (1818).

Matthew Arnold

... Once more I return to the early poetry of France, with which our own poetry, in its origins, is indissolubly connected. In the twelfth and thirteenth centuries, that seed-time of all modern language and literature, the poetry of France had a clear predominance in Europe. Of the two divisions of that poetry, its productions in the *langue d'oil* and its productions in the *langue d'oc*, the poetry of the *langue d'oc*, of southern France, of the troubadours, is of importance because of its effect on Italian literature; – the first literature of modern Europe to strike the true and grand note, and to bring forth, as in Dante and Petrarch it brought forth, classics. But the predominance of French poetry in Europe, during the twelfth and thirteenth centuries, is due to its poetry of the *langue d'oil*, the poetry of northern France and of the tongue which is now the French language. In the twelfth century the bloom of this romance-poetry was earlier and stronger in England, at the court of our Anglo-Norman kings, than in France itself. But it was a bloom of French poetry; and as our native poetry formed itself, it formed itself out of this. The romance-poems which took possession of the heart and imagination of Europe in the twelfth and thirteenth centuries are French; 'they are', as Southey justly says, 'the pride of French literature, nor have we anything which can be placed in competition with them.' Themes were supplied from all quarters; but the romance-setting which was common to them all, and which gained the ear of Europe, was French. This constituted for the French poetry, literature, and language, at the height of the Middle Age, an unchallenged predominance. The Italian Brunetto Latini, the master of Dante, wrote his *Treasure* in French because, he says, 'la parleure en est plus délitable et plus commune à toutes gens.' In the same century, the thirteenth, the French romance-writer, Christian of Troyes, formulates the claims, in chivalry and letters, of France, his native country, as follows:

> Or vous ert par ce livre apris,
> Que Gresse ot de chevalerie
> Le premier los et de clergie;
> Puis vint chevalerie à Rome,
> Et de la clergie la some,
> Qui ore est en France venue.
> Diex doinst qu'ele i soit retenue,
> Et que li lius li abelisse
> Tant que de France n'isse
> L'onor qui s'i est arestée !

'Now by this book you will learn that first Greece had the renown for chivalry and letters: then chivalry and the primacy in letters passed to Rome, and now it is come to France. God grant it may be kept there; and that the place may please it so well, that the honour which has come to make stay in France may never depart thence !'

Yet it is now all gone, this French romance-poetry, of which the weight of substance and the power of style are not unfairly represented by this extract from Christian of Troyes. Only by means of the historic estimate can we persuade ourselves now to think that any of it is of poetical importance.

But in the fourteenth century there comes an Englishman nourished on this poetry, taught his trade by this poetry, getting words, rhyme, metre from this poetry; for even of that stanza which the Italians used, and which Chaucer derived immediately from the Italians, the basis and suggestion was probably given in France. Chaucer (I have already named him) fascinated his contemporaries, but so too did Christian of Troyes and Wolfram of Eschenbach. Chaucer's power of fascination, however, is enduring; his poetical importance does not need the assistance of the historic estimate; it is real. He is a genuine source of joy and strength, which is flowing still for us and will flow always. He will be read, as time goes on, far more generally than he is read now. His language is a cause of difficulty for us; but so also, and I think in quite as great a degree, is the language of Burns. In Chaucer's case, as in that of Burns, it is a difficulty to be unhesitatingly accepted and overcome.

If we ask ourselves wherein consists the immense superiority of Chaucer's poetry over the romance-poetry – why it is that in passing from this to Chaucer we suddenly feel ourselves to be in another world, we shall find that his superiority is both in the substance of his poetry and in the style of his poetry. His superiority in substance is given by his large, free, simple, clear yet kindly view of human life – so unlike the total want, in the romance-poets, of all intelligent command of it. Chaucer has not their helplessness; he has gained the power to survey the world from a central, a truly human point of view. We have only to call to mind the Prologue to *The Canterbury Tales*. The right comment upon it is Dryden's : 'It is sufficient to say, according to the proverb, that *here is God's plenty*.' And again : 'He is a perpetual fountain of good sense.' It is by a large, free, sound representation of things, that poetry, this high criticism of life, has truth of substance; and Chaucer's poetry has truth of substance.

Of his style and manner, if we think first of the romance-poetry and then of Chaucer's divine liquidness of diction, his divine fluidity of movement, it is difficult to speak temperately. They are irresistible, and justify all the rapture with which his successors speak of his 'gold dew-drops of speech'. Johnson misses the point entirely when he finds fault with Dryden for ascribing to Chaucer the first refinement of our numbers, and says that Gower also can show smooth numbers and easy rhymes. The refinement of our numbers means something far more than this. A nation may have versifiers with smooth numbers and easy rhymes, and yet may have no real poetry at all. Chaucer is the father of our splendid English poetry; he is our 'well of English undefiled', because by the lovely charm of his diction, the lovely charm of his movement, he makes an epoch and founds a tradition. In Spenser, Shakespeare, Milton, Keats, we can follow the tradition of the liquid diction, the fluid movement, of Chaucer; at one time it is his liquid diction of which in these poets we feel the virtue, and at another time it is his fluid movement. And the virtue is irresistible.

Bounded as is my space, I must yet find room for an example of Chaucer's virtue, as I have given examples to show the virtue of the great classics. I feel disposed to say that a single line is enough to show the charm of Chaucer's verse; that merely one line like this –

O martyr souded* in virginitee!

has a virtue of manner and movement such as we shall not find
in all the verse of romance-poetry; but this is saying nothing. The
virtue is such as we shall not find, perhaps, in all English poetry,
outside the poets whom I have named as the special inheritors of
Chaucer's tradition. A single line, however, is too little if we
have not the strain of Chaucer's verse well in our memory; let us
take a stanza. It is from *The Prioress's Tale*, the story of the
Christian child murdered in a Jewry:

> My throte is cut unto my nekke-bone
> Saidè this child, and as by way of kinde
> I should have deyd, yea, longè time agone;
> But Jesu Christ, as ye in bookès finde,
> Will that his glory last and be in minde,
> And for the worship of his mother dere
> Yet may I sing O Alma loud and clere.

Wordsworth has modernised this Tale, and to feel how delicate
and evanescent is the charm of verse, we have only to read Wordsworth's first three lines of this stanza after Chaucer's –

> My throat is cut unto the bone, I trow,
> Said this young child, and by the law of kind
> I should have died, yea, many hours ago.

The charm is departed. It is often said that the power of liquidness and fluidity in Chaucer's verse was dependent upon a free, a
licentious dealing with language, such as is now impossible; upon
a liberty, such as Burns too enjoyed, of making words like *neck*,
bird, into a dissyllable by adding to them, and words like *cause*
rhyme, into a dissyllable by sounding the *e* mute. It is true that
Chaucer's fluidity is conjoined with this liberty, and is admirably
served by it; but we ought not to say that it was dependent upon
it. It was dependent upon his talent. Other poets with a like

---

* The French *soudé*: soldered, fixed fast.

liberty do not attain to the fluidity of Chaucer; Burns himself
does not attain to it. Poets, again, who have a talent akin to
Chaucer's, such as Shakespeare or Keats, have known how to
attain to his fluidity without the like liberty.

And yet Chaucer is not one of the great classics. His poetry
transcends and effaces, easily and without effort, all the
romance-poetry of Catholic Christendom; it transcends and
effaces all the English poetry contemporary with it; it transcends
and effaces all the English poetry subsequent to it down to the
age of Elizabeth. Of such avail is poetic truth of substance, in its
natural and necessary union with poetic truth of style. And yet,
I say, Chaucer is not one of the great classics. He has not their
accent. What is wanting to him is suggested by the mere mention of the name of the first great classic of Christendom, the
immortal poet who died eighty years before Chaucer – Dante.
The accent of such verse as

In la sua volontade è nostra pace . . .

is altogether beyond Chaucer's reach; we praise him, but we feel
that this accent is out of the question for him. It may be said
that it was necessarily out of the reach of any poet in the England of that stage of growth. Possibly; but we are to adopt a real,
not a historic, estimate of poetry. However we may account for
its absence, something is wanting, then, to the poetry of Chaucer,
which poetry must have before it can be placed in the glorious
class of the best. And there is no doubt what that something is. It is the σπουδαιότης, the high and excellent seriousness,
which Aristotle assigns as one of the grand virtues of poetry. The
substance of Chaucer's poetry, his view of things and his criticism
of life, has largeness, freedom, shrewdness, benignity; but it has
not this high seriousness. Homer's criticism of life has it, Dante's
has it, Shakespeare's has it. It is this chiefly which gives to our
spirits what they can rest upon; and with the increasing demands of our modern ages upon poetry, this virtue of giving us
what we can rest upon will be more and more highly esteemed.
A voice from the slums of Paris, fifty or sixty years after Chaucer,
the voice of poor Villon out of his life of riot and crime, has at its
happy moments (as, for instance, in the last stanza of *La Belle*

*Heaulmière**) more of this important poetic virtue of seriousness than all the productions of Chaucer. But its apparition in
Villon, and in men like Villon, is fitful; the greatness of the
great poets, the power of their criticism of life, is that their virtue
is sustained.

To our praise, therefore, of Chaucer as a poet there must be
this limitation; he lacks the high seriousness of the great classics,
and therewith an important part of their virtue. Still, the main
fact for us to bear in mind about Chaucer is his sterling value
according to that real estimate which we firmly adopt for all
poets. He has poetic truth of substance, though he has not high
poetic seriousness, and corresponding to his truth of substance
he has an exquisite virtue of style and manner. With him is born
our real poetry. . . .

S O U R C E : 'The Study of Poetry' (1880), reprinted in *Essays
in Criticism, Second Series* (1888).

* The name *Heaulmière* is said to be derived from a head-dress (helm) worn as a
mark by courtesans. In Villon's ballad, a poor old creature of this class laments
her days of youth and beauty. The last stanza of the ballad runs thus:

> Ainsi le bon temps regretons
> Entre nous, pauvres vieilles sottes.
> Assises bas, à croppetons,
> Tout en ung tas comme pelottes;
> A petit feu de chenevottes
> Tost allumées, tost estainctes.
> Et jadis fusmes si mignottes!
> Ainsi en prend à maintz et maintes.

'Thus amongst ourselves we regret the good time, poor silly old things, low-seated
on our heels, all in a heap like so many balls, by a little fire of hemp-stalks, soon
lighted, soon spent. And once we were such darlings! So fares it with many and
many a one.'

PART TWO

Twentieth-century Criticism

G. L. Kittredge

CHAUCER'S DISCUSSION
OF MARRIAGE (1912)

We are prone to read and study the *Canterbury Tales* as if each
tale were an isolated unit and to pay scant attention to what we
call the connecting links – those bits of lively narrative and dialogue that bind the whole together. Yet Chaucer's plan is clear
enough. Structurally regarded, the *Canterbury Tales* is a kind of
Human Comedy. From this point of view, the Pilgrims are the
dramatis personae, and their stories are only speeches that are
somewhat longer than common, entertaining in and for themselves (to be sure), but primarily significant, in each case, because they illustrate the speaker's character and opinions, or
show the relations of the travellers to one another in the pro-
gressive action of the Pilgrimage. In other words, we ought not
merely to consider the general appropriateness of each tale to
the character of the teller : we should also inquire whether the
tale is not determined, to some extent, by the circumstances – by
the situation at the moment, by something that another Pilgrim
has said or done, by the turn of a discussion already under way.

Now and then, to be sure, this point is too obvious to be over-
looked, as in the squabble between the Summoner and the Friar
and that between the Reeve and the Miller, in the Shipman's
intervening to check the Parson, and in the way in which the
gentles head off the Pardoner when he is about to tell a ribald
anecdote. But, despite these unescapable instances, the general
principle is too often blinked or ignored. Yet its temperate application should clear up a number of things which are
traditionally regarded as difficulties, or as examples of heedless-
ness on Chaucer's part.

Without attempting to deny or abridge the right to study and
criticize each tale in and for itself – as legend, romance,
exemplum, fabliau, or what-not – and without extenuating the

results that this method has achieved, let us consider certain tales in their relation to Chaucer's structural plan – with reference, that is to say, to the Pilgrims who tell them and to the Pilgrimage to which their telling is incidental. We may begin with the story of Griselda.

This is a plain and straightforward piece of edification, and nobody has ever questioned its appropriateness to the Clerk, who, as he says himself, has traveled in Italy and had heard it from the lips of the laureate Petrarch. The Clerk's 'speech', according to the General Prologue, was 'sowning in moral vertu', so that this story is precisely the kind of thing which we should expect from his lips. True, we moderns sometimes feel shocked or offended at what we style the immorality of Griselda's unvarying submission. But this feeling is no ground of objection to the appropriateness of the tale to the Clerk. The Middle Ages delighted (as children still delight) in stories that exemplify a single human quality, like valor, or tyranny, or fortitude. In such cases, the settled rule (for which neither Chaucer not the Clerk was responsible) was to show to what lengths this quality may conceivably go. Hence, in tales of this kind, there can be no question of conflict of duties, no problem as to the point at which excess of goodness becomes evil. It is, then, absurd to censure a fourteenth-century Clerk for telling (or Chaucer for making him tell) a story which exemplifies in this hyperbolical way the virtue of fortitude under affliction. Whether Griselda could have put an end to her woes, or ought to have put an end to them, by refusing to obey her husband's commands is *parum ad rem*. We are to look at her trials as inevitable, and to pity her accordingly, and wonder at her endurance. If we refuse to accept the tale in this spirit, we are ourselves the losers. We miss the pathos because we are aridly intent on discussing an ethical question that has no status in this particular court, however pertinent it may be in the general forum of morals.

Furthermore, in thus focusing attention on the morality or immorality of Griselda's submissiveness, we overlook what the Clerk takes pains to make as clear as possible – the real lesson that the story is meant to convey – and thus we do grave injustice to that austere but amiable moralist. The Clerk, a student of 'Aristotle and his philosophye', knew as well as any of us that every virtue may be conceived as a mean between two extremes.

Even the Canon's Yeoman, an ignorant man, was aware of this principle:

> That that is overdoon, it wol nat preve
> Aright, as clerkes seyn, – it is a vyce.   (G. 645–6)

Chaucer had too firm a grasp on his *dramatis personae* to allow the Clerk to leave the true purport of his parable undefined. 'This story is not told,' says the Clerk in substance, 'to exhort wives to imitate Griselda's humility, for *that* would be beyond the capacity of human nature. It is told in order that every man or woman, in whatever condition of life, may learn fortitude in adversity. For, since a woman once exhibited such endurance under trials inflicted on her by a mortal man, a fortiori ought *we* to accept patiently whatever tribulation God may send us. For God is not like Griselda's husband. He does not wantonly experiment with us, out of inhuman scientific curiosity. God *tests* us, as it is reasonable that our Maker should test his handiwork, but he does not *tempt* us. He allows us to be beaten with sharp scourges of adversity, not, like the Marquis Walter, to see if we can stand it, for he knoweth our frame, he remembereth that we are dust: all *his* affliction is for our better grace. Let us live, therefore, in manly endurance of the visitations of Providence.'

And then, at verse 1163, comes that matchless passage in which the Clerk (having explained the *universal* application of his parable – having provided with scrupulous care against any mis-interpretation of its serious purport) turns with gravely satiric courtesy to the Wife of Bath and makes the *particular* applica-tion of the story to her 'life' and 'all her sect'.

Here one may appreciate the vital importance of considering the *Canterbury Tales* as a connected Human Comedy – of tak-ing into account the Pilgrims in their relations to one another in the great drama to which the several narratives are structurally incidental. For it is precisely at this point that Professor Skeat notes a difficulty. 'From this point to the end', he remarks, 'is the work of a later period, and in Chaucer's best manner, though unsuited *to the coy Clerk*.' This is as much as to say that, in the remaining stanzas of the Clerk's Tale and in the Envoy, Chaucer has violated dramatic propriety. And, indeed, many

readers have detected in these concluding portions Chaucer's own
personal revulsion of feeling against the tale that he had suffered
the Clerk to tell.

Now the supposed difficulty vanishes as soon as we study vss.
1163–1212, not as an isolated phenomenon, but in their relation
to the great drama of the Canterbury Pilgrimage. It disappears
when we consider the lines in what we may call their dramatic
context, that is (to be specific), when we inquire what there was
in the situation to prompt the Clerk, after emphasizing the
serious and universal moral of Griselda's story, to give his tale a
special and peculiar application by annexing an ironical tribute
to the Wife of Bath, her life, her 'sect', and her principles. To
answer this question we must go back to the Wife of Bath's
Prologue.

The Wife of Bath's Prologue begins a group in the *Canterbury
Tales*, or, as one may say, a new act in the drama. It is not connected with anything that precedes. Let us trace the action from
this point down to the moment when the Clerk turns upon the
Wife with his satirical compliments.

The Wife had expounded her views at great length and with
all imaginable zest. Virginity, which the Church glorifies, is not
required of us. Our bodies are given us to use. Let saints be
continent if they will. She has no wish to emulate them. Nor does
she accept the doctrine that a widow or a widower must not
marry again. Where is bigamy forbidden in the Bible, or octo-
gamy either? She has warmed both hands before the fire of
life, and she exults in the recollection of her fleshly delights:

> But lord Crist! whan that it remembreth me
> Upon my youthe and on my iolitee,
> It tikleth me aboute myn herte rote;
> Unto this day it doth myn herte bote
> That I have had my world as in my time!   (D. 469–73)

True, she is willing to admit, for convention's sake, that chastity
is the ideal state. But it is not *her* ideal. On the contrary, her ad-
mission is only for appearances. In her heart she despises virginity. Her contempt for it is thinly veiled, or rather, not veiled at
all. Her discourse is marked by frank and almost obstreperous

animalism. Her whole attitude is that of scornful, though good-humored, repudiation of what the Church teaches in that regard.

Nor is the Wife content with this single heresy. She maintains also that wives should rule their husbands, and she enforces this doctrine by an account of her own life, and further illustrates it by her tale of the knight of King Arthur who learned that

> Wommen desiren to have sovereyntee
> As wel over hir housband as hir love,
> And for to been in maistrie him above, (D. 1038–40)

and who accepted the lesson as sound doctrine. Then, at the end of her discourse, she sums up in no uncertain words:

> And Iesu Crist us sende
> Housbandes meke, yonge, and fresshe abedde,
> And grace to overbyde hem that we wedde;
> And eek I preye Iesu shorte her lyves
> That wol nat be governed by her wyves. (D. 1258–62)

Now the Wife of Bath is not *bombinans in vacuo*. She addresses her heresies not to *us* or to the world at large, but to her fellow-pilgrims. Chaucer has made this point perfectly clear. The words of the Wife were of a kind to provoke comment – and we have the comment. The Pardoner interrupts her with praise of her noble preaching:

> 'Now, dame,' quod he, 'by God and by seint Iohn,
> Ye been a noble prechour in this cas!' (D. 164–5)

The adjective is not accidental. The Pardoner was a judge of good preaching: the General Prologue describes him as 'a noble ecclesiaste' (A. 708), and he shows his ability in his own sermon on Covetousness. Furthermore, it is the Friar's comment on the Wife's preamble that provokes the offensive words of the Summoner, and that becomes thereby the occasion for the two tales that immediately follow in the series. It is manifest, then, that Chaucer meant us to imagine the *dramatis personae* as taking a lively interest in whatever the Wife says. This being so, we ought to inquire what effect her Prologue and Tale would have upon the Clerk.

Of course the Clerk was scandalized. He was unworldly and an ascetic – he 'looked holwe and therto sobrely'. Moral virtue was his special study. He had embraced the celibate life. He was grave, devout, and unflinchingly orthodox. And now he was confronted by the lust of the flesh and the pride of life in the person of a woman who flouted chastity and exulted that she had 'had her world as in her time'. Nor was this all. The woman was an heresiarch, or at best a schismatic. She set up, and aimed to establish, a new and dangerous sect, whose principle was that the wife should rule the husband. The Clerk kept silence for the moment. Indeed, he had no chance to utter his sentiments, unless he interrupted – something not to be expected of his quiet ('coy') and sober temperament. But it is not to be imagined that his thoughts were idle. He could be trusted to speak to the purpose whenever his opportunity should come.

Now the substance of the Wife's false doctrines was not the only thing that must have roused the Clerk to protesting answer. The very manner of her discourse was a direct challenge to him. She had garnished her sermon with scraps of Holy Writ and rags and tatters of erudition, caught up, we may infer, from her last husband. Thus she had put herself into open competition with the guild of scholars and theologians, to which the Clerk belonged. Further, with her eye manifestly upon this sedate philosopher, she had taken pains to gird at him and his fellows. At first she pretends to be modest and apologetic – 'so that the clerkes be nat with me wrothe' (D. 125) – but later she abandons all pretense and makes an open attack:

> 'For trusteth wel, it is an impossible
> That any clerk wol speken good of wyves,
> But-if it be of holy seintes lyves,
> Ne of noon other wommen never the mo.   (D. 688–91)
>
> .   .   .   .
>
> The clerk, whan he is old, and may noght do
> Of Venus werkes worth his olde sho,
> Than sit he doun, and writ in his dotage
> That wommen can not kepe hir mariage.'   (D. 707–10)

And there was more still that the Wife made our Clerk endure. Her fifth husband was, like him, 'a clerk of Oxenford' – surely this is no accidental coincidence on Chaucer's part. He had abandoned his studies ('had left scole'), and had given up all thought of taking priest's orders. The Wife narrates, with uncommon zest, how she intrigued with him, and cajoled him, and married him (though he was twenty and she was forty), and how finally she made him utterly subservient to her will – how she got 'by maistrie al the soveraynetee'. This was gall and wormwood to our Clerk. The Wife not only trampled on his principles in her theory and practice, but she pointed her attack by describing how she had subdued to her heretical sect a clerk of Oxenford, an alumnus of our Clerk's own university. The Wife's discourse is not malicious. She is too jovial to be ill-natured, and she protests that she speaks in jest ('For myn entente nis but for to pleye', D. 192). But it none the less embodies a rude personal assault upon the Clerk, whose quiet mien and habitual reticence made him seem a safe person to attack. She had done her best to make the Clerk ridiculous. He saw it; the company saw it. He kept silent, biding his time.

All this is not speculation. It is nothing but straightforward interpretation of the text in the light of the circumstances and the situation. We can reject it only by insisting on the manifest absurdity (shown to be such in every headlink and endlink) that Chaucer did not visualize the Pilgrims whom he had been at such pains to describe in the Prologue, and that he never re- garded them as associating, as looking at each other and think- ing of each other, as becoming better and better acquainted as they jogged along the Canterbury road.

Chaucer might have given the Clerk a chance to reply to the Wife immediately. But he was too good an artist. The drama of the Pilgrimage is too natural and unforced in its development under the master's hand to admit of anything so frigidly schematic. The very liveliness with which he conceived his individual *dramatis personae* forbade. The Pilgrims were interested in the Wife's harangue, but it was for the talkative members of the company to thrust themselves forward. The Pardoner had already interrupted her with humorous comments before she was fully under way and had exhorted her to con-

tinue her account of the 'praktike' of marriage. The Friar, we
may be confident, was on good terms with her before she began :
she was one of those 'worthy wommen of the toun' whom he
especially cultivated. He, too, could not refrain from comment :

> The Frere lough, whan he had herd al this :
> 'Now, dame,' quod he, 'so have I ioye or blis,
> This is a long preamble of a tale !'   (D. 829–31)

The Summoner reproved him, in words that show not only his
professional enmity but also the amusement that the Pilgrims
in general were deriving from the Wife's disclosures. They
quarreled, and each threatened to tell a story at the other's expense. Then the Host intervened roughly, calling for silence and
bidding the Wife go ahead with her story. She assented, but not
without a word of good-humored, though ironical, deference to
the Friar :

> 'Al redy, sir,' quod she, 'right as yow lest,
> If I have licence of this worthy Frere.'   (D. 854–5)

And, at the very beginning of her tale, she took humorous vengeance for his interruption in a characteristic bit of satire at the
expense of 'limitours and other holy freres' (D. 864–81). This
passage, we note, has nothing whatever to do with her tale. It
is a side-remark in which she is talking at the Friar, precisely as
she has talked at the Clerk in her Prologue.

The quarrel between the Summoner and the Friar was in abey-
ance until the Wife finished her tale. They let her end her story
and proclaim her moral in peace – the same heretical doctrine
that we have already noted, that the wife should be the head of
the house. Then the Friar spoke, and his words are very much to
our present purpose. He adverts in significant terms both to the
subject and to the manner of the Wife's discourse – a discourse,
we should observe, that was in effect a doctrinal sermon illustrated (as the fashion of preachers was) by a pertinent *exemplum* :

> 'Ye have here touched, al-so moot I thee,
> In scole-matere greet difficultee.'   (D. 1271–2)

She has handled a hard subject that properly belongs to scholars. She has quoted authorities, too, like a clerk. Such things, he says, are best left to ecclesiastics:

> 'But, dame, here as we ryden by the weye,
>   Us nedeth nat to speken but of game,
>   And lete auctoritees, on Goddes name,
>   To preching and to scole eek of clergye.' (D. 1274-7)

This, to be sure, is but a device to 'conveyen his matere' – to lead up to his proposal to 'telle a game' about a summoner. But it serves to recall our minds to the Wife's usurpation of clerkly functions. If we think of the Clerk at all at this point (and assuredly Chaucer had not forgotten him), we must feel that here is another prompting (undesigned though it be on the Friar's part) to take up the subject which the Wife has (in the Clerk's eyes) so shockingly maltreated.

Then follows the comic interlude of the Friar and the Summoner, in the course of which we may perhaps lose sight of the serious subject which the Wife had set abroach – the status of husband and wife in the marriage relation. But Chaucer did not lose sight of it. It was a part of his design that the Host should call on the Clerk for the first story of the next day.

This is the opportunity for which the Clerk has been waiting. He has not said a word in reply to the Wife's heresies or to her personal attack on him and his order. Seemingly she has triumphed. The subject has apparently been dismissed with the Friar's words about leaving such matters to sermons and to school debates. The Host, indeed, has no idea that the Clerk purposes to revive the discussion; he does not even think of the Wife in calling upon the representative of that order which has fared so ill at her hands.

> 'Sir clerk of Oxenford,' our hoste sayde,
>   'Ye ryde as coy and stille as doth a mayde
>   Were newe spoused, sitting at the bord;
>   This day ne herde I of your tonge a word.
>   I trowe ye studie aboute som sophyme.' (E. 1-5)

Even here there is a suggestion (casual, to be sure, and, so far as the Host is concerned, quite unintentional) of *marriage*, the subject which is occupying the Clerk's mind. For the Host is mistaken. The Clerk's abstraction is only apparent. He is not pondering syllogisms; he is biding his time.

'Tell us a tale,' the unconscious Host goes on, 'but don't preach us a Lenten sermon – tell us som mery thing of aventures.' 'Gladly,' replies the demure scholar. 'I will tell you a story that a worthy *clerk* once told me at Padua – Francis Petrarch, God rest his soul !'

At this word *clerk*, pronounced with grave and inscrutable emphasis, the Wife of Bath must have pricked up her ears. But she has no inkling of what is in store, nor is the Clerk in any hurry to enlighten her. He opens with tantalizing deliberation, and it is not until he has spoken more than sixty lines that he mentions marriage. 'The Marquis Walter,' says the Clerk, 'lived only for the present and lived for pleasure only' –

> 'As for to hauke and hunte on every syde,
> Wel ny al othere cures leet he slyde;
> And eek he nolde, and that was worst of alle,
> Wedde no wyf, for noght that may bifalle.'   (E. 821–4)

These words may or may not have appeared significant to the company at large. To the Wife of Bath, at all events, they must have sounded interesting. And when, in a few moments, the Clerk made Walter's subjects speak of 'soveraynetee', the least alert of the Pilgrims can hardly have missed the point :

> 'Boweth your nekke under that blisful yok
> Of soveraynetee, noght of servyse,
> Which that men clepeth spousaille or wedlok.'
>
> (E. 113–15)

'Sovereignty' had been the Wife's own word :

> 'And whan that I hadde geten unto me
> By maistrie al the soveraynetee.'   (D. 817–18)

'Wommen desyren to have sovereyntee
As wel over hir housband as hir love,
And for to been in maistrie him above.'   (D. 1038–40)

Clearly the Clerk is catching up the subject proposed by the Wife. The discussion is under way again.

Yet, despite the cheerful view that Walter's subjects take of the marriage yoke, it is by no means yet clear to the Wife of Bath and the other Pilgrims what the Clerk is driving at. For he soon makes Walter declare that 'liberty is seldom found in marriage', and that, if he weds a wife, he must exchange freedom for servitude. Indeed, it is not until vss. 351–7 are reached that Walter reveals himself as a man who is determined to rule his wife absolutely. From that point to the end there is no room for doubt in any Pilgrim's mind : *the Clerk is answering the Wife of Bath*; he is telling of a woman whose principles in marriage were the antithesis of hers; he is reasserting the orthodox view in opposition to the heresy which she had expounded with such zest and with so many flings and jeers at the clerkly profession and character.

What is the tale of Griselda? Several things, no doubt – an old *märchen*, an *exemplum*, a *novella*, what you will. Our present concern, however, is primarily with the question what it seemed to be to the Canterbury Pilgrims, told as it was by an individual Clerk of Oxford at a particular moment and under the special circumstances. The answer is plain. To them it was a retort (indirect, impersonal, masterly) to the Wife of Bath's heretical doctrine that the woman should be the head of the man. It told them of a wife who had no such views – who promised ungrudging obedience and kept her vow. The Wife of Bath had railed at her husbands and badgered them and cajoled them : Griselda never lost her patience or her serenity. On its face, then, the tale appeared to the Pilgrims to be a dignified and scholarly narrative, derived from a great Italian clerk who was dead, and now ulitized by their fellow-pilgrim, the Clerk of Oxford, to demolish the heretical structure so boisterously reared by the Wife of Bath in her prologue and her tale.

But Chaucer's Clerk was a logician – 'unto logik hadde he longe ygo'. He knew perfectly well that the real moral of his story was

not that which his hearers would gather. He was aware that
Griselda was no model for literal imitation by ordinary woman-
kind. If so taken, his tale proved too much; it reduced his argument *ad absurdum*. If he let it go at that, he was playing into his
opponent's hands. Besides, he was a conscientious man. He could
not misrepresent the lesson which Petrarch had meant to teach
and had so clearly expressed – the lesson of submissive fortitude
under tribulation sent by God. Hence he does not fail to explain
this moral fully and in unmistakable terms, and to refer distinctly
to Petrarch as authority for it :

> And herkeneth what this auctor seith therfore.
>
> This storie is seyd, nat for that wyves sholde
> Folwen Griselde as in humilitee,
> For it were importable, though they wolde;
> But for that every wight, in his degree,
> Sholde be constant in adversitee
> As was Grisilde; therfor Petrark wryteth
> This storie, which with heigh style he endyteth.
>
> For, sith a womman was so pacient
> Un-to a mortal man, wel more us oghte
> Receyven al in gree that God us sent;
> For greet skile is, he preve that he wroghte.
> But he ne tempteth no man that he boghte,
> As seith seint Iame, if ye his pistel rede;
> He preveth folk al day, it is no drede,
>
> And suffreth us, as for our exercyse,
> With sharpe scourges of adversitee
> Ful ofte to be bete in sondry wyse;
> Nat for to knowe our wil, for certes he,
> Er we were born, knew al our freletee;
> And for our beste is al his governaunce :
> Lat us than live in vertuous suffrance.   (E. 1141–62)

Yet the Clerk has no idea of failing to make his point against
the Wife of Bath. And so, when the tale is finished and the proper

Petrarchan moral has been duly elaborated, he turns to the Wife (whom he has thus far sedulously refrained from addressing) and distinctly applies the material to the purpose of an ironical answer, of crushing force, to her whole heresy. There is nothing inappropriate to his character in this procedure. Quite the contrary. Clerks were always satirizing women – the Wife had said so herself – and this particular Clerk had, of course, no scruples against using the powerful weapon of irony in the service of religion and 'moral vertu'. In this instance, the satire is peculiarly poignant for two reasons : first, because it comes with all the suddenness of a complete change of tone (from high seriousness to biting irony, and from the impersonal to the personal); and secondly, because, in the tale which he has told, the Clerk has incidentally refuted a false statement of the Wife's, to the effect that

> 'It is an impossible
> That any clerk wol speke good of wyves,
> But if it be of holy seintes lyves,
> Ne of noon other womman never the mo.' (D. 688–91)

Clerks *can* 'speak well' of women (as our Clerk has shown), when women deserve it; and he now proceeds to show that they can likewise speak well (with biting irony) of women who do *not* deserve it – such women as the Wife of Bath and all her sect of domestic revolutionists.

It now appears that the form and spirit of the conclusion and the Envoy are not only appropriate to clerks in general, but peculiarly and exquisitely appropriate to this particular clerk under these particular circumstances and with this particular task in hand – the duty of defending the orthodox view of the relations between husband and wife against the heretical opinions of the Wife of Bath : 'One word in conclusion, gentlemen. There are few Griseldas now-a-days. Most women will break before they will bend. Our companion, the Wife of Bath, is an example, as she has told us herself. Therefore, though I cannot sing, I will recite a song in honor, not of Griselda (as you might perhaps expect), but of the Wife of Bath, of the sect of which she aspires to be a doctor, and of the life which she exemplifies in practice –

> '. . . . for the wyves love of Bathe,
>   Whos lif and al hir secte God mayntene
>   In high maistrye, and elles were it scathe.'   (E. 1170–2)

Her *way of life* – she had set it forth with incomparable zest. Her
sect – she was an heresiarch or at least a schismatic. The terms
are not accidental : they are chosen with all the discrimination
that befits a scholar and a rhetorician. They refer us back (as
definitely as the words 'Wife of Bath' themselves) to that prologue in which the Wife had stood forth as an opponent of the
orthodox view of subordination in marriage, as the upholder of
an heretical doctrine, and as the exultant practicer of what she
preached.

And then comes the Clerk's Envoy, the song that he recites
in honor of the Wife and her life and her sect, with its polished
lines, its ingenious rhyming, and its utter felicity of scholarly
diction. Nothing could be more in character. To whom in all the
world should such a masterpiece of rhetoric be appropriate
if not to the Clerk of Oxenford? It is a mock encomium,
a sustained ironical commendation of what the Wife has
taught :

'O noble wives, let no clerk ever have occasion to write such a
story of you as Petrarch once told me about Griselda. Follow your
great leader, the Wife of Bath. Rule your husbands, as she did; rail
at them, as she did; make them jealous, as she did; exert your-
selves to get lovers, as she did. And all this you must do whether you
are fair or foul [with manifest allusion to the problem of beauty or
ugliness presented in the Wife's story]. Do this, I say, and you will
fulfil the precepts that she has set forth and achieve the great end
which she has proclaimed as the object of marriage : that is, *you
will make your husbands miserable, as she did!*'

>   'Be ay of chere as light as leef on linde,
>   And lat him care and wepe and wringe and waille !'
>   (E. 1211–12)

And the Merchant (hitherto silent, but not from inattention)
catches up the closing words in a gust of bitter passion :

> 'Weping and wayling, care and other sorwe
> *I* know ynough on even and amorwe,'
> Quod the Merchant, 'and so don othere mo
> That wedded ben.' (E. 1213–16)

The Clerk's Envoy, then, is not only appropriate to his character and to the situation : it has also a marked dynamic value. For it is this ironical tribute to the Wife of Bath and her dogmas that, with complete dramatic inevitability, calls out the Merchant's *cri du cœur*. The Merchant has no thought of telling a tale at this moment. He is a stately and imposing person in his degree, by no means prone (so the Prologue informs us) to expose any holes there may be in his coat. But he is suffering a kind of emotional crisis. The poignant irony of the Clerk, following hard upon the moving story of a patient and devoted wife, is too much for him. He has just passed through his honeymoon (but two months wed !) and he has sought a respite from his thraldom under color of a pilgrimage to St. Thomas.

> 'I have a wyf, the worste that may be !' (E. 1218)

She would be an overmatch for the devil himself. He need not specify her evil traits : she is bad in every respect.

> 'There is a long and large difference
> Bitwix Grisildis grete pacience
> And of my wyf the passing crueltee.' (E. 1223–5)

The Host, as ever, is on the alert. He scents a good story :

> 'Sin ye so muchel knowen of that art,
> Ful hertely I pray yow tell us part.' (E. 1241–2)

The Merchant agrees, as in duty bound, for all the Pilgrims take care never to oppose the Host, lest he exact the heavy forfeit established as the penalty for rebellion. But he declines to relate his own experiences, thus leaving us to infer, if we choose – for nowhere is Chaucer's artistic reticence more effective – that his bride has proved false to him, like the wife of the worthy Knight of Lombardy.

Ans so the discussion of marriage is once more in full swing. The Wife of Bath, without intending it, has opened a debate in which the Pilgrims have become so absorbed that they will not leave it till the subject is 'bolted to the bran'.

The Merchant's Tale presents very noteworthy features, and has been much canvassed, though never (it seems) with due attention to its plain significance in the Human Comedy of the Canterbury Pilgrimage. In substance, it is nothing but a tale of bawdry, one of the most familiar of its class. There is nothing novel about it except its setting, but that is sufficiently remarkable. Compare the tale with any other version of the Pear-Tree Story – their name is legion – and its true significance comes out in striking fashion. The simple fabliau devised by its first author merely to make those laugh whose lungs are tickle o' the sere, is so expanded and overlaid with savage satire that it becomes a complete disquisition on marriage from the only point of view which is possible for the disenchanted Merchant. Thus considered, the cynicism of the Merchant's Tale is seen to be in no way surprising, and (to answer another kind of comment which this piece has evoked) in no sense expressive of Chaucer's own sentiments, or even of Chaucer's momentary mood. The cynicism is the Merchant's. It is no more Chaucer's than Iago's cynicism about love is Shakspere's.

In a word, the tale is the perfect expression of the Merchant's angry disgust at his own evil fate and at his folly in bringing that fate upon himself. Thus, its very lack of restraint – the savagery of the whole, which has revolted so many readers – is dramatically inevitable. The Merchant has schooled himself to hide his debts and his troubles. He is professionally an adept at putting a good face on matters, as every clever business man must be. But when once the barrier is broken, reticence is at an end. His disappointment is too fresh, his disillusion has been too abrupt, for him to measure his words. He speaks in a frenzy of contempt and hatred. The hatred is for women; the contempt is for himself and all other fools who will not take warning by example. For we should not forget that the satire is aimed at January rather than at May. That egotistical old dotard is less excusable than his young wife, and meets with less mercy at the Merchant's hands.

That the Merchant begins with an encomium on marriage

which is one of the most amazing instances of sustained irony in all literature, is not to be wondered at. In the first place, he is ironical because the Clerk has been ironical. Here the connection is remarkably close. The Merchant has fairly snatched the words out of the Clerk's mouth ('And lat him care and wepe and wringe and waile' – 'Weping and wayling, care and other sorwe'), and his mock encomium on the wedded state is a sequel to the Clerk's mock encomium on the Wife of Bath's life and all her sect. The spirit is different, but that is quite proper. For the Clerk's satire is the irony of a logician and a moral philosopher, the irony of the intellect and the ethical sense : the Merchant's is the irony of a mere man, it is the irony of passion and personal experience. The Clerk is a theorist – he looks at the subject from a point of philosophical detachment. The Merchant is an egotist – he feels himself to be the dupe whose folly he depicts. We may infer, if we like, that he was a man in middle age and that he had married a young wife.

There is plenty of evidence that the Merchant has been an attentive listener. One detects, for instance, a certain similarity between January and the Marquis Walter (different as they are) in that they have both shown themselves disinclined to marriage. Then again, the assertion that a wife is never weary of attending a sick husband –

> 'She nis nat wery him to love and serve,
> Thogh that he lye bedrede til he sterve' –   (E. 1291–2)

must have reminded the Pilgrims of poor Thomas, in the Summoner's Tale, whose wife's complaints to her spiritual visitor had precipitated so tremendous a sermon. But such things are trifles compared with the attention which the Merchant devotes to the Wife of Bath.

So far, in this act of Chaucer's Human Comedy, we have found that the Wife of Bath is, in a very real sense, the dominant figure. She has dictated the theme and inspired or instigated the actors; and she has always been at or near the center of the stage. It was a quarrel over her prologue that elicited the tale of the Friar and that of the Summoner. It was she who caused the Clerk to tell of Griselda – and the Clerk satirizes her in his Envoy. 'The art' of which the Host begs the Merchant to tell is *her* art, the art of marriage on which she has discoursed so learnedly. That the Merchant, therefore, should allude to her, quote her words, and finally mention her in plain terms is precisely what was to be expected.

The order and method of these approaches on the Merchant's part are exquisitely natural and dramatic. First there are touches, more or less palpable, when he describes the harmony of wedded life in terms so different from the Wife's account of what her husbands had to endure. Then – after a little – comes a plain enough allusion (put into January's mouth) to the Wife's character, to her frequent marriages, and to her inclination to marry again, old as she is:

> 'And eek thise olde widwes, God it wot,
> They conne so muchel craft on Wades boot,
> So muchel broken harm, whan that hem leste,
> That with hem sholde I never live in reste!
> For sondry scoles maken sotil clerkis:
> Wommen of many scoles half a clerk is.'   (E. 1423–8)

Surely the Wife of Bath was a woman of many schools, and her emulation of clerkly discussion had already been commented on by the Pardoner and the Friar. Next, the Merchant lets Justinus quote some of the Wife's very words – though without naming her: 'God may apply the trials of marriage, my dear January, to your salvation. Your wife may make you go straight to heaven without passing through purgatory.'

> 'Paraunter she may be your purgatorie!
> She may be Goddes mene, and Goddes whippe;
> Than shal your soule up to hevene skippe
> Swifter than doth an arwe out of the bowe.'
>
>   (E. 1670–3)

This is merely an adaptation of the Wife of Bath's own language in speaking of her fourth husband:

> 'By God, in erthe I was his purgatorie,
> For which I hope his soule be in glorie.'   (D. 489–90)

Compare also another phrase of hers, which Justinus echoes:
'Myself have been the whippe' (D. 175). And finally, when all
the Pilgrims are quite prepared for such a thing, there is a frank
citation of the Wife of Bath by name, with a reference to her exposition of marriage :

> 'My tale is doon : – for my wit is thinne.
> Beth not agast herof, my brother dere.
> *But lat us waden out of this matere:*
> *The Wyf of Bathe, if ye han understonde,*
> *Of marriage, which we have on honde,*
> *Declared hath ful wel in litel space.*
> Fareth now wel, God have yow in his grace.'
>
> (E. 1682–8)

Are the italicized lines a part of the speech of Justinus, or are
they interpolated by the Merchant, in his own person, in order to
shorten Justinus' harangue? Here is Professor Skeat's comment :
'These four parenthetical lines interrupt the story rather awkwardly. They obviously belong to the narrator, the Merchant,
as it is out of the question that Justinus had heard of the Wife of
Bath. Perhaps it is an oversight.' Now it makes no difference
whether we assign these lines to Justinus or to the Merchant, for
Justinus, as we have seen, has immediately before quoted the
Wife's very words, and he may as well mention her as repeat her
language. Either way, the lines are exquisitely in place. *Chaucer*
is not speaking, and there is no violation of dramatic propriety
on *his* part. It is not Chaucer who is telling the story. It is the
Merchant. And the Merchant is telling it as a part of the discussion which the Wife has started. It is dramatically proper, then,
that the Merchant should quote the Wife of Bath and that he
should refer to her. And it is equally proper, from the
dramatic point of view, for Chaucer to let the Merchant make
Justinus mention the Wife. In that case it is the Merchant – *not*
Chaucer – who chooses to have one of his characters fall out of his
part for a moment and make a 'local allusion'. Chaucer is responsible for making the *Merchant* speak in character; the
Merchant, in his turn, is responsible for *Justinus*. That the Merchant should put into the mouth of Justinus a remark that

Justinus could never have made is, then, not a slip on Chaucer's
part. On the contrary, it is a first-rate dramatic touch, for it is
precisely what the Merchant might well have done under the circumstances.

Nor should we forget the exquisitely comic discussion between
Pluto and Proserpine which the Merchant has introduced near
the end of his story. This dialogue is a flagrant violation of
dramatic propriety – not on Chaucer's part, however, but on the
Merchant's. And therein consists a portion of its merit. For the
Merchant is so eager to make his point that he rises superior to
all artistic rules. He is bent, not on giving utterance to a masterpiece of narrative construction, but on enforcing his lesson in
every possible way. And Chaucer is equally bent on making him
do it. Hence the Queen of the Lower World is brought in, discoursing in terms that befit the Wife of Bath (the presiding
genius of this part of the *Canterbury Tales*), and echoing some
of her very doctrines. The Wife had said :

> 'Thus shal ye speke and bere hem wrong on honde;
> For half so boldely can ther no man
> Swere and lyen as a womman can.
> I say nat this by wyves that ben wyse,
> But-if it be whan they hem misavyse.
> A wys wyf, if that she can hir good,
> Shal beren him on hond the cow is wood,
> And take witnesse of his owene mayde.'   (D. 226–33)

Now hear Proserpine :

> 'Now, by my modres sires soule I swere,
> That I shal yeven hir suffisaunt answere,
> And alle wommen after, for hir sake;
> That, though they be in any gilt ytake,
> With face bold they shulle hemself excuse,
> And bere hem doun that wolden hem accuse.
> For lakke of answere noon of hem shal dyen.
> Al hadde man seyn a thing with bothe his yen,
> Yit shul we wommen visage it hardily,
> And wepe, and swere, and chyde subtilly,
> So that ye men shul been as lewed as gees.'   (E. 2265–75)

And note that Pluto (who is as fond of citing authorities as the Wife's last husband) yields the palm of the discussion to Proserpine :

> 'Dame,' quod this Pluto, 'be no lenger wrooth;
> I yeve it up.'   (E. 2311-12)

This, too, was the experience of the Wife's husbands :

> 'I ne owe hem nat a word that is not quit.
> I broghte it so aboute by my wit
> That they moste yeve it up, as for the beste.'   (D. 425-7)

The tone and manner of the whole debate between Pluto and his queen are wildly absurd if regarded from the point of view of gods and goddesses, but in that very incongruity resides their dramatic propriety. What we have is not Pluto and Proserpine arguing with each other, but the Wife of Bath and one of her husbands attired for the nonce by the cynical Merchant in the external semblance of King Pluto and his dame.

The end of the Merchant's Tale does not bring the Marriage Chapter of the *Canterbury Tales* to a conclusion. As the Merchant had commented on the Clerk's Tale by speaking of his own wife, thus continuing the subject which the Wife had begun, so the Host comments on the Merchant's story by making a similar application :

> 'Ey, Goddes mercy,' seyde our Hoste tho,
> 'Now such a wyf I pray God kepe me fro!'   (E. 2419-20)

'See how women deceive us poor men, as the Merchant has shown us. However, *my* wife is true as any steel; but she is a shrew, and has plenty of other faults.' And just as the Merchant had referred expressly to the Wife of Bath, so also does the Host refer to her expressly : 'But I must not talk of these things. If I should, it would be told to her by some of this company. I need not say by whom, "sin wommen connen outen swich chaffare".' (E. 2419-40). Of course the Host points this remark by looking at the Wife of Bath. There are but three women in the company. Neither the highborn and dainty Prioress nor the pious nun who accompanies her is likely to gossip with Harry Baily's spouse. It is the Wife, a woman of the Hostess's own rank and temper, who will tattle when the party returns to the Tabard. And so we find the Wife of Bath still in the foreground, as she has been, in one way or another, for several thousand lines.

But now the Host thinks his companions have surely had enough of marriage. It is time they heard something of love, and with this in view he turns abruptly to the Squire, whom all the Pilgrims have come to know as 'a lovyer and a lusty bachiler'.

> 'Squier, com neer, if it your wille be,
> And sey somewhat of *love*; for certes ye
> Connen theron as muche as any man.'   (F. 1–3)

The significance of the emphasis on *love*, which is inevitable if the address to the Squire is read (as it should be) continuously with the Host's comments on marriage, is by no means accidental.

There is no psychology about the Squire's Tale – no moral or social or matrimonial theorizing. It is pure romance, in the mediaeval sense. The Host understood the charm of variety. He did not mean to let the discussion drain itself to the dregs.

But Chaucer's plan in this Act is not yet finished. There is still something lacking to a full discussion of the relations between husband and wife. We have had the wife who dominates her husband; the husband who dominates his wife; the young wife who befools her dotard January; the chaste wife who is a scold and stirs up strife. Each of these illustrates a different kind of marriage – but there is left untouched, so far, the ideal relation, that in which love continues and neither party to the contract strives for the mastery. Let this be set forth, and the series of views of wedded life begun by the Wife of Bath will be rounded off; the Marriage Act of the Human Comedy will be concluded. The Pilgrims may not be thinking of this; but there is at least *one* of them (as the sequel shows) who has the idea in his head. And who is he? The only pilgrims who have not already told their tales are the yeoman, two priests, the five tradesmen (haberdasher, carpenter, weaver, dyer, and tapicer), the parson, the plowman, the manciple, and the franklin. Of all these there is but one to whom a tale illustrating this ideal would not be inappropriate – the Franklin. To him, then, must Chaucer assign it, or leave the debate unfinished.

At this point, the dramatic action and interplay of characters are beyond all praise. The Franklin is not brought forward in formal fashion to address the company. His summons is incidental to the dialogue. No sooner has the Squire ended his chivalric romance, than the Franklin begins to compliment him :

> 'In feyth, squier, thou hast thee well yquit
> And gentilly. I preise wel thy wit,'
> Quod the frankeleyn, 'considering thy youthe.
> So felingly thou spekest, sir, I allow the !
> As to my doom, there is noon that is here
> Of eloquence that shal be thy pere,
> If that thou live : God yeve thee good chaunce
> And in vertu sende thee continuance,
> For of thy speche I have great deyntee !'   (F. 673–81)

'You have acquitted yourself well and *like a gentleman* !' *Gentillesse*, then, is what has most impressed the Franklin in the tale that he has just heard. And the reason for his enthusiasm soon appears. He is as we know, a rich freeholder, often sheriff in his county. Socially, he is not quite within the pale of the gentry, but he is the kind of man that mayhope to found a family, the kind of man from whose ranks the English nobility has been constantly recruited. And that such is his ambition comes out naïvely and with a certain pathos in what he goes on to say : 'I wish my son were like you' :

> 'I have a sone, and, by the Trinitee,
> I hadde lever than twenty pound worth lond,
> Though it right now were fallen in myn hond,
> He were a man of swich discrecioun
> As that ye been ! Fy on possessioun
> But-if a man be vertuous with-al !
> I have my sone snibbed, and yet shal,
> For he to vertu listeth nat entende;
> But for to pleye at dees, and to despende,

> And lese al that he hath, in his usage;
> And he hath lever talken with a page
> Than to commune with any gentil wight
> Ther he mighte lerne gentillesse aright.'   (F. 682–94)

It is the contrast between the Squire and his own son, in whom his hopes are centered, that has led the Franklin's thoughts to *gentillesse*, a subject which is ever in his mind.

But the Host interrupts him rudely: 'Straw for your gentillesse! It is your turn to entertain the company':

> 'Telle on thy tale withouten wordes mo!'   (F. 702)

The Franklin is, of course, very polite in his reply to this rough and unexpected command. Like the others, he is on his guard against opposing the Host and incurring the forfeit:

> 'I wol yow nat contrarien in no wise,
> As fer as that my wittes wol suffise.'   (F. 705–6)

Here, then, as in the case of the Merchant, the Host has taken advantage of a spontaneous remark on some Pilgrim's part to demand a story. Yet the details of the action are quite different. On the previous occasion, the Merchant is requested to go on with an account of his marriage, since he has already begun to talk about it; and, though he declines to speak further of his own troubles, he does continue to discuss and illustrate wedlock from his own point of view. In the present instance, on the contrary, the Host repudiates the topic of *gentillesse*, about which the Franklin is discoursing to the Squire. He bids him drop the subject and tell a story. The Franklin pretends to be compliant, but after all, he has his own way. Indeed, he takes delicate vengeance on the Host by telling a tale which thrice exemplifies *gentillesse* – on the part of a knight, a squire, and a clerk. Thus he finishes his interrupted compliment to the Squire, and incidentally honors two other Pilgrims who have seemed to him to possess the quality that he values so highly. He proves, too, both that *gentillesse* is an entertaining topic and that it is not (as the Host has roughly intimated) a theme which he, the Franklin, is ill-equipped to handle.

For the Franklin's Tale is a gentleman's story, and he tells it like a gentleman. It is derived, he tells us, from 'thise olde *gentil* Britons' (F. 709–15). Dorigen lauds Arveragus' *gentillesse* toward her in refusing to insist on soveraynetee in marriage (F. 754–5). Aurelius is deeply impressed by the knight's *gentillesse* in allowing the lady to keep her word, and emulates it by releasing her:

> Fro his lust yet were him lever abyde
> Than doon so heigh a churlish wrecchednesse
> Agaynes franchyse and alle gentillesse.   (F. 1522–4)

> I see his grete gentillesse.   (F. 1527)

> Thus can a squyer don a gentil dede
> As wel as can a knyght, withouten drede.   (F. 1543–4)

> Arveragus, of gentillesse,
> Had lever dye in sorwe and in distresse
> Than that his wyf were of her trouthe fals.
> (F. 1595–7)

And finally, the clerk releases Aurelius, from the same motive of generous emulation:

> This philosophre answerde, 'Leve brother,
> Everich of yow dide gentilly til other.
> Thou art a squyer, and he is a knight;
> But God forbede, for his blisful might,
> But-if a clerk coude doon a gentil dede
> As wel as any of yow, it is no drede!'   (F. 1607–12)

Thus it appears that the dramatic impulse to the telling of the Franklin's Tale is to be found in the relations among the Pilgrims and in the effect that they have upon each other – in other words, in the circumstances, the situation, and the interplay of character.

It has sometimes been thought that the story, either in subject or in style, is too fine for the Franklin to tell. But this objection Chaucer foresaw and forestalled. The question is not whether this tale, thus told, would be appropriate to a typical or 'average' fourteenth-century franklin. The question is whether it is appropriate to this particular Franklin, under these particular circumstances, and at this particular juncture. And to this question there can be but one answer. Chaucer's Franklin is an individual, not a mere type-specimen. He is rich, ambitious socially, and profoundly interested in the matter of *gentillesse* for personal and family reasons. He is trying to bring up his son as a gentleman, and his position as 'St. Julian in his country' has brought him into intimate association with first-rate models. He has, under the special circumstances, every motive to tell a gentleman's story and to tell it like a gentleman. He is speaking under the immediate influence of his admiration for the Squire and of his sense of the inferiority of his own son. If we choose to conceive the Franklin as a mediaeval Squire Western and then to allege that he could not possibly have told such a story, we are making the difficulty for ourselves. We are considering – not Chaucer's Franklin (whose character is to be inferred not merely from the description in the General Prologue but from all the other evidence that the poet provides) – not Chaucer's Franklin, but somebody quite different, somebody for whom Chaucer has no kind of responsibility.

In considering the immediate occasion of the Franklin's Tale, we have lost sight for a moment of the Wife of Bath. But she was not absent from the mind of the Franklin. The proper subject of his tale, as we have seen, is *gentillesse*. Now that (as well as marriage) was a subject on which the Wife of Bath had descanted at some length. Her views are contained in the famous harangue delivered by the lady to her husband on the wedding night : 'But for ye speken of swich gentillesse', etc. (D. 1109–76). Many readers have perceived that this portentous curtain-lecture clogs the story, and some have perhaps wished it away, good as it is in itself. For it certainly seems to be out of place on lips of the *fée*. But its insertion is (as usual in such cases) exquisitely appropriate to the teller of the tale, the Wife of Bath, who cannot help dilating on subjects which interest her, and who has had the advantage of learned society in the person of her fifth husband. Perhaps no *fée* would have talked thus to her knightly bridegroom on such an occasion; but it is quite in character for the Wife of Bath to use the *fée* (or anybody else) as a mouthpiece for her own ideas, as the Merchant had used Proserpine to point his satire. Thus the references to Dante, Valerius, Seneca, Boethius, and Juvenal – so deliciously absurd on the lips of a *fée* of King Arthur's time – are perfectly in place when we remember who it is that is reporting the monologue. The Wife was a citer of authorities – she makes the *fée* cite authorities. How comical this is the Wife did not know, but Chaucer knew, and if we think he did not, it is our own fault for not observing how dramatic in spirit is the *Canterbury Tales*.

A considerable passage in the curtain-lecture is given to the proposition that 'such gentillesse as is descended out of old richesse' is of no value: 'Swich arrogance is not worth an hen' (D. 1109 ff.). These sentiments the Franklin echoes:

> 'Fy on possessioun
> But-if a man be vertuous withal!'   (F. 686–7)

But, whether or not the Wife's digression on *gentillesse* is lingering in the Franklin's mind (as I am sure it is), one thing is perfectly clear: the Franklin's utterances on marriage are spoken under the influence of the discussion which the Wife has precipitated. In other words, though everybody else imagines that the subject has been finally dismissed by the Host when he calls on the Squire for a tale of *love*, it has no more been dismissed in fact than when the Friar attempted to dismiss it at the beginning of his tale. For the Franklin has views, and he means to set them forth. He possesses, as he thinks, the true solution of the whole difficult problem. And that solution he embodies in his tale of *gentillesse*.

The introductory part of the Franklin's Tale sets forth a theory of the marriage relation quite different from anything that has so far emerged in the debate. And this theory the Franklin arrives at by taking into consideration both *love* (which, as we remember, was the subject that the Host had bidden the Squire treat of) and *gentillesse* (which is to be the subject of his own story).

Arveragus had of course been obedient to his lady during the period of courtship, for obedience was well understood to be the duty of a lover. Finally, she consented to marry him –

> To take him for hir housbande and hir lord,
> Of swich lordshipe as men han over her wyves.
>
> (F. 742–3)

Marriage, then, according to the orthodox doctrine (as held by Walter and Griselda) was to change Arveragus from the lady's servant to her master. But Arveragus was an enlightened and chivalric gentleman, and he promised the lady that he would never assert his marital authority, but would content himself with the mere name of sovereignty, continuing to be her servant and lover as before. This he did because he thought it would ensure the happiness of their wedded life.

> And for to lede the more in blisse hir lyves,
> Of his free wil he swoor hir as a knight,
> That never in al his lyf he, day ne night,
> Ne sholde up-on him take no maistrye
> Agayn hir wil, ne kythe hir ialousye,
> But hir obeye, and folwe hir wil in al,
> As any lovere to his lady shal;
> Save that the name of soveraynetee,
> That wolde he have for shame of his degree.
>
> (F. 744–52)

But, just as Arveragus was no disciple of the Marquis Walter, so Dorigen was not a member of the sect of the Wife of Bath. She promised her husband obedience and fidelity in return for his *gentillesse* in renouncing his sovereign rights.

> She thanked him, and with ful greet humblesse
> She seyde, 'Sire, sith, of your gentillesse,
> Ye profre me to have so large a reyne,
> Ne wolde never God bitwixe us tweyne,
> As in my gilt, were outher werre or stryf.
> Sir, I wol be your humble trewe wyf,
> Have heer my trouthe, till that myn herte breste.'
>
> (F. 753–9)

This, then, is the Franklin's solution of the whole puzzle of matrimony, and it is a solution that depends upon love and *gentillesse* on both sides. But he is not content to leave the matter in this purely objective condition. He is determined that there shall be no misapprehension in the mind of any Pilgrim as to his purpose. He wishes to make it perfectly clear that he is definitely and formally offering this theory as the only satisfactory basis of happy married life. And he accordingly comments on the relations between his married lovers with fulness, and with manifest reference to certain things that the previous debaters have said.

The arrangement, he tells the Pilgrims, resulted in 'quiet and rest' for both Arveragus and Dorigen. And, he adds, it is the only arrangement which will ever enable two persons to live together in love and amity. Friends must 'obey each other if they wish to hold company long'.

> 'Love wol nat ben constreyned by maistrye;
> Whan maistrie comth, the god of love anon
> Beteth hise winges, and farewel! he is gon!
> Love is a thing as any spirit free;
> Wommen of kinde desiren libertee,
> And nat to ben constreyned as a thral;
> And so don men, if I soth seyen shal.
> Loke who that is most pacient in love,
> He is at his avantage al above.
> Pacience is an heigh vertu certeyn;
> For it venquisseth, as thise clerkes seyn,
> Thinges that rigour sholde never atteyne.
> For every word men may nat chyde or pleyne.
> Lerneth to suffre, or elles, so moot I goon,
> Ye shul it lerne, wher-so ye wole or noon.'   (F. 764-78)

Hence it was that this wise knight promised his wife 'suffraunce' and that she promised him never to abuse his goodness.

> Heer may men seen an humble wys accord;
> Thus hath she take hir servant and hir lord,
> Servant in love, and lord in mariage;
> Than was he bothe in lordship and servage;

> Servage? nay, but in lordshipe above,
> Sith he hath bothe his lady and his love;
> His lady, certes, and his wyf also,
> The which that lawe of love accordeth to.   (F. 791-8)

The result, the Franklin adds, was all that could be desired. The knight lived 'in blisse and in solas'. And then the Franklin adds an encomium on the happiness of true marriage :

> 'Who coude telle, but he had wedded be,
> The ioye, the ese, and the prosperitee
> That is bitwixe an housbonde and his wyf?'   (F. 803-5)

This encomium echoes the language of the Merchant :

> 'A wyf! a Seinte Marie! *benedicite!*
> How mighte a man han any adversitee
> That hath a wyf? Certes, I can nat seye!
> The blisse which that is bitwixe hem tweye
> Ther may no tonge telle or herte thinke.' (E. 1337-41)

The Franklin's praise of marriage is sincere; the Merchant's had been savagely ironical. The Franklin, we observe, is answering the Merchant, and he answers him in the most effective way – by repeating his very words.

And just as in the Merchant's Tale we noted that the Merchant has enormously expanded the simple *fabliau* that he had to tell, inserting all manner of observations on marriage which are found in no other version of the Pear-Tree Story, so also we find that the Franklin's exposition of the ideal marriage relation (including the pact between Arveragus and Dorigen) is all his own, occurring in none of the versions that precede Chaucer. These facts are of the very last significance. No argument is necessary to enforce their meaning.

It is hardly worth while to indicate the close connection between this and that detail of the Franklin's exposition and certain points that have come out in the discussion as conducted by his predecessors in the debate. His repudiation of the Wife of Bath's doctrine that men should be 'governed by their wives' is express, as well as his rejection of the opposite theory. Neither party should lose his liberty; neither the husband nor the wife should be a thrall. Patience (which clerks celebrate as a high virtue) should be mutual, not, as in the Clerk's Tale, all on one side. The husband is to be both servant and lord – servant in love and lord in marriage. Such servitude is true lordship. Here there is a manifest allusion to the words of Walter's subjects in the Clerk's Tale:

> That blisful yok
> Of sovereynetee, noght of servyse,   (E. 113–14)

as well as to Walter's rejoinder:

> 'I me reioysed of my libertee,
> That selde tyme is founde in mariage;
> Ther I was free, I moot been in servage.'
>
> (E. 145–7)

It was the regular theory of the Middle Ages that the highest type of chivalric love was incompatible with marriage, since marriage brings in mastery, and mastery and love cannot abide together. This view the Franklin boldly challenges. Love *can* be consistent with marriage, he declares. Indeed, without love (and perfect, *gentle* love) marriage is sure to be a failure. The difficulty about mastery vanishes when mutual love and forbearance are made the guiding principles of the relation between husband and wife.

The soundness of the Franklin's theory, he declares, is proved by his tale. For the marriage of Arveragus and Dorigen was a brilliant success:

> Arveragus and Dorigene his wyf
> In sovereyn blisse leden forth hir lyf.
> Never eft ne was ther angre hem bitwene;
> He cherisseth hir as though she were a quene;
> And she was to him trewe for evermore.
> Of this two folk ye gete of me na-more.   (F. 1551–6)

Thus the whole debate has been brought to a satisfactory conclusion, and the Marriage Act of the Human Comedy ends with the conclusion of the Franklin's Tale.

Those readers who are eager to know what Chaucer thought about marriage may feel reasonably content with the inference that may be drawn from his procedure. The Marriage Group of Tales begins with the Wife of Bath's Prologue and ends with the Franklin's Tale. There is no connection between the Wife's Prologue and the group of stories that precedes; there is no connection between the Franklin's Tale and the group that follows. Within the Marriage Group, on the contrary, there is close connection throughout. That act is a finished act. It begins and ends an elaborate debate. We need not hesitate, therefore, to accept the solution which the Franklin offers as that which Geoffrey Chaucer the man accepted for his own part. Certainly it is a solution that does him infinite credit. A better has never been devised or imagined.

S O U R C E : *Modern Philology*, IX (1911–12)

E. T. Donaldson

CHAUCER THE PILGRIM (1954)

Verisimilitude in a work of fiction is not without its attendant dangers, the chief of which is that the responses it stimulates in the reader may be those appropriate not so much to an imaginative production as to an historical one or to a piece of reporting. History and reporting are, of course, honorable in themselves, but if we react to a poet as though he were an historian or a reporter, we do him somewhat less than justice. I am under the impression that many readers, too much influenced by Chaucer's brilliant verisimilitude, tend to regard his famous pilgrimage to Canterbury as significant not because it is a great fiction, but because it seems to be a remarkable record of a fourteenth-century pilgrimage. A remarkable record it may be, but if we treat it too narrowly as such there are going to be certain casualties among the elements that make up the fiction. Perhaps first among these elements is the fictional reporter, Chaucer the pilgrim, and the role he plays in the Prologue to the *Canterbury Tales* and in the links between them. I think it time that he was rescued from the comparatively dull record of history and put back into his poem. He is not really Chaucer the poet – nor, for that matter, is either the poet, or the poem's protagonist, that Geoffrey Chaucer frequently mentioned in contemporary historical records as a distinguished civil servant, but never as a poet. The fact that these are three separate entities does not, naturally, exclude the probability – or rather the certainty – that they bore a close resemblance to one another, and that, indeed, they frequently got together in the same body. But that does not excuse us from keeping them distinct from one another, difficult as their close resemblance makes our task.

The natural tendency to confuse one thing with its like is perhaps best represented by a school of Chaucerian criticism, now outmoded, that pictured a single Chaucer under the guise of a wide-eyed, jolly, rolypoly little man who, on fine Spring mornings, used to get up early, while the dew was still on the grass, and go look at daisies. A charming portrait, this, so charming, indeed, that it was sometimes able to maintain itself to the exclusion of any Chaucerian other side. It has every reason to be charming, since it was lifted almost *in toto* from the version Chaucer gives of himself in the Prologue to the *Legend of Good Women*, though I imagine it owes some of its popularity to a rough analogy with Wordsworth – a sort of *Legend of Good Poets*. It was this version of Chaucer that Kittredge, in a page of great importance to Chaucer criticism, demolished with his assertion that 'a naïf Collector of Customs would be a paradoxical monster'. He might well have added that a naïve creator of old January would be even more monstrous.

Kittredge's pronouncement cleared the air, and most of us now accept the proposition that Chaucer was sophisticated as readily as we do the proposition that the whale is a mammal. But unhappily, now that we've got rid of the naïve fiction, it is easy to fall into the opposite sort of mistake. This is to envision, in the *Canterbury Tales*, a highly urbane, literal-historical Chaucer setting out from Southwark on a specific day of a specific year (we even argue somewhat acrimoniously about dates and routes), in company with a group of persons who existed in real life and whom Chaucer, his reporter's eye peeled for every idiosyncrasy, determined to get down on paper – down, that is, to the last wart – so that books might be written identifying them. Whenever this accurate reporter says something especially fatuous – which is not infrequently – it is either ascribed to an opinion peculiar to the Middle Ages (sometimes very peculiar), or else Chaucer's tongue is said to be in his cheek.

Now a Chaucer with tongue-in-cheek is a vast improvement over a simple-minded Chaucer when one is trying to define the whole man, but it must lead to a loss of critical perception, and in particular to a confused notion of Chaucerian irony, to see in the Prologue a reporter who is acutely aware of the significance of what he sees but who sometimes, for ironic emphasis, interprets the evidence presented by his observation in a fashion directly contrary to what we expect. The proposition ought to be expressed in reverse : the reporter is, usually, acutely unaware of the significance of what he sees, no matter how sharply he sees it. He is, to be sure, permitted his lucid intervals, but in general he is the victim of the poet's pervasive – not merely sporadic – irony. And as such he is also the chief agent by which the poet achieves his wonderfully complex, ironic, comic, serious vision of a world which is but a devious and confused, infinitely various pilgrimage to a certain shrine. It is, as I hope to make clear, a good deal more than merely fitting that our guide on such a pilgrimage should be a man of such naïveté as the Chaucer who tells the tale of 'Sir Thopas.' Let us accompany him a little distance.

It is often remarked that Chaucer really liked the Prioress very much, even though he satirized her gently – very gently. But this is an understatement: Chaucer the pilgrim may not be said merely to have liked the Prioress very much – he thought she was utterly charming. In the first twenty-odd lines of her portrait (A. 118 ff.) he employs, among other superlatives, the adverb *ful* seven times. Middle English uses *ful* where we use *very,* and if one translates the beginning of the portrait into a kind of basic English (which is what, in a way, it really is), one gets something like this: 'There was also a Nun, a Prioress, who was very sincere and modest in the way she smiled; her biggest oath was only "By saint Loy"; and she was called Madame Eglantine. She sang the divine service very well, intoning it in her nose very prettily, and she spoke French very nicely and elegantly' – and so on, down to the last gasp of sentimental appreciation. Indeed, the Prioress may be said to have transformed the rhetoric into something not unlike that of a very bright kindergarten child's descriptive theme. In his reaction to the Prioress Chaucer the pilgrim resembles another – if less – simple-hearted enthusiast: the Host, whose summons to her to tell a tale must be one of the politest speeches in the language. Not 'My lady prioresse, a tale now!' but, 'as curteisly as it had been a mayde',

> My lady Prioresse, by youre leve,
> So that I wiste I sholde yow nat greve,
> I wolde demen that ye tellen sholde
> A tale next, if so were that ye wolde.
> Now wol ye vouche sauf, my lady deere? (B.² 1637–41)

Where the Prioress reduced Chaucer to superlatives, she reduces the Host to subjunctives.

There is no need here to go deeply into the Prioress. Eileen Power's illustrations from contemporary episcopal records show with what extraordinary economy the portrait has been packed with abuses typical of fourteenth-century nuns. The abuses, to be sure, are mostly petty, but it is clear enough that the Prioress, while a perfect lady, is anything but a perfect nun; and attempts to whitewash her, of which there have been many, can only proceed from an innocence of heart equal to Chaucer the pilgrim's and undoubtedly directly influenced by it. For he, of course, is quite swept away by her irrelevant *sensibilité*, and as a result misses much of the point of what he sees. No doubt he feels that he has come a long way, socially speaking, since his encounter with the Black Knight in the forest, and he knows, or thinks he knows, a little more of what it's all about : in this case it seems to be mostly about good manners, kindness to animals, and female charm. Thus it has been argued that Chaucer's appreciation for the Prioress as a sort of heroine of courtly romance *manquée* actually reflects the sophistication of the living Chaucer, an urbane man who cared little whether amiable nuns were good nuns. But it seems a curious form of sophistication that permits itself to babble superlatives; and indeed, if this is sophistication, it is the kind generally seen in the least experienced people – one that reflects a wide-eyed wonder at the glamor of the great world. It is just what one might expect of a bourgeois exposed to the splendors of high society, whose values, such as they are, he eagerly accepts. And that is precisely what Chaucer the pilgrim is, and what he does.

If the Prioress's appeal to him is through elegant femininity, the Monk's is through imposing virility. Of this formidable and important prelate the pilgrim does not say, with Placebo,

> I woot wel that my lord kan moore than I :
> What that he seith, I holde it ferme and stable,
>
> (E. 1498–9)

but he acts Placebo's part to perfection. He is as impressed with the Monk as the Monk is, and accepts him on his own terms and at face value, never sensing that those terms imply complete condemnation of Monk *qua* Monk. The Host is also impressed by the Monk's virility, but having no sense of Placebonian propriety (he is himself a most virile man) he makes indecent jokes about it. This, naturally, offends the pilgrim's sense of decorum : there is a note of deferential commiseration in his comment, 'This worthy Monk took al in pacience' (B. 3155). Inevitably when the Monk establishes hunting as the highest activity of which religious man is capable, 'I seyde his opinion was good' (A. 183). As one of the pilgrim's spiritual heirs was later to say, Very like a whale; but not, of course, like a fish out of water.

Wholehearted approval for the values that important persons subscribe to is seen again in the portrait of the Friar. This amounts to a prolonged gratulation for the efficiency the deplorable Hubert shows in undermining the fabric of the Church by turning St. Francis' ideal inside out :

> Ful swetely herde he confessioun,
> And pleasaunt was his absolucioun.   (A. 221–2)

> For unto swich a worthy man as he
> Acorded nat, as by his facultee,
> To have with sike lazars aqueyntaunce.   (A. 243–5)

It is sometimes said that Chaucer did not like the Friar. Whether Chaucer the man would have liked such a Friar is, for our present purposes, irrelevant. But if the pilgrim does not unequivocally express his liking for him, it is only because in his humility he does not feel that, with important people, his own likes and dislikes are material : such importance is its own reward, and can gain no lustre from Geoffrey, who, when the Friar is attacked by the Summoner, is ready to show him the same sympathy he shows the Monk (see D. 1265–7).

Once he has finished describing the really important people on the pilgrimage the pilgrim's tone changes, for he can now concern himself with the bourgeoisie, members of his own class for whom he does not have to show such profound respect. In-

deed, he can even afford to be a little patronizing at times, and to
have his little joke at the expense of the too-busy lawyer. But
such indirect assertions of his own superiority do not prevent
him from giving substance to the old cynicism that the only
motive recognized by the middle class is the profit motive, for his
interest and admiration for the bourgeois pilgrims is centered
mainly in their material prosperity and their ability to increase it.
He starts, properly enough, with the out-and-out money-
grubber, the Merchant, and after turning aside for that *lusus
naturae*, the non-profit-motivated Clerk, proceeds to the
Lawyer, who, despite the pilgrim's little joke, is the best and
best-paid ever; the Franklin, twenty-one admiring lines on ap-
petite, so expensively catered to; the Gildsmen, cheered up the
social ladder, 'For catel hadde they ynogh and rente' (A. 373);
and the Physician, again the best and richest. In this series the
portrait of the Clerk is generally held to be an ideal one, containing no irony; but while it is ideal, it seems to reflect the pilgrim's
sense of values in his joke about the Clerk's failure to make
money: is not this still typical of the half-patronizing, half-ad-
miring *un*understanding that practical men of business display towards academics? But in any case the portrait is a fine
companion-piece for those in which material prosperity is the
main interest both of the characters described and of the
describer.

Of course, this is not the sole interest of so gregarious – if shy –
a person as Chaucer the pilgrim. Many of the characters have
the additional advantage of being good companions, a faculty
that receives a high valuation in the Prologue. To be good company might, indeed, atone for certain serious defects of character.
Thus the Shipman, whose callous cruelty is duly noted, seems
fairly well redeemed in the assertion, 'And certeinly he was a
good felawe' (A. 395). At this point an uneasy sensation that
even tongue-in-cheek irony will not compensate for the lengths
to which Chaucer is going in his approbation of this sinister
seafarer sometimes causes editors to note that *a good felawe*
means 'a rascal'. But I can find no evidence that it ever meant a
rascal. Of course, all tritely approbative expressions enter easily
into ironic connotation, but the phrase *means* a good companion,
which is just what Chaucer means. And if, as he says of the

Shipman, 'Of nyce conscience took he no keep' (A. 398), Chaucer the pilgrim was doing the same with respect to him.

Nothing that has been said has been meant to imply that the pilgrim was unable to recognize, and deplore, a rascal when he saw one. He could, provided the rascality was situated in a member of the lower classes and provided it was, in any case, somewhat wider than a barn door : Miller, Manciple, Reeve, Summoner, and Pardoner are all acknowledged to be rascals. But rascality generally has, after all, the laudable object of making money, which gives it a kind of validity; if not dignity. These portraits, while in them the pilgrim, prioress-like conscious of the finer aspects of life, does deplore such matters as the Miller's indelicacy of language, contain a note of ungrudging admiration for efficient thievery. It is perhaps fortunate for the pilgrim's reputation as a judge of men that he sees through the Pardoner, since it is the Pardoner's particular tragedy that, except in Church, every one can see through him at a glance; but in Church he remains to the pilgrim 'a noble ecclesiaste' (A. 708). The equally repellent Summoner, a practising bawd, is partially redeemed by his also being a good fellow, 'a gentil harlot and a kynde' (A. 647), and by the fact that for a moderate bribe he will neglect to summon : the pilgrim apparently subscribes to the popular definition of the best policeman as the one who acts the least policely.

Therefore Chaucer is tolerant, and has his little joke about the Summoner's small Latin – a very small joke, though one of the most amusing aspects of the pilgrim's character is the pleasure he takes in his own jokes, however small. But the Summoner goes too far when he cynically suggests that purse is the Archdeacon's hell, causing Chaucer to respond with a fine show of righteous respect for the instruments of spiritual punishment. The only trouble is that his enthusiastic defense of them carries *him* too far, so that after having warned us that excommunication will indeed damn our souls –

> But wel I woot he lyed right in dede :
> Of cursyng oghte ech gilty man him drede,
> For curs wol slee right as assoillyng savith –
>
> (A. 659–61)

he goes on to remind us that it will also cause considerable inconvenience to our bodies: 'And also war hym of a *Significavit*' (A. 662). Since a *Significavit* is the writ accomplishing the imprisonment of the excommunicate, the line provides perhaps the neatest – and most misunderstood – Chaucerian anticlimax in the Prologue.

I have avoided mentioning, hitherto, the pilgrim's reactions to the really good people on the journey – the Knight, the Parson, the Plowman. One might reasonably ask how his uncertain sense of values may be reconciled with the enthusiasm he shows for their rigorous integrity. The question could, of course, be shrugged off with a remark on the irrelevance to art of exact consistency, even to art distinguished by its verisimilitude. But I am not sure that there is any basic inconsistency. It is the nature of the pilgrim to admire all kinds of superlatives, and the fact that he often admires superlatives devoid of – or opposed to – genuine virtue does not inhibit his equal admiration for virtue incarnate. He is not, after all, a bad man; he is, to place him in his literary tradition, merely an average man, or mankind: *homo*, not very *sapiens* to be sure, but with the very best intentions, making his pilgrimage through the world in search of what is good, and showing himself, too frequently, able to recognize the good only when it is spectacularly so. Spenser's Una glows with a kind of spontaneous incandescence, so that the Red Cross Knight, mankind in search of holiness, knows her as good; but he thinks that Duessa is good, too. Virtue concretely embodied in Una or the Parson presents no problems to the well-intentioned observer, but in a world consisting mostly of imperfections, accurate evaluations are difficult for a pilgrim who, like mankind, is naïve. The pilgrim's ready appreciation for the virtuous characters is perhaps the greatest tribute that could be paid to their virtue, and their spiritual simplicity is, I think, enhanced by the intellectual simplicity of the reporter.

The pilgrim belongs, of course, to a very old – and very new – tradition of the fallible first person singular. His most exact modern counterpart is perhaps Lemuel Gulliver who, in his search for the good, failed dismally to perceive the difference between the pursuit of reason and the pursuits of reasonable horses: one may be sure that the pilgrim would have whinnied with the best of them. In his own century he is related to Long Will of *Piers Plowman*, a more explicit seeker after the good, but just as unswerving in his inability correctly to evaluate what he sees. Another kinsman is the protagonist of the *Pearl*, mankind whose heart is set on a transitory good that has been lost – who, for very natural reasons, confuses earthly with spiritual values. Not entirely unrelated is the protagonist of Gower's *Confessio Amantis*, an old man seeking for an impossible earthly love that seems to him the only good. And in more subtle fashion there is the teller of Chaucer's story of *Troilus and Cressida*, who, while not a true protagonist, performs some of the same functions. For this unloved 'servant of the servants of love' falls in love with Cressida so persuasively that almost every male reader of the poem imitates him, so that we all share the heartbreak of Troilus and sometimes, in the intensity of our heartbreak, fail to learn what Troilus did. Finally, of course, there is Dante of the *Divine Comedy*, the most exalted member of the family and perhaps the immediate original of these other first-person pilgrims.

Artistically the device of the *persona* has many functions, so integrated with one another that to try to sort them out produces both oversimplification and distortion. The most obvious, with which this paper has been dealing – distortedly, is to present a vision of the social world imposed on one of the moral world. Despite their verisimilitude most, if not all, of the characters described in the Prologue are taken directly from stock and recur again and again in medieval literature. Langland in his own Prologue and elsewhere depicts many of them : the hunting monk, the avaricious friar, the thieving miller, the hypocritical pardoner, the unjust stewards, even, in little, the all-too-human nun. But while Langland uses the device of the *persona* with considerable skill in the conduct of his allegory, he uses it hardly at all in portraying the inhabitants of the social world : these are described directly, with the poet's own voice. It was left to Chaucer to turn the ancient stock satirical characters into real people assembled for a pilgrimage, and to have them described, with all their traditional faults upon them, by another pilgrim who records faithfully each fault without, for the most part, recognizing that it is a fault and frequently felicitating its possessor for possessing it. One result – though not the only result –

is a moral realism much more significant than the literary realism which is a part of it and for which it is sometimes mistaken; this moral realism discloses a world in which humanity is prevented by its own myopia, the myopia of the describer, from seeing what the dazzlingly attractive externals of life really represent. In most of the analogues mentioned above the fallible first person receives, at the end of the book, the education he has needed: the pilgrim arrives somewhere. Chaucer never completed the *Canterbury Tales*, but in the Prologue to the Parson's Tale he seems to have been doing, rather hastily, what his contemporaries had done: when, with the sun nine-and-twenty degrees from the horizon, the twenty-nine pilgrims come to a certain – unnamed – *thropes ende* (I. 12), then the pilgrimage seems no longer to have Canterbury as its destination, but rather, I suspect, the Celestial City of which the Parson speaks.

If one insists that Chaucer was not a moralist but a comic writer (a distinction without a difference), then the device of the *persona* may be taken primarily as serving comedy. It has been said earlier that the several Chaucers must have inhabited one body, and in that sense the fictional first person is no fiction at all. In an oral tradition of literature the first person probably always shared the personality of his creator: thus Dante of the *Divine Comedy* was physically Dante the Florentine; the John Gower of the *Confessio* was also Chaucer's friend John Gower; and Long Will was, I am sure, someone named William Langland, who was both long and wilful. And it is equally certain that Chaucer the pilgrim, 'a popet in an arm t'enbrace' (B.[2] 1891), was in every physical respect Chaucer the man, whom one can imagine reading his work to a courtly audience, as in the portrait appearing in one of the MSS. of *Troilus*. One can imagine also the delight of the audience which heard the Prologue read in this way, and which was aware of the similarities and dissimilarities between Chaucer, the man before them, and Chaucer the pilgrim, both of whom they could see with simultaneous vision. The Chaucer they knew was physically, one gathers, a little ludicrous; a bourgeois, but one who was known as a practical and successful man of the court; possessed perhaps of a certain diffidence of manner, reserved, deferential to the socially imposing persons with whom he was associated; a bit absent-minded, but affable and, one supposes, very good company – a good fellow; sagacious and highly perceptive. This Chaucer was telling them of another who, lacking some of his chief qualities, nevertheless possessed many of his characteristics, though in a different state of balance, and each one probably distorted just enough to become laughable without becoming unrecognizable: deference into a kind of snobbishness, affability into an over-readiness to please, practicality into Babbittry, perception into inspection, absence of mind into dimness of wit; a Chaucer acting in some respects just as Chaucer himself might have acted but unlike his creator the kind of man, withal, who could mistake a group of stock satirical types for living persons endowed with all sorts of superlative qualities. The constant interplay of these two Chaucers must have produced an exquisite and most ingratiating humor – as, to be sure, it still does. This comedy reaches its superb climax when Chaucer the pilgrim, resembling in so many ways Chaucer the poet, can answer the Host's demand for a story only with a rhyme he 'lerned longe agoon' (B.² 1899) – 'Sir Thopas', which bears the same complex relation to the kind of romance it satirizes and to Chaucer's own poetry as Chaucer the pilgrim does to the pilgrims he describes and to Chaucer the poet.

Earlier in this paper I proved myself no gentleman (though I hope a scholar) by being rude to the Prioress, and hence to the many who like her and think that Chaucer liked her too. It is now necessary to retract. Undoubtedly Chaucer the man would, like his fictional representative, have found her charming and looked on her with affection. To have got on so well in so changeable a world Chaucer must have got on well with the people in it, and it is doubtful that one may get on with people merely by pretending to like them: one's heart has to be in it. But the third entity, Chaucer the poet, operates in a realm which is above and subsumes those in which Chaucer the man and Chaucer the pilgrim have their being. In this realm prioresses may be simultaneously evaluated as marvelously amiable ladies and as prioresses. In his poem the poet arranges for the moralist to define austerely what ought to be and for his fictional representative – who, as the representative of all mankind, is no mere fiction – to go on affirming affectionately what is. The two points of view, in strict moral logic diametrically opposed, are somehow made harmonious in Chaucer's wonderfully comic attitude, that double vision that is his ironical essence. The mere critic performs his etymological function by taking the Prioress apart and clumsily separating her good parts from her bad; but the poet's function is to build her incongruous and inharmonious parts into an inseparable whole which is infinitely greater than its parts. In this complex structure both the latent moralist and the naïve reporter have important positions, but I am not persuaded that in every case it is possible to determine which of them has the last word.

SOURCE: *PMLA*, LXIX (1954)

NOTE

Quotations from Chaucer in this paper are made from F. N. Robinson's text (Cambridge, Mass., 1933). Books referred to or cited are G. L. Kittredge, *Chaucer and His Poetry* (Cambridge, Mass., 1915) p. 45; Eileen Power, *Medieval People* (London, 1924) pp. 59–84. Robinson's note to A. 650 records the opinion that *a good felawe* means a 'rascal'. The medieval reader's expectation that the first person in a work of fiction would represent mankind generally and at the same time would physically resemble the author is commented on by Leo Spitzer in an interesting note in *Traditio*, IV (1946) 414–22.

Arthur W. Hoffman

CHAUCER'S PROLOGUE TO
PILGRIMAGE: THE TWO VOICES (1954)

Criticism of the portraits in Chaucer's General Prologue to the
Canterbury Tales has taken various directions: some critics have
praised the portraits especially for their realism, sharp in-
dividuality, adroit psychology, and vividness of felt life; others,
working in the genetic direction, have pointed out actual
historical persons who might have sat for the portraits; others,
appealing to the light of the medieval sciences, have shown the
portraits to be filled, though not burdened, with the lore of
Chaucer's day, and to have sometimes typical identities like case
histories. Miss Bowden,[1] in her recent study of the Prologue,
assembles the fruits of many earlier studies and gives the text an
impressive resonance by sketching historical and social norms and
ideals, the facts and the standards of craft, trade, and profession,
so that the form of the portraits can be tested in the light of possible conformities, mean or noble, to things as they were or to
things as they ought to have been.

It is not unlikely that the critics who have explored in these
various directions would be found in agreement on one commonplace, a metaphor which some of them indeed have used,
the designation of the portraits in the General Prologue as
figures in a tapestry. It is less likely that all of the critics would
agree as to the implications of this metaphor, but it seems to me
that the commonplace deserves to be explored and some of its
implications tested. The commonplace implies that the portraits
which appear in the General Prologue have a designed together-
ness, that the portraits exist as parts of a unity.

Such a unity, it may be argued, is partly a function of the
exterior framework of a pilgrimage to Canterbury; all the portraits are portraits of pilgrims:

> At nyght was come into that hostelrye
> Wel nyne and twenty in a compaignye,
> Of sondry folk, by aventure yfalle
> In felaweshipe, and pilgrimes were they alle. (A. 23–6)[2]

But the unity of the Prologue may be also partly a matter of internal relationships among the portraits, relationships which are many and various among 'sondry folk'. One cannot hope to survey all of these, but the modest objective of studying some of the aesthetically important internal relationships is feasible.

If one begins with the unity that is exterior to the portraits, the unity that contains them, one faces directly the question of the nature of pilgrimage as it is defined in this dramatic poem. What sort of framework does the Prologue in fact define? Part of the answer is in the opening lines, and it is not a simple answer because the definition there ranges from the upthrust and burgeoning of life as a seasonal and universal event to a particular outpouring of people, pilgrims, gathered briefly at the Tabard Inn in Southwark, drifting, impelled, bound, called to the shrine of Thomas a Becket at Canterbury. The pilgrimage is set down in the calendar of seasons as well as in the calendar of piety; nature impels and supernature draws. 'Go, go, go,' says the bird; 'Come,' says the saint.

In the opening lines of the Prologue springtime is characterized in terms of procreation, and a pilgrimage of people to Canterbury is just one of the many manifestations of the life thereby produced. The phallicism of the opening lines presents the impregnating of a female March by a male April, and a marriage of water and earth. The marriage is repeated and varied immediately as a fructifying of 'holt and heeth' by Zephirus, a marriage of air and earth. This mode of symbolism and these symbols as parts of a rite of spring have a long background of tradition; as Professor Cook[3] once pointed out, there are eminent passages of this sort in Aeschylus and Euripides, in Lucretius, in Virgil's *Georgics*, in Columella, and in the *Pervigilium Veneris*, and Professor Robinson cites Guido delle Colonne, Boccaccio, Petrarch, and Boethius. Zephirus is the only overt mythological figure in Chaucer's passage, but, in view of the instigative role generally assigned to Aphrodite in the rite of spring, she is perhaps to be recognized here, as Professor Cook suggested, in the name of April, which was her month both by traditional association and by one of the two ancient etymologies.[4] Out of this context of the quickening of the earth presented naturally and symbolically in the broadest terms, the Prologue comes to pilgrimage and treats pilgrimage first as an event in the calendar of nature, one aspect of the general springtime surge of human energy and longing. There are the attendant suggestions of the renewal of human mobility after the rigor and confinement of winter, the revival of wayfaring now that the ways are open. The horizon extends to distant shrines and foreign lands, and the attraction of the strange and faraway is included before the vision narrows and focusses upon its English specifications and the pilgrimage to the shrine at Canterbury with the vows and gratitude that send pilgrims there. One way of regarding the structure of this opening passage would emphasize the magnificent progression from the broadest inclusive generality to the firmest English specification, from the whole western tradition of the celebration of spring (including, as Cook pointed out, such a non-English or very doubtfully English detail as 'the droghte of March') to a local event of English society and English Christendom, from natural forces in their most general operation to a very specific and Christian manifestation of those forces. And yet one may regard the structure in another way, too; if, in the calendar of nature, the passage moves from general to particular, does it not, in the calendar of piety, move from nature to something that includes and oversees nature? Does not the passage move from an activity naturally generated and impelled to a governed activity, from force to *telos*? Does not the passage move from Aphrodite and *amor* in their secular operation to the sacred embrace of 'the hooly blisful martir' and of *amor dei*?

The transition from nature to supernature is emphasized by the contrast between the healthful physical vigor of the opening lines and the reference to sickness that appears in l. 18. On the one hand, it is physical vitality which conditions the pilgrimage; on the other hand, sickness occasions pilgrimage. It is, in fact, rather startling to come upon the word 'seeke' at the end of this opening passage, because it is like a breath of winter across the landscape of spring. 'Whan that they were seeke' may, of course, refer literally to illnesses of the winter just past, but, in any event, illness belongs symbolically to the inclement season. There is also, however, a strong parallelism between the beginning and end of this passage, a parallelism that has to do with restorative power. The physical vitality of the opening is presented as restorative of the dry earth; the power of the saint is presented as restorative of the sick. The seasonal restoration of nature parallels a supernatural kind of restoration that knows no season; the supernatural kind of restoration involves a wielding and directing of the forces of nature. The Prologue begins, then, by presenting a double view of the Canterbury pilgrimage : the pilgrimage is one tiny manifestation of a huge tide of life, but then, too, the tide of life ebbs and flows in response to the power which the pilgrimage acknowledges, the power symbolized by 'the hooly blisful martir'.

After l. 18 the process of particularizing is continued, moving from 'that seson' just defined to a day and to a place and to a person in Southwark at the Tabard, and thence to the portraits of the pilgrims. The double view of pilgrimage is enhanced and extended by the portraits where it appears, in one aspect, as a range of motivation. This range of motivation is from the sacred to the secular and on to the profane – 'profane' in the sense of motivations actually subversive of the sacred. All the pilgrims are, in fact, granted an ostensible sacred motive; all of them are seeking the shrine. The distances that we are made aware of are both *within* some of the portraits, where a gulf yawns between ostensible and actual motivation, and *between* the portraits, where the motivation of the Knight and the Parson is near one end of the spectrum, and the motivation of the Summoner and the Pardoner near the other end. There is such an impure but blameless mixture as the motivation of the Prioress; there is the secular pilgrimage of the Wife of Bath, impelled so powerfully and frankly by Saint Venus rather than drawn by Saint Thomas, and goaded by a Martian desire to acquire and dominate another husband; in the case of the Prioress, an inescapable doubt as to the quality of *amor* hesitates between the sacred and secular, and in the case of the thoroughly secular Wife of Bath, doubt hesitates between the

secular and the profane while the portrait shows the ostensible
motive that belongs to all the pilgrims shaken without ever
being subverted, contradicted perhaps, brazenly opposed, but
still acknowleged and offered, not, at any rate, hypocritically betrayed. In the area of motivation, the portraits seem to propose,
ultimately, a fundamental, inescapable ambiguity as part of the
human condition; prayer for the purification of motive is valid
for all the pilgrims. And the pilgrims who move, pushed by impulse and drawn by vows, none merely impelled and none
perfectly committed, reflect, in their human ambiguity, the broad
problem of origins and ends, the stubbornness of matter and the
power of spirit, together with ideas of cosmic resolution and harmony in which source and end are reconciled and seen to be the
same, the purposes of nature and supernature found to be at one,
the two restorative powers akin, the kinds of love not discon-
tinuous, Saint Venus and Saint Thomas different and at odds yet
not at war, within the divine purpose which contains both.

The portraits of the Knight and the Squire have a
particular interest. The relationships between these two
portraits are governed by and arise out of the natural relationship of father and son. Consanguinity provides the base for a
dramatic relationship, and at the same time is the groundwork
for a modestly generalized metaphor of age and youth. Each
portrait is enhanced and defined by the presence of the other :
the long roll of the Knight's campaigns, and the Squire's little
opportunity ('so litel space'), a few raids enumerated in one
line; a series of past tenses, a history, for the Knight, and for the
Squire a present breaking forth in active participles; the
Knight not 'gay', wearing fustian soiled by his coat of mail,
'bismotered', the Squire bright and fresh and colorful; the
Knight meek and quiet – or so the portrait leaves him – beside the
Squire, who sings and whistles all the day. The Knight's love is
an achieved devotion, a matter of pledges fulfilled and of values,
if not completely realized, yet woven into the fabric of experience (ideals – 'trouthe', 'honour', 'fredom', 'curteisie'). The
Squire is a lover, a warm and eager lover, paying court to his
lady and sleeping no more than the nightingale. In the one, the
acquired, tutored, disciplined, elevated, enlarged love, the piety;
and in the other, the love channelled into an elaborate social

ritual, a parody piety, but still emphatically fresh and full of
natural impulse. One cannot miss the creation of the Squire in
conventional images of nature, the meadow, the flowers, the
freshness like May, the lover like the nightingale – comparisons
that are a kind of re-emergence of the opening lines of the Prologue, the springtime surge of youthful, natural energy that ani-
mates the beginning. 'Go, go, go', the bird's voice, is a major
impulse in the portrait of the Squire and in the Squire's pilgrimage; the Knight's pilgrimage is more nearly a response to the
voice of the saint. Yet the Squire is within the belt of rule, and
learning the calendar of piety. The concluding couplet of the
portrait

> Curteis he was, lowely and servysable,
> And carf biforn his fader at the table.   (A. 99–100)

has the effect of bending all the youth, energy, color, audible-
ness, and high spirit of the Squire to the service of his father,
the Knight, and to attendance on his pilgrimage, with perhaps
a suggestion of the present submitting to the serious and res-
pected values served and communicated by the past, the natural
and the imposed submitting of the son to his natural father, and
beyond him to the supernatural goal, the shrine to which the
father directs his pilgrimage.

The portraits of the Knight and the Squire represent one of
the ways in which portraiture takes into account and develops
the double definition of pilgrimage which is established at the
beginning. The double definition of pilgrimage is involved in a
different way in the portrait of the Prioress; there it appears as a
delicately poised ambiguity. Two definitions appear as two faces
of one coin. Subsequently, when the portrait of the Prioress is
seen together with the portraits of the Monk and the Friar, a
sequence is realized, running from ambiguity to emphatic discrepancy, and the satire that circles the impenetrable duality of
sacred and secular impulse in the case of the Prioress, knifes in
as these impulses are drawn apart in the case of the Monk and
strikes vigorously in the still wider breach that appears in the case
of the Friar. What is illustrated within the portraits is amplified
by a designed sequence.

The delicate balance in the picture of the Prioress has been generally recognized and has perhaps been only the more clearly exhibited by occasional seesawing in the critical interpretation of the portrait in which the satiric elements are sometimes represented as heavy, sometimes as slight, sometimes sinking the board, and sometimes riding light and high. There is, perhaps, no better illustration of the delicacy of the balance than the fact that the Prioress's very presence on a pilgrimage, as several commentators have pointed out, may be regarded as the first satiric touch. The very act of piety is not free from the implication of imperfection; the Prioress is obligated to a cloistered piety that serves and worships God without going on a journey to seek a shrine, and prioresses were specifically and repeatedly enjoined from going on pilgrimages. Prioresses did, nevertheless, go as pilgrims, so that Chaucer's Prioress is not departing from the norm of behavior of persons in her office so much as she is departing from the sanctioned ideal of behavior.[5] In the case of the Prioress, the blemish is sufficiently technical to have only faint satiric coloring; it is not the notable kind of blemish recognized in all times and all places. Nevertheless, it is precisely this kind of hint of a spot that places the Prioress at one end of a sequence in which the more obviously blemished Monk and Friar appear. If we pose a double question – What kind of woman is the Prioress, and what kind of prioress is the woman? – the portrait responds more immediately to the first part of the question, and leaves the answer to the second part largely in the area of implication. The portrait occupies forty-five lines, and more than three-fourths of the lines have to do with such matters as the Prioress's blue eyes, her red mouth, the shape of her nose and width of her forehead, her ornaments and dress, her table manners, her particular brand of French, her pets and what she fed them, and her tenderness about mice. It is, of course, one of the skilful arts of these portraits to work with surfaces and make the surfaces convey and reveal what lies beneath, but it should be observed that in the case of the Parson – or even in the case of the Knight – a character is arrived at almost entirely without physical and superficial detail. One need not take the emphatic surface in the portrait of the Prioress as necessarily pejorative in its implication; it need not follow that the Prioress is a shallow and super-

ficial person, and, in consequence, sharply satirized. But the
portrait does seem, by means of its emphasis on surfaces, to
define the Prioress as woman, and strongly enough so that tension between the person and her office, between the given human
nature and the assumed sacred obligation is put vividly before
us, and rather as the observation of a fact than as the instiga-
tion of a judgment. In the cases of the Monk and the Friar, the
tension is so exacerbated that judgment is, in the case of the
Monk, incited, and in the case of the Friar, both incited and in-
flamed to severity.

In the portrait of the Prioress the double view of pilgrimage
appears both in an ambiguity of surfaces, and in an implied inner
range of motivation. In the surfaces there is a sustained hovering effect: the name, Eglentyne, is romance, and 'simple and
coy' is a romance formula, but she *is* a nun, by whatever name,
and 'simple' and 'coy', aside from their romance connotations,
have meanings ('simple' and 'modest') appropriate enough to a
nun; there are the coral beads and the green gauds, but they *are*
a rosary; there are the fluted wimple and the exposed forehead,
but the costume *is* a nun's habit; there is the golden brooch shining brightly, but it *is* a religious emblem. Which shall be taken as
principal, which as modifying and subordinate? Are the departures or the conformities more significant of her nature? Are
her Stratford French and her imitation of court manners more
important than the fact that she sings well and properly the
divine service? Do we detect vanity in her singing well, or do we
rely on what she sings and accept her worship as well performed – to the glory of God? The ambiguity of these surface
indications leads into the implied range of motivation; this implied range has been generally recognized in the motto – '*Amor
vincit omnia*' – on the Prioress's golden brooch, and the implications set up in the portrait as a whole seem to be clustered and
tightly fastened in this ornament and symbol.

The motto itself has, in the course of history, gone its own
double pilgrimage to the shrine of Saint Venus and to sacred
shrines; the original province of the motto was profane, but it
was drawn over to a sacred meaning and soon became complexly
involved with and compactly significant of both. Professor Lowes
comments on the motto as it pertains to the Prioress:

Now is it earthly love that conquers all, now heavenly; the phrase plays back and forth between the two. And it is precisely that happy ambiguity of the convention – itself the result of an earlier transfer – that makes Chaucer's use of it here . . . a master stroke. *Which of the two loves does 'amor' mean to the Prioress?* I do not know; but I think she thought she meant love celestial.[6]

Professor Lowes, presumably, does not really expect to see the matter concluded one way or the other and finds this very inconclusiveness, hovering between two answers, one of the excellences of the portrait. There is, however, a certain amount of illumination to be gained, though not an answer to the question as formulated by Professor Lowes, by asking the question another way and considering an answer in terms that lie outside of the Prioress's motivation. Put the question in this form : Which of the two loves does the *portrait* in the context of the Prologue mean by *amor*? The answer to this question, of course, is *both*. On the one hand, profane love or the love of earthly things does overcome all; the little vanities and pretensions, the love of color and decoration and dress, the affection squandered in little extravagances towards pets, the pity and tender emotion wasted upon a trapped mouse – the multiplicity of secular, impulsive loves threatens to and could ultimately stifle the dedication to the celestial love. This answer is, in fact, a version of the Prioress's character and motivation sometimes offered. It actually implies one half of the view of pilgrimage – the natural powers that move people and that may usurp the whole character. But the other answer – celestial love conquers all things – also applies to the portrait, though it is not very easily arrived at in terms of the Prioress's motivation. Here we are dealing with the ostensible meaning of the motto, the ideal meaning of the motto as worn by a prioress – what it ought to mean in terms of her office. And, no matter what the impurity of the Prioress's motives, no matter what she means or thinks she means by the motto, the motto does, in the calendar of piety, mean that God's love is powerful over all things, powerful in this case over the vanity that may be involved in the wearing of the brooch, powerful over all the shallowness and limitation and reduction and misdirection of love that the Prioress may be guilty of, powerful over all her departures from or misunderstandings of discipline and obligation and vow, powerful over all inadequacy, able to overcome the faults of God's human instruments and make this woman's divine office valid. The motto, and the portrait of which it is the conclusion, appreciate both the secular impulses and the sacred redemptive will, but there is no doubt which love it is that is crowned with ultimate power.

Chaucer has found ways, as in the case of the Prioress, of making an ideal or standard emerge within a portrait. The standard may be ambiguously stated or heavily involved in irony, but it is almost always present, and nowhere with greater effectiveness than in the most sharply satiric portraits. This, I take it, is the effect of the formula of worthiness which is applied to so many of the pilgrims. A character is declared to be 'worthy' or 'the best that ever was' of his craft or profession or office, and frequently under circumstances that make the statement jarring and the discrepancy obvious. There is a definite shock, for example, when Friar Huberd is declared to be a 'worthy lymytour', or the Pardoner 'a noble ecclesiaste'. Even when the satiric thrust has two directions, striking both at the individual and at the group to which he belongs, the implication has nevertheless been lodged in the portrait that there could be, for example, a worthy friar, or a pardoner who was indeed a noble ecclesiastic. The reader is, as it were, tripped in the act of judging and reminded that if he condemns these figures, if they appear culpable, there must be some sort of standard by which they are so judged, by which they appear so.

Chaucer has also adopted the method of including ideal or nearly ideal portraits among the pilgrims. There are, for example, the Knight and the Plowman, figures at either end of the secular range, and among the clerical figures there is the Parson. A host of relative judgments, of course, are set up by devices of sequence and obvious pairing and contrasting of portraits. It is the ideal portraits, however, that somehow preside over all these judgments and comparisons, and it is to them that the relative distinctions are presented for a kind of penultimate judgment. Prioress, Monk, and Friar, and all the other clerical figures are reckoned with the Parson who is, in fact, made to speak in an accent of judgment upon the clerical figures who go astray – '. . . if gold ruste, what shal iren do?' (We may remember the

Prioress's shining gold brooch, the Monk's gold pin, and, among the secular figures, the Physician who so doubly regarded gold as a sovereign remedy.)

Chaucer has used an interesting device for undergirding the ideal portrait of the Parson. He employs consanguinity with metaphorical effect. After the assertions which declare that the Parson 'first . . . wroghte, and afterward . . . taughte', the actualizing of Christian ideals is supported by the representation of the Parson as brother to the Plowman. It is the Parson's Christian obligation to treat men as brothers, and the portrait abundantly affirms that he does so. Making him actually the brother of the Plowman brilliantly insists that what supernature calls for is performed by the Parson and, more than that, comes by nature to him.[7] The achieved harmony both comes from above and rises out of the ground; sacred and secular are linked, the shepherd of souls and the tiller of the soil. This is a vantage point from which the conflicts of secular and sacred, of nature and supernature, are seen in a revealing light, a point at which one sees reflected in the clear mirror of ideal characters and an actual–ideal relationship the fundamental double view of pilgrimage established in the beginning.

The double definition of pilgrimage is differently but nonetheless revealingly illuminated by the portraits of another fraternizing pair, the Summoner and Pardoner, who conclude the sequence of pilgrims. The illumination here is not clarified by way of ideal characters but somehow refracted and intensified by the dark surfaces upon which it falls. The darkness is most visible in connection with the theme of love, which appears here in a sinister and terrible distortion. The hot and lecherous Summoner, the type of sexual unrestraint, is represented as harmonizing in song with the impotent Pardoner, the eunuch; the deep rumbling voice and the thin effeminate voice are singing, 'Com hider, love, to me!' The song, in this context, becomes both a promiscuous and perverted invitation and an unconscious symbolic acknowledgment of the absence of and the need for love, love that comes neither to the grasping physical endeavor of the Summoner nor to the physical incapacity of the Pardoner – nor to their perverted spirits. Love has been treated in the Prologue from the beginning as dual in character, a matter both of the body and the spirit, the *amor* symbolized by Venus, sung by the Squire, equivocally illustrated by the Prioress, lustily celebrated by the Wife of Bath; and the *amor dei*, the love shadowily there beyond all the secular forms of love, a hovering presence among the pilgrims and sometimes close, as to the Knight and the Parson and the Plowman, and symbolized in the saint's shrine which is the goal of all of them. On this view, the song of the Summoner and the Pardoner is a superb dramatic irony acknowledging the full extent of their need and loss, the love of God which they ought to strive for, the love which they desperately need.

The office which each of these men is supposed to fulfill should be taken into account. The Summoner is, ostensibly, an instrument through whom divine justice, in a practical way, operates in the world. There are, in the portrait, a few touches that may be reminders of the ultimate source of his authority and function: his '*Questio quid iuris*', though it is represented satirically as the sum and substance of his knowledge, and posed as a question, *is* legitimately the substance of his knowledge – his province is law, especially the divine law; '*Significavit*' is the opening word of a legal writ, a dreaded worldly pronouncement of divine judgment, excommunication; he is physically a fearful figure from whom children run (not the divine love which suffers them to come), and some of the physical details may be reminders of noble and awesome aspects of divine justice – his 'fyr-reed cherubynnes face' and the voice described in a significant analogy as like a trumpet, 'Was nevere trompe of half so greet a soun'. The Pardoner, on the other hand, is the ostensible instrument of divine mercy and love. Many of the pardoners, as Miss Bowden points out, went so far as to pretend to absolve both *a poena* and *a culpa*, thereby usurping, in the pretended absolution *a culpa*, a function which theological doctrine reserved to God and His grace. In any case, their legitimate functions were an appeal for charity and an extension of God's mercy and love. The Pardoner, it should be observed, is, compared to the Summoner, an attractive figure. We may be reminded of the superior affinity of the Pardoner's office by the veil which he has sewed upon his cap, the copy of St. Veronica's veil which is supposed to have received the imprint of Christ's face.[8]

The justice and love[9] of which the Summoner and Pardoner are emissaries are properly complementary and harmoniously, though paradoxically and mysteriously, related, so that the advances that are being made both of persons and of values are, in a very serious sense, proper to this pair. The radical physical distinctness of Summoner and Pardoner is at this level the definition of two aspects of supernature; there is the same employment of physical metaphor here that there is in the portraits of the Parson and the Plowman, but with the difference that light comes out of darkness, and out of the gravest corruption of nature the supernatural relationship emerges clarified in symbol. The Summoner cannot finally pervert, and the Pardoner's impotence cannot finally prevent; the divine justice and love are powerful even over these debased instruments – *Amor vincit omnia*. Beyond their knowing, beyond their power or impotence, impotently both Pardoner and Summoner appeal for the natural love – melody of bird-song and meadows of flowers – and both pray for the celestial love, the ultimate pardon which in their desperate and imprisoned darkness is their only hope: 'Com hider, love, to me!'

The exterior unity achieved by the realistic device and broadly symbolic framework of pilgrimage is made stronger and tighter in the portraits, partly by local sequences and pairings, but most impressively by the illustration, the variation and enrichment by way of human instances, of a theme of love, earthly and celestial, and a general complex intermingling of the consideration of nature with the consideration of supernature. The note of love is sounded in different keys all through the portraits:

The Knight	. . . he loved chivalrie, Trouthe and honour, fredom and curteisie (A. 45–6)
The Squire	A lovyere and a lusty bacheler . . . (A. 80)
	So hoote he lovede that by nyghtertale He sleep namoore than dooth a nyghtyngale. (A. 97–8)
The Prioress	. . . *Amor vincit omnia.* (A. 162)

The Monk	A Monk . . . that lovede venerie, . . . (A. 166)
	He hadde of gold ywroght a ful curious pyn; A love-knotte in the gretter ende ther was. (A. 196–7)
	A fat swan loved he best of any roost. (A. 206)
The Friar	In love-dayes ther koude he muchel help . . . (A. 258)
	Somewhat he lipsed, for his wantownesse, . . . (A. 264)
The Clerk	For hym was levere have at his beddes heed Twenty bookes, clad in blak or reed, Of Aristotle and his philosophie, Than robes riche, or fithele, or gay sautrie. (A. 293–6)
The Frankelyn	Wel loved he by the morwe a sop in wyn; To lyven in delit was evere his wone, For he was Epicurus owene sone . . . (A. 334–6)
The Physician	He kepte that he wan in pestilence. For gold in phisik is a cordial, Therefore he lovede gold in special. (A. 442–4)
The Wife of Bath	Of remedies of love she knew per chaunce, For she koude of that art the olde daunce. (A. 475–6)
The Parson	But rather wolde he yeven, out of doute, Unto his povre parisshens aboute Of his offryng and eek of his substaunce. (A. 487–9)
	. . . Cristes loore and his apostles twelve He taughte, but first he folwed it hymselve. (A. 527–8)
The Plowman	With hym ther was a Plowman, was his brother, . . . (A. 529)

> Lyvynge in pees and parfit charitee.
> God loved he best with al his hoole herte
> At alle tymes, thogh him gamed or smerte,
> And thanne his neighebor right as hymselve.
>
> (A. 532–5)

The Summoner
      and
the Pardoner   . . . 'Com hider, love, to me!' (A. 672)

The theme of restorative power attends upon the theme of love. It is, of course, announced at the beginning and defined in terms both of nature and supernature. Both the Physician, concerned with natural healing, and the Pardoner, the agent of a supernatural healing, appear under the rubric of 'Physician, heal thyself'. The worldly Physician is disaffected from God; the Pardoner is naturally impotent. Serious inadequacy in either realm appears as counterpart of inadequacy in the other. It is the Parson who both visits the sick and tends properly to the cure of souls; he works harmoniously in both realms, and both realms are in harmony and fulfilled in him.

The pilgrims are represented as affected by a variety of destructive and restorative kinds of love. Their characters and movement can be fully described only as mixtures of the loves that drive and goad and of the love that calls and summons. The pilgrims have, while they stay and when they move, their worldly host. They have, too, their worldly Summoner and Pardoner who, in the very worst way, move and are moved with them. Nevertheless, the Summoner and Pardoner, who conclude the roll of the company, despite and beyond their appalling personal deficiency, may suggest the summoning and pardoning, the judgment and grace which in Christian thought embrace and conclude man's pilgrimage and which therefore, with all the corrosions of satire and irony, are also the seriously appropriate conclusion to the tapestry of Chaucer's pilgrims.

S o u r c e : *Journal of English Literary History*, xxi (1954).

NOTES

1. Muriel Bowden, *A Commentary on the General Prologue to the Canterbury Tales* (New York, 1948).

2. All references to the text of the *Canterbury Tales* are to *The Poetical Works of Chaucer*, ed. F. N. Robinson (Cambridge, Mass., 1933).

3. Albert S. Cook, 'Chaucerian Papers – 1 : 1 Prologue 1–11', *Transactions of the Connecticut Academy of Arts and Sciences*, XXIII (New Haven, 1919) 5–21.

4. Cook, 5–10.

5. The relevance of the ideal sanctioned character of an office to the portrait of a person will appear again strikingly in the case of the Summoner and the Pardoner.

6. John Livingston Lowes, *Convention and Revolt in Poetry* (Boston and New York, 1919) p. 66.

7. There is, of course, plenty of actual basis for representing a parson as a son of the soil; the connection is not merely an artistic and symbolic device.

8. Later, in telling his story, the Pardoner acknowledges that his pardons are inferior versions of the supreme pardon which is Christ's. See the Pardoner's Tale, C. 915–18.

9. This statement of the symbolic values behind the Summoner and the Pardoner is not a disagreement with, but merely an addition to, the point made by Kellogg and Haselmayer (Alfred L. Kellogg and Louis A. Haselmayer, 'Chaucer's Satire of the Pardoner', *PMLA*, LXVI (1951) 215–77, when they assert : 'In this paradox, this ironic portrait of justice and crime singing in close harmony, we reach the center of Chaucer's satire' (p. 275). There is, indeed, the strongest satiric impact in this affiliation of the man who should apprehend the wrongdoer with the criminal. In addition, however, if we are to see beyond the Summoner's disabilities to his representation of justice, we see in parallel vision beyond the Pardoner's disabilities a representation of love.

William Frost

AN INTERPRETATION OF CHAUCER'S KNIGHT'S TALE (1949)

In his recent article, 'A Reinterpretation of Chaucer's Theseus'
[*Review of English Studies*, XXIII (1947) 289–96], Professor
Henry J. Webb undertakes to demonstrate that the Theseus of
the Knight's Tale is more of a villain that has commonly been
believed. It is his contention that Chaucer, in reworking his
source material, emphasized or added to 'those traits in the
character of Theseus which were ignoble or cruel'; and that the
poet's frequent use of the adjective 'noble' in conjunction with
Theseus's name is to be interpreted as ironic (pp. 289, 296).
Part of Mr. Webb's argument is based on Theseus's actions in
the Tale (his destruction of Thebes, pillaging of the Theban
country-side, imprisonment of Palamon and Arcite without asking ransom, and release of Arcite without releasing Palamon);
part is based on the character of Theseus as it appears in other
legends about him (notably in the story of his desertion of
Ariadne, which Chaucer recounts in *The Legend of Good
Women*).

   Mr. Webb's reinterpretation appears to me partial, mislead-
ing, and incomplete. To deal with the second class of evidence
first, it is a moot question how closely the Theseus of the Knight's
Tale is to be identified with the Theseus of the Ariadne story.
Mr. Webb, if I understand him correctly, supposes that the
Ariadne episode occurred *later* in Theseus's life than the events
of the Tale; thus he says that Theseus's character 'soon suffered
a change' (p. 289), and speaks of Arcite's release as having 'foreshadowed the deed which eventually damned the duke' (p. 294).
But it is clear from l. 980 of the Knight's Tale that the conquest
of the Minotaur, which led immediately to the betrayal of
Ariadne, had taken place *before* the Palamon and Arcite story.
Probably long before; for in the Knight's Tale Theseus is no
longer a young man [he says that he has been a lover 'ful yore

agon' (1813)]; while according to Chaucer's version of the
Ariadne story he was sent to Crete at the age of twenty-three
(*L.G.W.* 2075).

But even setting chronology aside, how closely are we to
identify the Theseuses of the two stories? I would suggest that
they be kept quite distinct. In the Legend of Ariadne, one more
woeful tale of a woman abandoned by her lover, Chaucer is using
the figure of Theseus for a purpose utterly unlike his purpose in
the Knight's Tale; and, furthermore, the circumstances of the
two stories are not compatible with each other if the two are
taken as relating episodes in the life of the same man. Egeus,
Theseus's father, drowns at the end of Chaucer's Ariadne legend
(*L.G.W.* 2178), probably as a kind of poetic penalty for his
son's faithlessness to that heroine; but in the Knight's Tale –
many years later – Egeus is still alive, though aged, and has a
speaking part (2837–52). All that remains, in the Knight's
Tale, of the whole Cretan business is a single passing reference
to the heroic glories of Theseus's early youth.

As for Theseus's actions in the Tale, Mr. Webb reviews several
of them in the light of various medieval treatises on chivalry with
the object of showing that the Duke was at times an abnormally
cruel and arbitrary ruler. Here his argument would have more
point, I think, if Theseus were an historical English duke rather
than a figure in a poem. As a figure in a poem he is entitled
to be regarded first of all in the light of the full literary context
in which he appears; but Mr. Webb omits entirely any consideration of such an important part of that context as, for example, Theseus's 'cheyne of love' speech (2987 ff.). When
Chaucer calls his Friar 'noble' in his description of him in the
Prologue (208 ff.) it is clear from the preceding lines (which
have strongly implied that the Friar is a great seducer of women)
that the praise is ironic; but we have no corresponding reason,
in the text of the Knight's Tale itself, for interpreting the praise
of Theseus in a similarly ambiguous light.

I agree entirely with Mr. Webb when he calls (Theseus one
of the most complex characters delineated anywhere in the
Canterbury Tales) but for an understanding of his complexities
nothing less than a review of the entire poem as an artistic unit
will adequately serve.[1]

The labours of modern medievalists have clarified for us much of the intellectual, historical, and literary materials which went into the creation of the poem Chaucer put into the mouth of his Knight and dignified as the first of the *Canterbury Tales*. Thanks to historical scholarship we now know not only that its immediate source was in Boccaccio rather than 'Stace of Thebes and thise bookes olde' (as the Knight rather vaguely puts it) but also just what Chaucer imitated from the Italian's *Teseide*, what he left out, and where he got much of what he added. Arcite's 'maladye of Hereos' has been diagnosed by Professor Lowes with an erudition no doubt few fourteenth-century physicians could have commanded; Chaucer's use of the *Teseide* (in the Knight's Tale and elsewhere) has been related to his general development as a poet by Professor R. A. Pratt; Professor B. A. Wise has traced the inspiration of some passages in the Tale back to 'Stace of Thebes' himself; Professors B. L. Jefferson and H. R. Patch have derived many ideas in the poem from the tradition of Boethius. The mysteries of Chaucerian astrology have been clarified by Professor W. C. Curry; a number of writers have dealt with the conventions of courtly love embodied in the story; and the close relation of the military aspects of the Tale to actual fourteenth-century warfare has been established: indeed, the latest suggestion is that the tournament at the climax of the plot may have been inspired by a real tournament Chaucer probably witnessed in London.[2]

In short, we know something of Chaucer's experiences, library, tastes, opinions, and methods of composition; as well as, by inference, something of the point of view of his earliest audience – we can dimly imagine how it felt to read the Knight's Tale in the 1390s. But on the Tale as a tale – except for widespread comments that it is, generally speaking, a good one – much less has been written and very little agreement been reached. What may be the point of the story is frequently debated, votes having been registered for the Tale as allegory, as a riddle, as a pseudo-epic (marred by omission of too much of Boccaccio's material), and as a piece of realism (marred by an excess of epic machinery). Who should be considered the hero is even questioned, some preferring Palamon, some Arcite, others finding little to choose between them. Among these latter is Professor Root,[3] who feels that the descriptions (of battles, temples, May, &c.), 'with occasional passages of noble reflection', are the 'flesh and blood' of the poem, 'of which the characters and action are merely the skeleton framework'.[4] 'What is the Knight's Tale', he asks, 'but a splendidly pictured tapestry, full of color and motion?'[5] It is my purpose to attempt, in terms of the Tale itself, an answer to Mr. Root's question.

I

The Knight's Tale develops from three widening concentric circles of interest : the merely human interest of the rivalry between two young heroes, both noble and both in love, for the hand of a heroine who has no apparent preference between them; the ethical interest of a conflict of obligations between romantic love and military comradeship; and finally the theological interest attaching to the method by which a just providence fully stabilizes a disintegrating human situation.

As important as the problems of the plot is the atmosphere in which they are worked out, the world of the Knight's Tale. This world, being an amalgam of legendary Athens, fourteenth-century England, and the never-never land of chivalric romance, presents to us that curious double relationship to any imaginable real world which most great art – the *Odyssey, Hamlet, Paradise Lost, Faust* – seems to attain; that is, a simultaneous relationship (the delight of readers and despair of historians) of nearness and distance. Anyone called 'Theseus, Duke of Athens' must surely be a classical hero refracted through a medieval lens; so we suppose, only to discover that there was a living 'Duke of Athens' at the time Chaucer wrote.[6] But whether classical, realistic, or chivalric, the atmosphere of the Tale has three abiding attributes : it is predominantly noble, predominantly tragic, and deeply infused with a sense of significance transcending both human beings and their material environment. In this essay I shall consider first the problems of the story, then the general characteristics of the universe in which the story happens.

II

The problem of who shall win the hand of the fair Emelye, Duke Theseus's young sister, is intensified throughout the Knight's Tale by systematic and delicately balanced parallelism in the presentation of the rival heroes, Palamon and Arcite. At no point is either allowed to take the centre of the stage or the initiative in setting the plot in motion without the other at once having an equal opportunity. If the two knights are together they are spoken of as a pair: 'This Palamon and his felawe Arcite' (1031); if events separate them the spotlight shifts impartially from one to the other:

> Now wol I stynte of Palamon a lite,
> And lete hym in his prisoun stille dwelle,
> And of Arcita forth I wol yow telle. . . .   (A. 1334–6)

> . . . And in this blisse lete I now Arcite
> And speke I wole of Palamon a lite. . . .   (A. 1449–50)

Moreover, the two knights have much in common: besides being noble, young, and passionately in love, besides being kinsmen, compatriots, and sworn blood-brothers, they are equally valorous:

> There nas no tygre in the vale of Galgopheye
> Whan that hir whelp is stole whan it is lite,
> So crueel on the hunte as is Arcite
> For jelous herte upon this Palamon.
> Ne in Belmarye ther nys so fel leon,
> That hunted is, or for his hunger wood,
> Ne of his praye desireth so the blood,
> As Palamon to sleen his foo Arcite. . . .   (A. 2626–33)

If Arcite despairs at being exiled from Athens and the sight of Emelye, Palamon despairs at being still imprisoned and help-

less to win her. If Palamon breaks faith with Theseus by escaping
from prison, Arcite merits equal punishment for returning to
Athens in disguise. At the final tourney, for which each has prepared by prayer and sacrifice to a patron deity, each is seconded
by a confederate champion, warlike and exotic : Palamon by
'Lygurge hymself, the grete kyng of Trace' (2129), with his white
wolfhounds; Arcite by 'the grete Emetreus, the kyng of Inde'
(2156), an eagle on his wrist and tame lions and leopards all
about him.

So ostensibly impartial is the presentation of the heroes, in fact,
that it is no wonder that some Chaucerians – Professor Hulbert,
for example[7] – have failed to see any significant distinction between them. The teller of the tale himself never obviously sides
with one or the other; to Theseus they are an identical pair of
infatuated fools; and even Emelye expresses no preference between 'Palamon, that hath swich love to me' (2314) and 'Arcite,
that loveth me so soore' (2315). Finally, as the lines I have been
quoting demonstrate, the concurrent stories of the two heroes are
narrated in a poetry marked by all manner of rhetorical parallelism.[8]

I am sure myself that the heroes are significantly differentiated
from each other, and that a valid preference between them is
implied by the poem; but they are certainly not individualized
in the manner of such rival protagonists of later storytelling as
Richard II and Bolingbroke, or Dobbin and George Osborne.
Much of the beauty of the Knight's Tale, and of its appropriateness to the man who tells it, resides in a certain formal regula-
rity of design. Thus the May-songs of Emelye and Arcite, re-
dolent of youth, freshness, and spontaneity, come at two crucial
points in the plot; while early May is also the time of the final
contest that will make one hero happy and the other glorious.
Thus the Tale begins with a wedding, a conquest, and a funeral;
and ends with a tournament, a funeral, and a wedding.

III

A conflict between love and comradeship in the hearts of the two
knights is the emotional focus of the story, the poetry of which

develops each of the conflicting elements as a constituent of the world in which the story takes place. Comradeship implies war : Palamon and Arcite are first introduced, side by side, 'both in oon armes', on the field of battle. Chaucer created the military elements of the poem by fusing his own knowledge of contemporary warfare with a classical tradition that stretches back through Boccaccio and Statius to the ancient Greeks. The mixture is rich, allusive, and concrete :

> The rede statue of Mars, with spere and targe,
> So shyneth in his white baner large,
> That alle the feeldes glyteren up and doun;
> And by his baner born is his penoun
> Of gold ful riche, in which there was ybete
> The Mynotaur, which that he slough in Crete.
> Thus rit this duc, thus rit this conquerour,
> And in his hoost of chivalrie the flour . . .   (A. 975–82)

These lines are from a description of Theseus, the dominant figure of the poem and, significantly, the man who unites in his person successes in war and love alike. 'He conquered al the regne of Femenye' (866), symbolic homeland of Ypolita, Amazon queen and Theseus's bride. For neither of the two knights, it finally develops, will such a double triumph be possible; one is to have victory in battle, the other to marry Emelye.

In a drama involving conquest, tourneying, and hand-to-hand combat ankle-deep in blood, comradely loyalty is, of course, a fitting plot-motif; and the outward similarity between Palamon and Arcite enhances the violence of their rupture. They are, moreover, sworn blood-brothers – into Palamon's mouth is put a picture of the relation between them as it has been up to the beginning of the tale and ought, ideally, to continue (1129–40). Since the re-establishment of this normal, desirable, and exemplary relation is to be a part of the denouement, it is noteworthy that immediately after the break between the two knights there occurs a symbolic allusion to one of the most famous instances of fellowship in ancient legend. Scarcely have Palamon and Arcite quarrelled for the first time than Perotheus arrives in Athens and is described as follows :

> A worthy duc that highte Perotheus,
> That felawe was unto duc Theseus
> Syn thilke day that they were children lite. . . .
> So wel they lovede, as olde bookes sayn,
> That whan that oon was deed, soothly to telle,
> His felawe went and soughte hym doun in helle. . . .
>
>   (A. 1191–3, 1198–1200)

And we are reminded of a great myth celebrated in classical
poetry – in Horace, for example :

> . . . Theseus leaves Pirithöus in the chain
> The love of comrades cannot take away.[9]

This reference to Theseus's journey to the underworld is, by the
way, one classical detail Chaucer *added* to what he took from the
Teseide.[10]

Romantic love, which drives Palamon and Arcite apart, enters
the poem most notably in the praise each lover accords Emelye,
the illness and despair each undergoes, and Palamon's prayer
in the temple of Venus. Romantic love, however, implying as it
does chivalry, courts of love, and the idealization of woman, in-
vests the figure of Theseus also. Despite his mockery of the lovers
the Duke has been, he says, a 'servant' in his time. He is, moreover, a general who undertakes a new war to avenge insults done
to ladies; an absolute ruler who allows his punishment of self-
acknowledged culprits to be deflected by the merciful intervention of his wife and sister; a devastator of 'wall and sparre and
rafter' in conquered Thebes, but also an umpire who forbids
fatal bloodshed at the tournament over which he presides. Thus
if the Knight's Tale develops a conflict between an ethic of battle
and an ethic of love, nevertheless in the figures of Theseus,
Ypolita, and Perotheus we are presented with an emblem of the
two kinds of value reconciled and in accord.

We are also presented, in the minds of Palamon and Arcite,
with two views of the same situation, Palamon being the spokes-
man of the greater idealism.[11] The contrast comes first in the
way each regards Emelye. In Boccaccio both saw her as Venus;
in Chaucer Palamon alone, in the following metaphor charged
with religious overtones, makes that identification :

> Venus, if it be thy wil
> Yow in this gardyn thus to transfigure,
> Bifore me, sorweful, wrecched creature . . .
>
> (A. 1104–6)

Arcite emphatically differs, and seeks to use the difference as an argument for his own priority; he says to Palamon,

> Thyn is affeccioun of hoolynesse,
> And myn is love, as to a creature . . . . (A. 1158–9)

Or, as Dryden translated the lines :

> Thine was devotion to the blest above;
> I saw the woman, and desired her love. . . .
>
> (*Palamon and Arcite*, i, 319–20)

It is a conflict, not between love and love, but between devotion and desire.[12]

This is the first instance of a significant divergence between the rivals; a second follows at once in their attitude toward the law of comradeship. Each, naturally, cites this law as binding on the other; but it is Arcite, not Palamon, who ultimately repudiates it for them both, in the lines :

> And therfore, at the kynges court, my brother,
> Ech man for hymself, ther is noon other. (A. 1181–2)

The third and crucial divergence comes on the morning of the tournament when Arcite prays to Mars for a victory in arms which he thinks will be the means of possessing Emelye, while Palamon prays to Venus for Emelye herself.

Thus to Arcite the situation presents itself throughout as a practical problem of satisfying a desire by pursuit of the logical means to attain it. When he compares himself and Palamon, quarrelling in prison over Emelye, to the two dogs who fought over a bone till both lost it (1177–80) he resembles Theseus at the latter's most pragmatic moment (1798–1812); and on his return to Athens as Philostrate Arcite sets on foot the most elaborate scheme either lover ever conceives of to gain his object. Palamon, on the other hand, though fully as fervent as his rival, includes his passion in a wider conception of Venus-worship; and, far from prizing victory or any other means of success, puts his love for Emelye above life itself (2254–8). In thus extending beyond the grave his love resembles the devoted comradeship of Theseus and Perotheus.

Even the language used about him by the teller of the Tale distinguishes Palamon's experience from that of his comrade: his imprisonment while Arcite is free is spoken of as a 'martyrdom' (1460),[13] and with 'hooly herte' he makes a 'pilgrymage' to the temple of Venus (2214–15).[14]

It seems to me, then, that the outcome of the tale is fully justified by what has gone before – that Palamon wins Emelye because he is worthier of her, in terms of the story, than is Arcite. By this I would not imply either that Arcite is base or that the loser wins nothing; half the interest of the final solution is in the reconciliation between the two knights and the comments of Theseus on Arcite's fate. If it be thought that the evidence on which I have sought to make a distinction between the knights is too slender to support one, then I can plead in defence that the slightest parts of the poem are often charged with a significance only apparent in the light of the whole. When Arcite, for example, on being given his liberty complains that 'We witen nat what thing we preyen heere' (1260), his words are full of an irony (because of his later prayer to Mars) greater than his immediate circumstances presuppose.

IV

The justice of the solution in relation to the two knights would be incomplete, however, if that solution were not brought by justifiable procedure. The course of events is determined to some extent by the knights themselves, more largely by Theseus, and ultimately by the various divinities, especially Saturn, and the supernatural power that they represent. Of the human figures in the story that of Theseus is most dominant – indeed, so much so as to seem, in comparison to Palamon, Arcite, and Emelye, almost superhuman. Theseus is both the guardian of Emelye and the legal possessor of the persons of the knights from the moment they are brought before him, more dead than alive, after the battle at Thebes. Later he releases Arcite, and Palamon escapes; but before either has had a chance to advance his cause with Emelye the Duke comes upon them and takes them prisoner again. At this point the poem implicitly associates him with the destiny and divine foreknowledge which, according to the teller of the Tale, lie behind all human events and situations:

> . . . And forth I wole of Theseus yow telle.
> The destinee ministre general,
> That executeth in the world over al
> The purveiaunce that God hath seyn biforn
> So strong it is that, though the world had sworn
> The contrarie of a thing by ye or nay,
> Yet sometyme it shall fallen on a day
> That falleth nat eft withinne a thousand yeer. . . .
> This mene I now by myghty Theseus. . . .   (A. 1662 ff.)

Theseus is the executant of destiny. On the morning of the final tourney he sits in a window of his palace overlooking the crowd and 'arrayed right as he were a god in trone' (2529). As a personality he is appropriately impressive: terrifying in action, philosophical in outlook; richly experienced yet detached in point of view; warmly sympathetic to misfortune[15] yet mockingly ironical at the expense of youthful enthusiasm. From the moment when he gives orders that the captured knights be imprisoned to the moment when he arranges the final nuptials of Emelye and Palamon he dominates the plot without ever being a partisan. Thus his pronouncements, and especially his long speech in the final scene, carry peculiar weight.

Destiny proper is represented first by the three divinities to whom the rivals, and Emelye, appeal; then by Saturn, who settles the issue among the divinities; and ultimately by a Divinity – 'the sighte above' (1672), 'the Firste Moevere' (2987) – beyond all particular divinities. This ultimate godhead, 'the which is prince and cause of alle thing' (3036), is identified by Theseus with 'Juppiter'; but the conception of him given by Theseus's speech as a whole sets him significantly apart from those other representatives of the classical pantheon who figure in the Knight's Tale. These – Mars, Diana, and the rest – are as much stars as gods;[16] and being stars they are the particular manifestations of Fortune, or Destiny, which is the agent, ultimately, of Providence. In *Paradise Lost* the pagan deities are assimilated to Christian story by their banishment to hell as rebel angels; in the Knight's Tale they still reign in the physical heavens, but reign as deputies of a transcendent sovereign.[17]

v

When the Knight had finished his Tale Chaucer records that it won the general applause of the pilgrims, and the unanimous approval of the gentlefolk among them : 'And namely the gentils everichon' (3113). This last statement we can readily believe; for the Tale is wholeheartedly aristocratic, both in subject-matter and attitude. All the principal figures are of high birth; Arcite, for example, mortified by his disguise as a poor squire, reflects on his lineage in the following lines :

> Allas, ybroght is to confusioun
> The blood roial of Cadme and Amphioun, –
> Of Cadmus, which that was the firste man
> That Thebes bulte, or first the toun bigan,
> And of the citee first was crouned kyng.
> Of his lynage am I and his ofspryng
> By verray ligne, as of the stok roial. . . .   (A. 1545–51)

Theseus represents the full exercise of a sovereignty the material prerogatives of which are made, at several points, very explicit. 'Ful lik a lord' the Duke rides to the lists through a city which is said to be 'Hanged with clooth of gold, and nat with sarge' (2568–9). For the building of the temples beside the 'noble theatre' he has employed all the architects and artisans in the country, regardless of expense : the temple of Mars 'coste largely of gold a fother' (1908). The limitlessness of his wealth is initially apparent when he demands no ransom for his royal prisoners – a circumstance so remarkable in dukes that it is referred to more than once.

Even persons who appear only briefly in the action are of rank: the suppliant Theban women at the beginning of the poem are all duchesses and queens. Even disguised as Philostrate, a mere hewer of wood and bearer of water, Arcite

> . . . was so gentil of condicioun
> That thurghout al the court was his renoun.
>
> (A. 1431–2)

The recurrent occasions of life for people of such condition as this are ceremonious, their actions at such times being imbued with the piety of ancient ritual. Arcite, even though he has rejected the code that binds him to his blood-brother, insists on returning to Athens, after finding the escaped Palamon, for food and weapons for his rival. The poem as a whole presents in affectionate detail three major ceremonial events: the prayers at the temples, the elaborate formalities of the tournament, and Arcite's funeral. Even the period of mourning for Arcite is apparently of prescribed duration (2967–8).

The action takes place, then, in an idealized aristocratic universe, magnanimous, munificent, and ceremonial. Theseus is the ideal conquering governor, Palamon the ideal lover, Emelye the emblem of vernal innocence. The story ends, too, with its ideal lover at last

> . . . in alle wele,
> Lyvynge in blisse, in richesse, and in heele. . . .
>
> (A. 3101–2)

Yet the view of the universe taken by the Tale is a tragic view, and the condition of man presented by the teller is also tragic.

The most direct, simple, and uncompromising expression of this tragic view comes in the words of Egeus, Theseus's father, after the accident to Arcite proves fatal. Egeus (who makes only this single brief appearance in the story) has been taken by some critics for a dotard; however that may be, his speech, of which I will quote the final lines, has central importance:

> This world nys but a thurghfare ful of wo,
> And we been pilgrymes, passynge to and fro.
> Deeth is an ende of every worldly soore.   (A. 2847–9)

The sentiment is a commonplace, of course, which could doubtless be matched, if not duplicated, a thousand times in the
literature of Chaucer's age and of preceding periods; it nevertheless has power in the Knight's Tale because that poem, although its plot is concerned with success in love and its setting
pictures aristocratic splendours, presents on the whole such an
abiding and various image of 'every worldly soore'. Man, the
teller might be saying, whatever his station in life, is the victim of
arbitrary, cruel, and often ironical mischance. The Theban ladies
are summarily widowed by civil wars; Thebes sacked by Athens;
the knights jailed by Theseus; while noble Arcite slowly and painfully dies of a fall from his horse because, nature having abandoned him, medicine is consequently useless –

> And certeinly, ther Nature wol nat wirche,
> Fare wel phisik! go ber the man to chirche!
>
> (A. 2759–60)

It is not only the events of the story which provide a rich reference for Palamon's bitter questioning of the 'crueel goddes' in
the following lines:

> What is mankynde moore unto you holde
> Than is the sheep that rouketh in the folde?
> For slayn is man right as another beest
> And dwelleth eek in prison and arreest,
> And hath siknesse and greet adversitee. . . .
>
> (A. 1307–11)

As tragically impressive as the events I have mentioned is the
image of the human condition implied by the great descriptions
of the temples of Venus, Mars, and Diana (especially by that of
Mars) and by the speech of Saturn detailing his own influence
on mortal affairs. These passages, among the most admired in
Chaucer, are generally treated as set-pieces, in detachment from

context. Actually they are an organic part of the Tale, for they symbolically extend the misfortunes and griefs of the central characters and at the same time provide a background against which these same misfortunes and griefs will seem less extraordinary. This extension supports the view of human life taken by Egeus and Palamon in the lines I have just quoted, and by Arcite and Theseus in lines I shall presently discuss.

The picture of the temple of Venus refers, it is true, to both the delights and the sorrows she causes; but it begins and ends with the sorrows – 'ful pitous to biholde' – and it emphasizes the follies of lovers : 'the folye of kyng Salomon. . . . The riche Cresus, kaytyf in servage' (1942, 1946). The temple of Diana, which represents innocence and a kind of divine beneficence and is associated with Emelye, is described more naïvely as a collection of wonders merely; but even here the most vivid pictures are of the hounds devouring Actaeon 'for that they knewe hym naught' (2068), and of a woman in the throes of a difficult childbirth. The images inspired by Mars and Saturn give an inclusive and uncompromising panorama of existence as a moral hell and a cosmic chaos. The sow devours the baby 'right in the cradel' (2019); the man-eating wolf rends his victim at the foot of Mars's statue, to the glory of the god; the glance of Saturn is 'the fader of pestilence' (2469); images of manslaughter, arson, suicide, treason, murder, and rapine make up the decorations of Mars's temple.

This last edifice is built like a dungeon, as the following lines show :

> The dore was al of adamant eterne,
> Yclenched overthwart and endelong
> With iren tough; and for to make it strong,
> Every pyler, the temple to sustene,
> Was tonne-greet, of iren bright and shene . . .
>
> (A. 1990–4)

Imprisonment is a symbol of great importance to the poem; it is significant that Arcite's long-desired release from captivity leads first to exile and then despair, then to a strenuous life of practical expedients crowned by illusive victory and sudden death. His epitaph is spoken by Theseus (the original imprisoner of the knights) in these words :

> ... goode Arcite, of chivalrie the flour,
> Departed is with duetee and honour
> Out of this foule prisoun of this lyf. . . .
>
> (A. 3059–61)

For Arcite release from prison has been no more than escape into a larger prison, until the final release of death. 'What is this world?' asks the dying knight, whom devices and expedients can help no longer –

> What is this world? What asketh men to have?
> Now with his love, now in his colde grave
> Allone, withouten any compaignye?   (A. 2777–9)

But although the picture of 'this world' implied by the Mars and Saturn passages is chaotic and hideous enough, such a view of human existence is by no means the total effect left by the Knight's Tale. To begin with, the very presence of the gods, whether astrological or theological, gives a degree of order and significance to the lives of mortals. A trio of divinities accounts for the misery of Palamon : as Palamon puts it,

> ... I moot been in prisoun thurgh Saturne,
> And eek thurgh Juno, jalous and eek wood,
> That hath destroyed wel ny al the blood
> Of Thebes with his waste walles wyde;
> And Venus sleeth me on that oother syde
> For jalousie and fere of hym Arcite.   (A. 1328–33)

And a conflict of divinities accounts for the death of Palamon's rival. Nothing exists in this human world but has its source, significance, and guidance from above – a kind of guidance symbolized most concretely by the traditional device of Mercurie's appearance to advise Arcite to go to Athens. Thus the very vicissitudes of life fall into an ultimate pattern decipherable by wisdom and philosophy; even the destructive divinities are still divine.

More important still, beyond these destructive divinities governs the Firste Moevere of Theseus's final elegy. This speech is the climax of the poem. Here Theseus sets forth in general terms what the particulars of the story have been leading to. Human decay and corruption (the accident to Arcite, the violence and pestilence symbolized by Mars and Saturn, the follies in which Venus has a share) proceed under the laws of an ultimate Providence, which has fixed a term to the existence of finite things. Man's proper wisdom is not to cry out against the 'faire cheyne of love' which binds the universe, but nobly to accept his destiny – to 'take it weel . . . that to us alle is due' (3043–4). Hence the importance of Arcite: his nobility, his education, his tragedy. His death was not meaningless to him since it empowered him to reassert his proper relation to Palamon and to do his friend the service he might have done at the beginning. As Theseus says,

> . . . And certeinly a man hath moost honour
> To dyen in his excellence and flour,
> Whan he is siker of his goode name;
> Thanne hath he doon his freend, ne hym, no shame.
>
> (A. 3047–50)

And after Arcite's funeral, the decent period of mourning, and Theseus's elegy, stability can be established by the harmonious union of Emelye and Palamon, who incidentally represent the formerly warring countries, Thebes and Athens.

VI

Such a tale is clearly suited to the Knight of Chaucer's prologue who tells it, a man of high rank, wide travel, and ingenuous loyalty to the ideas of his class and age. The lessons of the Tale, if such they may be called, imply a pious and logical mind in the instructor, a deep acceptance of Christian faith and chivalric standards, and an heroic disposition to face the vicissitudes and disasters of a dangerous calling. That they had been faced in fact we have been assured by the prologue:

> At Alisaundre he was whan it was wonne.
> Ful ofte tyme he hadde the bord bigonne
> Aboven alle nacions in Pruce;
> In Lettow hadde he reysed and in Ruce,
> No Cristen man so ofte of his degree.
> In Gernade at the seege eek hadde he be
> Of Algezir, and riden in Belmarye.
> At Lyeys was he and at Satalye,
> Whan they were wonne; and in the Grete See
> At many a noble armee hadde he be.   (A. 51–60)

To present the mind and heart of this Knight is an important function of the Tale. Though hardly a dramatic monologue in the Shakespearian or Browningesque sense of the term, the Tale is nevertheless a dramatic utterance both externally (in the light of its setting) and internally. Scarcely has the Knight finished his story of Palamon and Arcite, and won the applause of all the pilgrims (especially of the gentlefolk), than the drunken Miller is pushing forward, interrupting the Host's attempted introduction of the Monk as second narrator, and insisting loudly on *his* tale instead. The Miller's Tale (as everyone knows) is perhaps the most elaborate improper story in English literature – the most elaborate and in many ways the grossest. It represents an artistic antithesis to the Knight's Tale, being also a tale of the rivalry of two suitors for a young woman. But whereas Palamon and Arcite worshipped the maiden Emelye with an introspective ardour that seemed almost its own reward, Nicholas and Absolon pursue the lickerish Alisoun for the simple object of cuckoldry just (to use Chaucer's simile) as a cat pursues a mouse. Instead of the international and even cosmological background of the Knight's Tale, the scene of the Miller's Tale is small-town, domestic, and bourgeois. Its plot embodies a kind of crude justice meted out by circumstances both to successful and to attempted adultery. The manners of chivalry are burlesqued in the figure of the genteel parish-clerk-and-barber Absolon; while Christianity enters the story as a ready means of duping an illiterate and credulous husband. The contrast to the Knight's Tale could hardly be more complete. It is as if the Miller, growing more and more restive in the moral stratosphere as the leisurely Knight's Tale winds to its ceremonious and philosophical conclusion, were unable to keep silent after the Knight's final words about the young couple :

> For now is Palamon in alle wele,
> Lyvynge in blisse, in richesse, and in heele,
> And Emelye hym loveth so tendrely,
> And he hire serveth al so gentilly,
> That nevere was ther no word hem bitwene
> Of jalousie or any oother teene. . . .   (A. 3101–6)

What a picture of married life ! The Miller will show that there is another side to *that* story ! –

> By armes, and by blood and bones,
> I kan a noble tale for the nones,
> With which I wol now quite the Knyghtes tale
>
> (A. 3125–7)

says the Miller.

The Miller's Tale, then, is the principal external means by which the Knight's Tale is made dramatic and given a certain artistic distance both from the reader and from the poet of the *Canterbury Tales*. There are also internal and ironical means of accomplishing the same object, and they are fully employed. I refer, of course, to such occasions as when Theseus remarks that the lover who loses Emelye may as well 'go pipen in an yvy leef' (1838); or when the women of Athens (with all the sensibilities of modern cinema addicts) lament the death of Arcite because, as they put it, he had 'gold ynough, and Emelye' (2836); or when the species of trees that make up Arcite's funeral pyre are listed with no more ceremony of adjective than it is now customary to give the names in a telephone directory. The very ingenuousness of the Knight as a commentator on his own story may sometimes give rise to the pleasantest irony : the reader must smile at the speaker, while his heart warms to him. I shall close this essay with one example of such irony, an example which illustrates also the pitfalls into which even a learned Chaucerian may occasionally slip.

The pathetic death of Arcite is a matter of intense grief to his comrade-in-arms and his intended bride. 'Shrighte Emelye, and howleth Palamon' (2817); and Theseus carries away the prostrate heroine. At this point the Knight who tells the story embarks on a generalization, in the following terms:

> What helpeth it to tarien forth the day
> To tellen how she weep bothe eve and morwe?
> For in swich cas wommen have swich sorwe,
> Whan that hir housbondes ben from hem ago,
> That for the moore part they sorwen so,
> Or ellis fallen in swich maladye,
> That at the laste certeinly they dye.   (A. 2820–6)

'Coming from the author of the Wife of Bath,' remarks H. B. Hinckley in his *Notes on Chaucer*,[18] 'these words can only be construed as satire, or as insincerity. Was it such a passage as this – a passage which is certainly out of place – that prompted Matthew Arnold's celebrated saying that Chaucer lacked "high seriousness"?'

The Knight, however, is neither insincere, satirical, nor the author of the Wife of Bath; and it is probably a measure of our present distance from the Victorian critics that the irony of Chaucer, his constant perception of personal and spiritual incompatibilities in a complex humanity, is the very quality that gives him, in our eyes, his seriousness as a poet and a critic of life.

S o u r c e : *Review of English Studies*, xxv (1949).

NOTES

1. A method of critical procedure similar to Mr. Webb's (namely, examination of selected parts divorced from any treatment of the poem as a whole) renders equally open to attack, in my judgement, the conclusions about the personalities of Palamon and Arcite reached recently by Professor A. H. Marckwardt, *Characterization in Chaucer's Knight's Tale*, University of Michigan Contributions in Modern Philology, No. 5 (1947).

2. See the notes to the Tale in *The Complete Works of Chaucer*,

ed. F. N. Robinson (Cambridge, Mass., 1933) pp. 770 ff. for Lowes, Wise, Patch, and Curry; also B. L. Jefferson, *Chaucer and . . . Boethius* (Princeton, 1917); Johnstone Parr, 'The Date and Revision of Chaucer's Knight's Tale', *PMLA* LX (1945) 307–24; and R. A. Pratt, 'Chaucer's Use of the *Teseide*'. *PLMA*, LXII (1947) 598–621, especially 613–20.

3. See R. K. Root, *Poetry of Chaucer* (Cambridge, Mass., 1922) pp. 163–73. Mr. Root discriminates between the temperaments of the two knights, but concludes that 'the reader of the tale . . . is unable to decide on which he would wish the ultimate success to light' (p. 170).

4. Root, p. 172.

5. Root, p. 37.

6. See H. R. Patch, 'Chauceriana', *Englische Studien*, LXV (1930–1) 354 *n.*; cited by Robinson in a note on A. 860.

7. J. R. Hulbert, 'What was Chaucer's Aim in the Knight's Tale?', *Studies in Philology*, XXVI (1929) 375 ff.

8. At one point rhetorical parallelism may possibly extend beyond the two knights and bracket Palamon and Emelye: compare ll. 2212 and 2273.

9. *Odes*, IV. 7. The translation is from Housman's *Collected Poems* (New York, 1940) p. 164.

10. See B. A. Wise, *Influence of Statius upon Chaucer* (Baltimore, 1911) p. 88.

11. For some aspects of the following comparison of Palamon and Arcite I am indebted to my friend Mr. Douglas Knight.

12. Contrast the language of Arcite's prayer to Mars (especially the verb 'usedest') : 'For thilke hoote fir / In which thow whilom brendest for desir,/Whan that thou usedest the beautee/Of faire yonge, fresshe Venus free' (2383–6) with that of Palamon's prayer to Venus : 'For thilke love thow haddest to Adoon' (2224).

13. Cf. also l. 1562, where Arcite says that Theseus 'martireth' Palamon in prison.

14. By far the most interesting discussion of Palamon and Arcite I have seen in print is that of Professor H. N. Fairchild in his article 'Active Arcite, Contemplative Palamon', *Journal of English and Germanic Philology*, XXVI (1927) 285–93. His allegorical interpretation has been called 'somewhat forced' by Robinson in his edition of Chaucer (p. 772), and it must be admitted that several of Fairchild's comments do not seem fully warranted by the text of the poem. We have no reason to suppose, for example, that Arcite goes a-maying because he is 'stirred by the vague uneasiness of the

active man' (Fairchild, p. 289), especially when the poem says that he 'litel wiste how ny that was his care' (1489). But Fairchild's article, in contrast to some other discussions of the subject, is fully alive to possible symbolic values in Chaucer's presentation of the knights.

15. I take his imprisonment of the two knights without asking ransom to be simply part of the *donnée* of the story as it came to Chaucer – and not, without further explanation of motive than the poet gives us, an implication that Theseus lacks chivalry.

16. See W. C. Curry, *Chaucer and the Medieval Sciences* (Oxford, 1926) chapter VI.

17. The position of 'Juppiter' is made ambiguous by his brief appearance during the quarrel between Venus and Mars, of which it is said that 'Juppiter was bisy it to stente' (2442); Saturn finally resolves the strife. In the light of the poem as a whole it appears that Saturn is the logical deity to devise the catastrophe which causes Arcite's death; and the passage in question need not be taken to imply either that Saturn is superior in power to the divine disputants or that Jupiter was, or would have been, unable to settle matters. Nothing in the passage seems inconsistent with the idea of Saturn representing one aspect, or agent, of Jupiter's omnipotence.

18. (Northampton, Mass., 1907) p. 113.

E. T. Donaldson

IDIOM OF POPULAR POETRY IN
THE MILLER'S TALE (1950)

A poet who abandons the poetic idiom of his time and nation
and devises one entirely new in its place creates for the would-be
critic of his language a difficult problem. Criticism of the language of poetry can exist only through comparison with contemporary and earlier writings, and when, as sometimes happens,
the critic cannot find between these and the work of the
innovator enough similarity even to reflect the differences, he has
to resort, in lieu of criticism, to merely quoting the innovator
admiringly. With Chaucer the problem is even greater than with
Milton, Shakespeare, Wordsworth, or Eliot. For while we may
at least be sure that they were brought up in an English
literary tradition from which they more or less consciously revolted, the disquieting suspicion always arises that Chaucer, bred
if not born in a culture predominantly continental, may not have
been very much aware of the literary tradition from which he was
presumably in revolt; and this means that anyone who, in search
of comparisons with Chaucer's diction, goes to the most pro-
lific of the vernacular literary traditions, the romance, or to the
closely related lyric, must consider himself to be in danger of
wasting his time.[1]

But Chaucer did, after all, write in English, however continental his background may have been, and it stands to reason
that diligent search will reveal at least a few correspondences with
the popular English poetic diction of his day. Complete analysis
of his own vocabulary is now – and has been for some time – possible through use of the Chaucer *Concordance*;[2] in this one can
study all the contexts of every word he ever used, and hence can
try to determine the values he placed upon the words he
appropriated from the conventional vocabulary of popular
poetry. It is the evaluation of these borrowings that I have under-

taken; but since the job is a tricky one at best, I have thought it advisable to begin with those words which, while common in contemporary romance and lyric, occur only a very few times in Chaucer and are therefore to be suspected of carrying a rather special sort of weight. Only by such drastic limitation of the subject can it be treated at all in the time allotted.

In approaching the problem of evaluation there are two subordinate poems that I have found to be of some help. The first is Fragment A of the Middle English translation of the *Roman de la Rose*. That this is really Chaucer's work cannot be entirely proved. Most scholars think it is,[3] and I have little doubt that it is. But even if it is not, it is at least the sort of poem we should suppose him to have written in his poetic immaturity. For while it is not nearly so free as Chaucer's mature works are from that conventional diction – those clichés – by which the whole vernacular tradition was infected,[4] it nevertheless frequently has that quality, common to all Chaucer's indisputable works, of uniting perfectly simple English words with extraordinary ease into genuinely poetic language of a kind that makes the phrase 'poetic diction' seem entirely too high-flown to be apt. Whether it is by Chaucer or not, its diction, occasionally but not consistently conventional, seems to represent a half-way point between popular English poetry and the *Canterbury Tales*. I find it critically illuminating, therefore, in comparing the Fragment with the *Canterbury Tales*, to observe how the mature Chaucer places in new and sometimes startling contexts words which a poet of somewhat less refined taste (probably the young Chaucer) had used flatly in time-honored contexts.

Rather firmer help is offered by Chaucer's 'Sir Thopas'. For this parody, while a criticism of vernacular conventions of every sort, is above all a criticism of standard English poetic diction. Therefore, if we find – as we do – words that Chaucer makes fun of in 'Sir Thopas' showing up in seemingly innocent contexts elsewhere in his work, we shall have at least a small area in which to exercise criticism of Chaucer's idiom. Let me confess at once that the total critical yield from the words of this sort that I have noticed is not great and that it makes possible, not a wider appreciation of Chaucer's more serious poetry, but of some of his comic effects. In this paper I shall deal largely with the effect upon

the Miller's Tale of certain words introduced from the vernacular poetic tradition. It goes almost without saying that this
effect is ironical and that more irony is not the sole product I
should have wished to achieve from my investigation. Still, this
is only a beginning, and 'after this I hope ther cometh moore' –
if not from me, from better critics. The following is therefore
presented as an example of a technique by which it may be possible to arrive at a better understanding of Chaucer's poetic
idiom.

Since in the Miller's Tale I shall be dealing with ironical context, I shall start with an illustration of an ironical use of conventional idiom that is, thanks to the brilliant work of Professor
Lowes, known to every Chaucerian. Lowes has demonstrated that
the key to the portrait of the Prioress is in the second line, which,
in describing her smiling as 'ful symple and coy', endows her with
a pair of qualities that were also those of innumerable heroines of
Old French romance.[5] It is, incidentally, a measure of Chaucer's
gallicization, as well as of his tact with a lady who likes to speak
at least a sort of French, that these conventional words, along
with most of the others in her characterization, are not commonly applied to ladies in Middle English romance. Furthermore, Lowes shows that in describing her person – gray eyes,
delicate soft red mouth, fair forehead, nose *tretys* – Chaucer borrows from stock French descriptions of ladies details that were
full of courtly reminiscences for the cultivated reader of the time,
though with impeccable taste he foregoes the complete physical
catalogue that an Old French heroine would feel herself entitled
to. If Lowes had wished to reinforce his point, whose delicacy
needs no reinforcement, he could have gone on to examine
Chaucer's own works for the reappearance of the words used to
describe the Prioress. He would have found, for instance, that
'coy' is used of no other woman in Chaucer, though it appears
in the stereotype 'as coy as a maid', used only of men. 'Simple', as
Lowes does observe, is also the attribute of Blanche the Duchess
– Chaucer's most serious conventional portrait; but it is applied
further to three romantic ladies in the first fragment of the
Roman, and, in Chaucer's mature work, it is used twice of
Criseide, perhaps in a delicate attempt to be suggestive about
her manner without being communicative about her character.

It is worthy of note that the Prioress' nose *tretys* is foreshadowed by the face *tretys* of Lady Beauty in the English *Roman*; but the word is otherwise non-Chaucerian. Further, while ladies' noses receive full treatment in the translation of the *Roman*, elsewhere the only female nose mentioned is the stubby one that the miller's daughter inherited from her father in the Reeve's Tale – 'With kamus nose, and eyen greye as glas', an interesting mutation, incidentally, on the Prioress, 'Hir nose tretys, hir eyen greye as glas'. And of all the women in Chaucer, only the Prioress and Alison, heroine of the Miller's Tale, have mouths or foreheads worthy of note : a case, perhaps, of the Colonel's Lady and Judy O'Grady. Finally, if one had time one might, I think, profitably investigate the words 'fetys' and 'fetisly', both used in describing the Prioress, but elsewhere appearing only in contexts which render highly suspect the particular sort of elegance they suggest.[6] In any case, the Prioress' portrait is a masterpiece of idiomatic irony, though the idiom is that of French poetry rather than of English.

With this much preliminary let us turn to the Miller's Tale. Upon this, Chaucer's worst ribaldry, it is generally agreed that he lavished his greatest skill, and in particular upon his description of the three principal characters – Alison, Absolon, and *hende* Nicholas, and upon their dialogue with one another. One of the devices he used most skillfully was that of sprinkling these characterizations and conversations with clichés borrowed from the vernacular versions of the code of courtly love – phrases of the sort we are accustomed to meet, on the one hand, in Middle English minstrel romances and, on the other, in secular lyrics such as those preserved in Harley MS 2253 – but phrases that are not encountered elsewhere in the serious works of Geoffrey Chaucer. The comic effect of this imported courtly diction will, I hope, be understood as we go along. At the start it is necessary to bear in mind only that by the fourteenth century at least, the aim and end of courtly love was sexual consummation, however idealized it may have been made to appear, and that of the various factors upon which the *ars honeste amandi* depended for its idealization the conventional language associated with it was not the least important.

The key to the matter, as one might expect, is in the constant epithet applied to the hero of the Miller's Tale – that is, in hende Nicholas' almost inseparable *hende*. Any one who has done even cursory reading in popular English poetry of Chaucer's time – and before and after – will heartily agree with the *Oxford Dictionary*'s statement that 'hende' is 'a conventional epithet of praise, very frequent in Middle English poetry'. Originally it seems to have meant no more than 'handy, at hand'; but it gradually extended its area of signification to include the ideas of 'skillful, clever' and of 'pleasant, courteous, gracious' (or 'nice', as the *Oxford Dictionary* says with what I take to be exasperated quotation marks); and it simultaneously extended its area of reference to include, under the general sense 'nice', almost every hero and heroine, as well as most of the rest of the characters siding with the angels, in Middle English popular poetry. Thus, the right of the Squire of Low Degree to the hand of the King's Daughter of Hungary is established by the minstrel poet's exclamation :

> The squir was curteous and hend,
> Ech man him loved and was his frend.

And another poet boasts of Sir Isumbras,

> Alle hym loffede, that hym seghe :
> Se hende a man was hee ![7]

Such examples could be multiplied indefinitely. Indeed, the average popular poet could no more do without 'hende' than he could do without the lovers whose endless misadventures gave him his plots, since unless a lover was 'hende', he or she was no proper exponent of courtly love. We should, therefore, have a right to expect the adjective to modify such Chaucerian characters as Troilus and Criseide, Arveragus and Dorigen, Palamon, Arcite, and Emily. But in Chaucer's indisputable works the word, while it is used eleven times with Nicholas, appears only twice elsewhere, and it is applied to none of the more serious characters, such as those just mentioned. The translator of Fragment A of the *Roman* had, to be sure, used it twice to describe amiable folk associated with the garden of the Rose; but thereafter it is spoken only by the Host, that distinguished exponent of bourgeois good manners, when he calls upon the Friar to be 'hende' to the Summoner; and by Alice of Bath, who expresses with it the charm possessed by her fifth-husband-to-be, jolly Jankin, who is a spiritual sibling of Nicholas' if there ever was one. It is clear from these usages, as well as from the even more eloquent lack of its use in any genuinely courtly context, that for Chaucer 'hende' had become so déclassé and shopworn as to be ineligible for employment in serious poetry.

But by the same token it was highly eligible for employment in the Miller's Tale. Nicholas is, after all, a hero of sorts, and he deserves to be as 'hende' as any other self-respecting hero-lover. But in the present context the word mocks the broad meaning 'nice' that is apparent in non-Chaucerian contexts. Indeed, its constant association with Nicholas encourages one to feel that here 'hende' does not so much define Nicholas as he defines it. Furthermore, he defines it in a way that is surprisingly true to the less usual senses of the word, for Nicholas turns out to be a good deal less romantically 'nice' than he is realistically 'clever, skillful'. He even represents the earliest meaning of the word, 'at hand, handy'; for the Miller, analyzing his love-triangle in proverbial terms, remarks that always the 'nye slye' (the sly dog at hand, Nicholas) displaces the 'ferre leeve' (the distant charmer, Absolon). But most important, in Nicholas as in other heroes, the quality of being 'hende' is the cause of his success in love. In the quotations given above we learn that it was because they were 'hende' that Sir Isumbras and the Squire of Low Degree were generally beloved. Nicholas is also lovable, but his lovableness is of the rather special sort that would appeal to a woman of Alison's tastes and morals. In short, the coupling of word and character suggests in Nicholas nothing more than a large measure of physical charm that is skillful at recognizing its opportunities and putting itself to practical sexual use; and this is a sorry degradation for an adjective that had been accustomed to modify some of the nicest people in popular poetry, who now, as a result of Nicholas, begin to suffer from guilt by association.

A somewhat similar aspect of Nicholas' character is reflected in the line that tells us,

Of deerne love he koude and of solas.   (A. 3200)

For his aptitude at *derne love*, 'secret love', Nicholas must have
been the envy of a good many young men in contemporary
English poetry. For instance, in the Harley MS we meet several
swains whose unsuccessful involvement in secret love affairs is their
chief source of poetic woe.

> Lutel wot hit any mon
> hou derne loue may stonde,

grumbles one of these before going on to explain with what
agonies and ecstasies it is attended.[8] Such lyricists were probably
apt to pretend to themselves that the secretive line of conduct
suggested by the phrase 'derne love', while it may have made
things difficult, was nevertheless one of the ennobling conditions
imposed upon them by the courtly code. Chaucer, however, seems
to have felt otherwise, for while many of his heroes experience
'secree love', none besides Nicholas is ever 'derne' about it. Elsewhere Chaucer does not even use the common adjective to
modify other nouns besides 'love', apparently feeling that its reputation had been ruined by the company it had kept so long.
Even in Old English, of course, the word was ambiguous,
reflecting sometimes justified secrecy and sometimes secret sin;
and among the moral lyrics of the Harley MS there is one whose
author makes it clear that for him 'derne dedes' are dirty deeds.[9]
From his avoidance of the adjective it appears that Chaucer also
subscribed to such an opinion. Moreover, the modern reader of
the Harley love lyrics will probably sympathize with him, for it
sometimes seems that, whatever the lovers pretended, they res-
pected the principle of 'derne love' more because of its value in
protecting them from outraged husbands or fathers than from
any courtly ideal of preserving their lady's good name.[10] Thus,
long before Chaucer's time 'derne love' was already in potential-
ity what it becomes in actuality in Nicholas, a device for getting
away with adultery, if not really a sort of excuse for indulging in
it. Therefore Nicholas' aptitude parodies an ideal already devalued through misuse in the vernacular; and since even at its
most exalted the courtly code of secrecy might be described as

crassly practical, his aptitude also parodies that of more genuinely
courtly lovers than the Harley lyricists.

Turning to Nicholas' rival, jolly Absolon, one may find
further instances of this technique of Chaucer's. What Absolon
lacks in the way of Nicholas' 'hendeness' he tries to make up with
his own 'joly-ness'. The epithet 'joly' is not as consistently used
with Absolon as 'hende' is with Nicholas, and since it has a wide
variety of meanings and is common in Chaucer, it may not be so
readily classified. Suffice it to say that it is generally in the
mouths of bourgeois characters and that in the senses 'handsome'
and 'pretty' it modifies men or women with equal frequency. But
it is, perhaps, the secret of Absolon's ill-success that all his
jollification makes rather for prettiness than for masculine effectiveness. One recalls that Sir Thopas, though a sturdy hero, possesses some of the charms of a typical medieval heroine, and the
Miller seems to suggest by several of the terms in his portrait of
Absolon that the latter had somehow or other fallen across the
fine line which in medieval poetry separated feminine beauty
from that of beardless youths. For in his description he uses
words that a minstrel poet would normally apply to a pretty
girl. For instance,

> His rode was reed, his eyen greye as goos,   (A. 3317)

and the gray eyes will remind us of the Prioress, as well as of
countless other medieval heroines and, it must be granted, a number of heroes, though not in Chaucer, who reserves gray eyes for
ladies. But in possessing a 'rode' – that is, a peaches-and-cream
complexion recommended by fourteenth-century Elizabeth
Ardens, Absolon places himself in the almost exclusive company
of Middle English damsels.[11] The complexion of truly manly
males of the time was, after all, generally obscured by a good
deal of beard, and hence apt to remain unsung. It is significant
that the only other 'rode' in all Chaucer belongs to Sir Thopas, a
feminine feature that contrasts startingly with the saffron beard
of that curiously constituted creature. Absolon further distinguishes himself (from his sex, I fear) by being the only
character in Chaucer to be associated with the adjective
'lovely', which is applied to the looks he casts upon the ladies of

the parish and to no other thing Chaucerian, though to hundreds of things, especially things feminine, in popular poetry.[12]

Readers of the latter would naturally expect the flesh of this pretty fellow to be

> As whit as is the blosme upon the rys,   (A. 3324)

and it comes as a surprise that it is not Absolon's flesh, but his surplice, that is described in these terms. But the line, either in much the same form or, if one wants pink flesh, with the variation 'as reed as rose on ris', is one of the clichés found almost inevitably in descriptions of women.[13] For instance, the variant form is applied to Lady Beauty's flesh in the *Roman* fragment. But in what we are sure is Chaucer's work there is elsewhere no such phrase – indeed, there is elsewhere no such thing as a 'ris', 'spray', at all. When he quietly transfers the conventional descriptive phrase from the body to the clothing that covers it – in this case Absolon's surplice – Chaucer is, of course, creating the humor of surprise; but more important, the trick enables him to evoke for the reader the hackneyed context, with all its associations, in which the phrase usually appears, while at the same time the poet can make literal use of the phrase's meaning in his own more realistic description. There is an even more effective example of this economy in the portrait of Alison, to which I shall now turn.

The pretty heroine of the tale exemplifies most brilliantly Chaucer's reduction of the worn-out ideal, expressed by the worn-out phrase, to its lowest common denominator of sexuality.

> Fair was this yonge wyf, and therwithal
> As any wezele hir body gent and smal.   (A. 3233–4)

Now the weasel, as Lowes has observed,[14] is Chaucer's own fresh image, and its effectiveness is obvious. But the fact that Alison's body is 'gent and smal' – shapely and delicate – makes her the sister of every contemporary vernacular heroine who is worthy of having a lover.[15] Lady Beauty, paragon of embraceable women in the *Roman*, is in a similar way shapely –

> Gente, and in hir myddill small –

and it is natural that Sir Thopas should be 'fair and gent'. Possibly with Sird Thopas 'gent' has its non-physical sense of 'high-born, noble', but in view of the fact that the poet later commends his 'sydes smale' – an item of female beauty – one may detect in the word at least a suggestion of ambiguity. On the other hand, while many lovely women in Chaucer's known works are 'gentil', none besides Alison is 'gent'. His third and last use of the adjective is in the *Parliament of Fowls*, where it describes, appropriately enough, the 'facounde gent', the 'noble' eloquence, of the down-to-earth goose (a sort of female Miller in feathers) who speaks so uncourtly of the tercel eagles' love dilemma. Thus, in applying the stale adjective 'gent' to Alison's body the Miller seems to be regarding her from a point of view less ideal and esthetic than realistic and pragmatic.

As in the case of the Prioress, Chaucer's restraint (I suspect that here it is only a teasing sort of restraint) prevents him from listing – except for one startling detail – the other conventional charms of Alison's body. We might expect from the Miller that our heroine would be – as Lowes has said – 'anatomized in good set similes as inescapable as death', as, for instance, is Annot of the Harley lyric 'Annot and John'.[16] But the reader who wants this is doomed to disappointment, for what he gets is less of Alison's body than of her wardrobe. Several of the conventional terms, however, that one expects to meet in corporeal catalogues are still present, even though they are applied only to her clothing. Her sides, to be sure, are not like the Harley Fair Maid of Ribblesdale's,

> Whittore then the moren-mylk,[17]

but her apron is, a quality it shares in Chaucer only with the silk purse of the pink-and-white fleshed Franklin. This same apron lies, moreover,

> Upon hir lendes, ful of many a goore.   (A. 3237)

Now 'gore', which meant originally a triangular piece of land and later (as here) a triangular strip of cloth, hence by synecdoche a skirt or apron, is obviously a technical word, and the fact that Chaucer used it only twice may not be significant. But when one recalls the number of vernacular ladies – including Alison's namesake in the Harley lyrics – who were 'geynest vnder gore', or 'glad vnder gore',[18] one may, perhaps, become suspicious. To be sure, scholars assure us that these phrases, along with such variants as 'worthy under wede', 'lovesome under line', 'semely under serk', are merely stereotyped superlatives and presumably have no sexual connotation.[19] But in their literal meanings they could have such a connotation, and in their origin they probably did have. For instance, the poet of *Gawain and the Green Knight* speaks of the lady of the castle as 'lufsum vnder lyne' only when Gawain is being subjected by her to the most powerful sexual temptation. And inasmuch as Chaucer, violating his self-imposed restraint, takes pains to mention the 'lendes' (the loins), a word that appears a little later in a frankly sexual context[20] – that are hidden beneath the 'gores' of Alison's apron, it is possible that his employment of the word 'gore' is evocative as well as technical; that he is, indeed, by providing a sort of realistic paraphrase of the conventional expression, insinuating what the lover of the Harley Alison really had in mind when he called his mistress 'geynest vnder gore'. This is only a possibility, and I should not want to insist upon it. But the possibility becomes stronger when we recall Chaucer's other use of the word[21] – in Sir Thopas' dream,

> An elf-queene shal my lemman be
> And slepe under my goore.   (B.² 1978–9)

Whatever 'gore' means here – presumably cloak – its context is unmistakable.

Nowhere does Chaucer's idiom devaluate with more devastating effect the conventional ideal to the level of flat reality than in two sentences occurring near the end of Alison's portrait. Like many a lyric and romance poet the Miller discovers that he is not clever enough to describe the total effect his lady produces – indeed, he doubts that any one is clever enough. The poet of the *Life of Ipomedon* was later to remark of a lady,

> In all this world is non so wyse
> That hir goodnesse kan devyse,

while the Harley Alison's lover had already asserted,

> In world nis non so wyter mon
> That al hire bounte telle con.[22]

True to the convention, the Miller exclaims of his Alison,

> In al this world, to seken up and doun,
> There nys no man so wys that koude thenche
> So gay a popelote, or swich a wenche.   (A. 3252–4)

But the Miller's mind is not on the 'bounte' (excellence) or 'goodnesse' of Alison; and his crashing anticlimax, ending with the word 'wenche', which, in Chaucer, when it does not mean servant-girl means a slut,[23] is a triumph of the whole process we have been examining. Another occurs a little later. Once more the Miller is following convention, this time comparing Alison to a flower. John had said of Annot in the Harley lyric,

> The primerole he passeth, the peruenke of pris,[24]

and the Miller also begins his comparison with the cowslip, the 'primerole':

> She was a prymerole, a piggesnye.   (A. 3268)

But the accompanying item is no longer a 'pervenke of pris', an excellent periwinkle, but a 'piggesneye', something which, while it may be also a flower (perhaps, appropriately enough, a cuckoo flower),[25] remains, unmistakably, a pig's eye. Beneath the Miller's remorseless criticism the Blanchefleurs and even the Emilys of Middle English romance degenerate into the complacent targets of a lewd whistle.

In their conversation with Alison the two clerks talk like a couple of Harley lyricists.[26] But Absolon, fated to accomplish more words than deeds, naturally has the richer opportunity to speak in the vernacular of love – or rather, to quote Absolon, of love-longing.

> Ywis, lemman, I have swich love-longynge,
> That lik a turtel trewe is my moornynge,   (A. 3705–6)

he laments outside her window. Love-longing was, of course, a common complaint, positively epidemic in the Middle Ages, and most of Chaucer's lovers have at least occasional attacks of it. But as with certain modern diseases, its name seems to have varied with the social status of its victim, and in Chaucer only Absolon and Sir Thopas are afflicted with it under that name. They are therefore in a tradition that includes knights as illustrious as Sir Tristram, not to mention those rustics the Harley lovers,[27] but fails to include Aurelius, Arcite, Troilus, or even the less admirable Damian. The inference is that for Chaucer the phrase 'love-longing' implied a desire of the flesh irreconcilable with courtly idealism, though fine for Absolon. Absolon is also following popular tradition when he introduces the figure of the legendarily amorous turtle-dove into his declaration : 'like a turtle true is my mourning.' Ordinarily, however, it is the lady who is the dove, a 'trewe tortle in a tour'[28] – faithful and remote in her tower, but curiously inarticulate, considering that she is a dove and that doves are rarely silent. Thus, the conventional image is reset in a context that is more natural and in this case more genuinely poetic. Another simile of Absolon's for conveying his distress –

I moorne as dooth a lamb after the tete –   (A. 3704)

is the Miller's own audacious contribution to the language of love, and demonstrates the ease with which Chaucer, employing a sort of merciless logic, can move from a wholly conventional image involving animals to one wholly original and wholly devastating.

Elsewhere, Absolon keeps closer to what we should expect. Alison, for instance is his 'swete brid' or 'brĭd' – that is, his sweet bird, bride, or possibly even 'burd' (maiden): as in the romances and love lyrics it is often difficult to tell which of the three the lover means, or whether he is himself altogether sure.[29] In the other works of Chaucer birds are clearly birds, brides clearly brides, and 'burd' does not occur except once of a lady in the *Roman*. Perhaps, however, it is only fair to observe that Chaucer's avoidance elsewhere of this trite form of endearment results in a use of 'dear heart' and of the substantive 'swete' so excessive as to amount to a triteness of Chaucer's own devising.

Continuing in the lyrical tradition even after the shame of his débacle, Absolon calls Alison his 'deerelyng' – the only instance in Chaucer of this indestructible term.[30] But Absolon's lyricism reaches its highest point, naturally, before his disillusionment when, close to what he mistakes for the Promised Land – in this case the shot-window of the carpenter's bower – he begs for Alison's favors – that is, for her 'ore' (mercy), as lyric poets usually expressed it. A Harley poet describing a similar crisis in his relations with his mistress reports,

> Adoun y fel to hire anon
> Ant cri[d]e, 'Ledy, thyn ore !'[31]

And much earlier, according to Giraldus Cambrensis, a priest of Worcestershire had so far forgotten himself at the altar as to displace the liturgical response 'Dominus vobiscum' with the lyrical refrain 'Swete lamman, dhin are'.[32] Thus, Absolon was conforming to a very old tradition when, about to receive his kiss, he

> doun sette hym on his knees,
> And seyde, 'I am a lord at alle degrees;
> For after this I hope ther cometh moore :
> Lemman, thy grace, and sweete bryd, thyn oore!'
>
> (A. 3723–6)

'Ore', the venerable word that is so often in the mouths of love-sick swains in Middle English, occurs in Chaucer only here. And the immediate similarity but impending difference between Absolon's situation and the situation of the average lyric lover epitomizes the technique we have been examining.

One final illustration of Chaucer's use – or abuse – of conventional idiom will suffice. Every reader of medieval romance knows that sooner or later the poet is going to describe a feast, if not a literal feast of food, at least a metaphorical one of love; and readers of English romances, including, in this case, Chaucer's own, can anticipate with some accuracy the terms in which the feast is going to be described – all the mirth and minstrelsy, or mirth and solace, or bliss and solace, or bliss and revelry, or revelry and melody by which the occasion will be distinguished. In the Miller's Tale the feast is, of course, of the metaphorical kind, consisting in the consummation of an adulterous love; and the obscene Miller, with his vast talent for realism, adapts the hackneyed old phrases most aptly to the situation. The carpenter, snug if uncomfortable in his kneading trough on high, is alternating groans with snores – 'for his head mislay' – while Alison and Nicholas are in his bed below.

> Ther was the revel and the melodye;
> And thus lith Alison and Nicholas
> In bisynesse of myrthe and of solas.   (A. 3652–4)

At this feast the carpenter's snores furnish the 'melodye', while his wife and her lover experience the 'solas' – that seemingly innocent word for delight which here receives the full force of Chaucer's genius for devaluation – the completion of a logical process that began when we first heard it said of 'hende' Nicholas that

> Of deerne love he koude and of solas.   (A. 3200)

It is, of course, true that the idiom I have been examining is just what we should expect of the Miller's cultural background – and of that of his characters[33] – and it would be possible to dispose of it by simply labeling it 'verisimilitude'. But verisimilitude seems to me among the least important of artistic criteria, and I refuse to believe that the courtly idiom in the Miller's Tale accomplishes nothing more than that. Perhaps I should have made a larger effort than I have to distinguish the Miller from Chaucer, and my interchanging of their names must have grated on some ears. But as I see it, much of Chaucer's irony in the *Canterbury Tales* becomes operative in the no man's land that exists between the poet Chaucer – who if he read his poems aloud must have been a very personal fact to his own audience – and the assigned teller of the tale, whether the Miller, the Knight, or, in 'Sir Thopas', Chaucer the pilgrim. The irony produced by the use of popular poetic idiom in the Miller's Tale becomes operative in this no man's land and operates in several directions. First, the idiom tends to make of the tale a parody of the popular romance, rather like 'Sir Thopas' in effect, though less exclusively literary. Then, too, it reinforces the connection between the Miller's Tale and the Knight's truly courtly romance that the Miller's Tale is intended to 'quite' (to repay); for it emphasizes the parallelism between the two different, though somehow similar, love-rivalries, one involving two young knights in remote Athens, the other two young clerks in contemporary Oxford. And in so far as it does this, it tends to turn the tale into a parody of all courtly romance, the ideals of which are subjected to the harshly naturalistic criticism of the fabliau. But finally, while doing its bit in the accomplishment of these things, the idiom Chaucer borrows from popular poetry contributes to the directly humorous effect of the Miller's Tale, and that is probably its chief function.[34]

S O U R C E : *English Institute Essays*, ed. A. S. Downer (New York, 1950).

NOTES

1. The researches of Laura H. Loomis in recent years have, however, done much to justify such comparison by demonstrating Chaucer's familiarity with the native romance tradition. See 'Chaucer and the Auchlinleck MS. . .', in *Essays and Studies in Honor of Carleton Brown* (New York, 1940) pp. 111–28; 'Chaucer and the Breton Lays of the Auchinleck MS', *Studies in Philology* XXXVIII (1941) 14–33; and her study of 'Sir Thopas' in *Sources and Analogues to Chaucer's Canterbury Tales*, ed. W. F. Bryan and Germaine Dempster (Chicago, 1941) pp. 485–559.

2. Ed. J. S. P. Tatlock and A. G. Kennedy (Washington, 1927).

3. For a summary of scholarly opinions on the authorship of the Fragment see Joseph Mersand, *Chaucer's Romance Vocabulary* (New York, 1939) p. 60, n. 7.

4. See, for instance, the old poetic word 'swire' (neck); and the conventional alliterative phrases *styf in stour* and *byrde in bour*. Quotations from Chaucer are from F. N. Robinson's edition (Cambridge, Mass., 1933).

5. J. L. Lowes, 'Simple and Coy . . .', *Anglia*, XXXIII (1910) 440–51.

6. Aside from Fragment A of the *Roman*, where the words are common, they are normally used only by lower-class speakers; the only exceptions are in the portraits of the Prioress and the Merchant.

7. *Squyr of Lowe Degre*, ed. W. E. Mead, ll. 3–4; *Sir Ysumbras*, ed. G. Schleich, ll. 17–18; for examples of many of the characteristics discussed here, see W. C. Curry, *The Middle English Ideal of Personal Beauty* (Baltimore, 1916).

8. See *The Harley Lyrics*, ed. G. L. Brook (Manchester, 1948) 32.1–2; also 3.36 and 9.43 (references are to poem and line numbers).

9. See *O.E.D.*, 'dern', and Brook, 2.5–11.

10. See Brook, 24.17–20.

11. For examples see Curry, pp. 92–4. In contexts not concerned with romantic love or lovers this word, as well as others discussed here, was commonly employed without regard to gender.

12. For an example see Brook, 14.32. *O.E.D.*, 'lovely', records the word at *Anel.* 142, but Skeat and Robinson read 'lowly'.

13. Curry, p. 94; also Brook, 3.11, 5.32.

14. *Geoffrey Chaucer* (Oxford, 1934) p. 177.

15. Curry, p. 102.

16. See Lowes, *Geoffrey Chaucer*, p. 177; Brook, 3.11–20.

17. Brook, 7.77; also Curry, p. 81.

18. Brook, 4.37, 3.16.

19. See *O.E.D.*, 'gore', *sb.* 2, 2; *Sir Gawain and the Green Knight*, ed. J. R. R. Tolkien and E. V. Gordon (rev. edn : Oxford, 1930) note on l. 1814.

20. 'And [Nicholas] thakked hire aboute the lendes weel.'

21. In MS Harley 7334, A. 3322 reads : 'Schapen with goores in the newe get', which Tatlock regarded as a possible Chaucerian revision : see Robinson's textual note on the line.

22. *Lyfe of Ipomydon*, ed. E. Koelbing, ll. 123–4; Brook, 4.26–7.

23. In his thorough study of the dialect of the Reeve's Tale in *Transactions of the Philological Society* (London) for 1934, p. 52, J. R. R. Tolkien observes that 'wench' 'was still a respectable and literary word for "girl" in Chaucer's time, and was probably in pretty general use all over the country.' But it was not a respectable word in Chaucer's eyes (except in the sense 'servant-girl'), as a study of his uses will quickly reveal; see the Manciple's definition, H. 211–22.

24. Brook, 3.13; cf. 14.51–3.

25. See J. M. Manly's note, citing an *English Dialect Dictionary* definition for Essex, in his edition of *C.T.* (New York, 1928) p. 560.

26. One is frequently tempted to suggest that Chaucer had the Harley lyrics in mind when he was composing *M.T.*, but in view of the poor conditions that existed for the preservation of secular lyrics, to associate Chaucer with a few survivals seems too large an economy. Particularly close correspondences may be noted with the lyric 'De Clerico et Puella' (Brook, 24), a dramatic dialogue in which a maiden initially repulses a clerk's plea of secret love : notice especially the third stanza, where she rebukes him ('Do wey, thou clerc, thou art a fol') and warns him of the consequences if he should be caught in her bower, and compare Alison's initial resistance ('Do wey youre handes') and her warning (A. 3294–7); further, the Harley lyric's window where the two had kissed 'fyfty sythe' (l. 23), and the carpenter's shot window. But the situation is, of course, a very old one (see *Dame Sirith*), and the Harley lyric may go back remotely to the same source from which Chaucer's immediate source stems.

27. See Brook, 4.5; *Sir Tristrem*, ed. E. Koelbing, l. 1860.

28. Brook, 3.22; cf. 9.3.

29. The Harley lyrics have 'burde', maiden (Brook, 3.1., 5.36), 'brudes', maidens (6.39), 'brid', maiden? (14.17), and 'brid', bird for maiden (6.40). In the *King's Quair*, stanza 65, 'bridis' rhymes with 'bydis' (abides), but clearly means 'birds'.

30. See, for instance, *William of Palerne*, ed. W. W. Skeat, l. 1538.

31. Brook, 32.16–17.

32. *Opera*, ed. J. S. Brewer, II (London, 1862) 120.

33. According to L. A. Haselmayer, 'The Portraits in Chaucer's Fabliaux', *Review of English Studies*, XIV (1938) 310–14, conventionalized portraits existed – though in only a vestigial form – in the French fabliaux with which Chaucer was acquainted. It was perhaps from these that Chaucer got the idea of using conventional poetic idiom in ironic contexts.

34. Since this was written, Fr. Paul E. Beichner has in a delightful paper fully demonstrated the effeminacy of Absolon and its traditional nature; see 'Absolon's Hair', *Mediaeval Studies*, XII (1950) 222–33.

Tony Slade

IRONY IN THE WIFE OF
BATH'S TALE (1969)

A feature of much criticism of the Wife of Bath's Tale has been a tendency to view it against a background of supposed Arthurian romances, and some critics have gone so far as to suggest that it is exactly this Arthurian element which gives the tale its appeal and interest.[1] Allied with this branch of Chaucerian criticism has been the suggestion that 'only a small part of [the tale's] significance lies in its expression of character'.[2] Yet although most discussions of the tale have centred on the analogues of the story and the loathly lady motif (often to such an extent that the Wife of Bath herself seems to have been forgotten), one or two critics have suggested that this interest in the background to the tale is not of much immediate use in evaluating the particularly literary appeal of the story as Chaucer tells it. J. F. Roppolo in particular makes out an interesting case for emphasizing the importance of the character of the knight in his attempt to suggest that the tale has more unity than some former critics have held.[3] Roppolo's discussion of the knight's role in the tale is continued by F. G. Townsend, who goes on to suggest the importance not only of the 'nameless knight' but also of the fact that the tale does illustrate the character of Dame Alison, and that moreover the tale cannot be properly understood unless we remember that it is Alison who is telling the story which 'is the expression of her hopes and dreams'.[4] Quite rightly in my opinion Townsend adds that it is unfortunate that 'Chaucer's use of the very common transformation motif has focussed attention on the tale and its analogues, and obscured its real function, which is to prolong the self-revelation of the Wife to the very end of the episode'. In this present discussion I wish to take Townsend's thesis a stage further to show that by looking at the tale as an example of the Wife's character the story does take on a unity which it might otherwise seem to lack, in that certain apparent irrelevancies in it (notably the sermon on 'gentilesse') have an essentially ironic function in a tale of superb comedy and character portrayal. My suggestion is that by interpreting the Wife of Bath's Tale primarily as an expression of her personality, and by playing down the Arthurian element, we shall be able to see in it an example of Chaucer's ironic genius at its very best.

To do this it is important to remember that although the tale is, as Townsend has argued, an expression of the Wife's character, it is ultimately told by Chaucer himself. That is, the Wife is telling the story on one level whilst Chaucer is telling it on another, so that the usual ironic situation of a statement being made which one audience takes at its face value, and another (more sophisticated) audience at its ironic level, is considerably complicated here by the fact that at times Dame Alison is commenting ironically on the story she is telling (for example, her comments on the friars at the beginning) while at other times Chaucer himself is commenting ironically on her views and reactions. The Wife's character has already been exposed in some detail in her Prologue, which rambles around the theme of 'sovereynetee' in marriage : her tone is coarse and garrulous, and there is little evidence of that sort of delicate poetic beauty which some critics have professed to find in the Tale itself (I shall refer to this in more detail later). The main features of her character are common sense and a pre-occupation with sex, and an important element in both Prologue and Tale is her desire to explain life in terms of her own values. This leads her to tell a traditional story of the 'loathly lady' in a wholly typical and individual way, which is totally distinct in tone from all the other surviving versions. The Wife's version has none of the naive and fairy-tale elements of the analogues, for on the contrary its tone is largely (though not entirely) adult, aggressive, matter-of-fact, and sexually pre-occupied. She is telling the story because she wishes to make a moral point which has relevance in the world as she sees it, but in telling it in the way she does she exposes much of her own character.

The tone of the whole story is well struck from the beginning. At the end of her Prologue the Friar has rudely (but perhaps understandably) called her to task for rambling on :

'Now dame,' quod he, 'so have I joye or blis,
This is a long preamble of a tale!'   (D. 830–1)

The Summoner comes to her aid and argues with the Friar, but
at the beginning of her tale the Wife shows that she is well able
to look after herself with a masterly attack on the friars in the
opening passage:

In th'olde dayes of the Kyng Arthour,
Of which that Britons speken greet honour,
Al was this land fulfild of fayerye.
The elf-queene, with hir joly compaignye,
Daunced ful ofte in many a grene mede.
This was the olde opinion, as I rede;
I speke of manye hundred yeres ago.
But now kan no man se none elves mo,
For now the grete charitee and prayeres
Of lymytours and othere hooly freres,
That serchen every lond and every streem,
As thikke as motes in the sonne-beem,
Blessynge halles, chambres, kichenes, boures,
Citees, burghes, castels, hye toures,
Thropes, bernes, shipnes, dayeryes –
This maketh that ther ben no fayeryes.
For ther as wont to walken was an elf,
Ther walketh now the lymytour hymself
In undermeles and in morwenynges,
And seyth his matyns and his hooly thynges
As he gooth in his lymytacioun.
Wommen may go now saufly up and doun.
In every bussh or under every tree
Ther is noon oother incubus but he,
And he ne wol doon hem but dishonour.

(D. 857–81)

It is worth looking closely at this whole introductory passage because it does appear to have been misconstrued by some critics.
Close textual analysis of Middle English poetry is notoriously
open to abuse because it is difficult to assess what overtones were
carried by words in Chaucer's time, but it does seem unjustifiable

to me to see in the passage 'a consciousness of the ancient
nature religion of Britain as having been desecrated, uprooted
and supplanted by the new ecclesiastical order' as John Speirs
asserts, nor is it by any means clear 'that the Wife's sympathy is
with the old nature cults, with "the elf-queene, with her joly
compaignye" . . .'.[5] It seems just as wrong to view this passage in
this way as it is to assume from the reference to the 'fayerye'
that the Wife's Tale is in any important sense a legendary tale of
wonder.[6] An important feature of the Tale is its bareness of description. The descriptive element is reduced to a minimum, and
we have only the bare essentials of the scene. The reference to
Arthur would seem at first to place the Tale firmly in the
tradition of Arthurian romance, but in reality this is simply a set
introduction similar to many folk-songs and ballads which
usually have little or nothing to do with any romance tradition.
In view of the imminent attack on the friars, however, there does
appear to be a sardonic touch in the phrase 'fulfild of fayerye',
where 'fulfild' could almost be rendered as 'filled to overflowing'
or even 'chock-a-block', and in the phrase 'ful ofte' with its
slightly comic suggestion of 'all the time, everywhere you looked'.
In any case, it seems wrong to regard these lines simply as the
Wife's expression of lament for the lost world of Faery Britain,
partly because this sort of sentimentality is not typical of her
character (her sentimentality is of a different sort, and is not
revealed until the end of the Tale), and partly because such an
interpretation implies a dramatic change of tone in the following lines with the attack on the sexual conduct of the friars. The
Wife in this case is consciously employing the irony, with the
magnificent, almost surrealist, image of the friars 'as thikke as
motes in the sonne-beem' searching for alms and women. At the
same time the Wife's own loquaciousness is implied by Chaucer
in the lines which seem at first to be merely a list –

> Blessynge halles, chambres, kichenes, boures,
> Citees, burghes, castels, hye toures,
> Thropes, bernes, shipnes, dayeryes . . .   (D. 869–71)

but which have the point of being those places which the friars
are 'blessing with their presence' because women will be found

in them. The friars have chased out the 'fayerye' (who has now become an incubus, in any case, with its additional sexual implication) and women can now go about safely, apart from the threat of dishonour posed by the friars themselves. Apart from this last sting in the tail, however, a notable feature of the tone of this section is that the irony is not vicious or hostile, and the Wife does not give the impression of being morally outraged by the friars' behaviour.

This tone of tolerant sexual irony is continued in the rape episode, which has received considerable attention from commentators. The late Professor G. H. Gerould has aptly emphasized the point of the 'grotesque absurdity of beginning a tale of "gentilesse" with rape',[7] and unless we remember the Wife's own character the episode does raise certain problems. Again it is the tone of the story as the Wife tells it which is all-important. Everything is described in a matter-of-fact way, and one gets the impression that she is not worried by the fact of rape in the sense that we might be : the woman is merely a figure in the piece, and she is 'fair game' to the 'lusty bacheler' (one can imagine the Wife's lips curling around the phrase). What is wrong in the Wife's eyes is not related necessarily to whether the woman is a peasant or a lady, but the fact that the act was committed 'maugree hir heed' (D. 887). In the Wife's eyes it is the domination of the man over the woman which is the knight's real offence, and it is for this that he has to undergo his test. We have to accept the episode in terms of the Wife's own values, which ironically appear humorous as the scene shifts to Arthur's court. This court is far removed from the world of Arthurian romance or 'gentilesse', however, for it is one where the women hold sway. Although the knight should have been beheaded for his offence 'the queene and othere ladyes mo' (D. 894) – almost certainly because he is a 'lusty bacheler' – persuade Arthur to hand him over to them. Arthur is a shadowy, unimportant figure in all this, but he knows his place according to the Wife's viewpoint, which is to give in to his wife's demands on the subject even if it involves ignoring the law of the land. The off-hand, matter-of-fact, way in which this is implied by the Wife should not blind us to the ironically humorous comment which Chaucer is implying all this time upon her assumptions and attitudes.

The Queen's motivation in saving the knight's life is not discussed by the Wife, who assumes it to be self-evident. The knight's reaction to his reprieve, however, is not one of joy or steadfast resolve to do better when he is told to go and search for the answer to the question of what it is that women most desire:

> Wo was this knyght, and sorwefully he siketh;
> But what! he may nat do al as hym liketh.

(D. 913–14)

Although he is a knight he has still to learn that he cannot do just as he pleases, but it is worth noting now that the lesson he is to be taught is hardly a profoundly moral one: it is that he has to accept women's 'sovereynetee' over men, and the lesson goes no deeper than this in spite of the discussions on 'gentilesse' and proper behaviour which are to follow later in the Tale. The ensuing search for an answer to the question is described very much in terms of the Wife's own values, and she is unable to keep her own views out of the discussion. The things which are suggested as answers to the knight are almost all accepted as serious answers by her: women want riches, honour, a good time, fine clothes, sex, to be often married and widowed, to be flattered, to be free and irresponsible, and lastly to be regarded as stable and capable of keeping a secret. Only with this last suggested answer does she seriously disagree, and it is in keeping with her argumentative and dogmatic nature that she should ramble off the main point of the narrative, just as it is in keeping with her character that in doing so she should misquote a story from Ovid in an attempt to prove her point. This illogicality is typical of her, and the digression (comparatively brief here) should also prepare us for a similar situation later in the Tale in the sermon on 'gentilesse'.

She then returns to the narrative with the description of the knight meeting with the old hag in what is for a moment a typical fairy-tale setting of a tale of wonder. Yet the 'wondrous' elements of the scene are not dwelt on, and the bareness of description is apparent in the economic handling of the episode (D. 989–99). The old hag and the knight strike a bargain in which he promises to do the next thing she asks him in return for the

answer to the question he has been set. Quickly the scene shifts
back to the Court of Love at Arthur's palace, where the assembled
wives, girls, and widows (the widows being especially wise, adds
the often-widowed Wife) are all immediately and without dispute satisfied with the knight's answer that women most of all
desire to have mastery over their men. In comparison with some
other versions of the story this section is hurried on by the narrator, for the knight does not experiment by suggesting other
possible answers before he states the right one, as there is only one
obvious answer according to the Wife in any case. Yet although
the knight has given the right answer it is apparent from his
shocked reaction to the old hag's request that he should marry
her that he has still not learnt his lesson. He tries to back out of
his earlier agreement in a realistic and understandable fashion :

> This knyght answerde, 'Allas ! and weylawey !
> I woot right wel that swich was my biheste.
> For Goddes love, as chees a newe requeste ! . . .
>
> (D. 1058–60)

Eventually, however, he is forced to marry the old hag, and in a
scene of rich comedy he is taken off to the marriage bed – 'he was
with his wyf abedde *ybroght*' (D. 1084). The humour of this
episode, which we are sharing with the Wife, is magnificent,
where the knight 'walweth and he turneth to and fro', whilst
his old wife lies smiling by his side. The comedy is aided by the
relish and understanding which the Wife has for the knight's
predicament, and the old hag taunts him with superb irony :

> 'Oh deere housebonde, *benedicitee* !
> Fareth every knyght thus with his wyf as ye ?
> Is this the lawe of kyng Arthures hous ?
> Is every knyght of his so dangerous ? . . .'
>
> (D. 1087–90)

Only a hundred lines have been used to get to this point from
the old hag's first introduction into the story (D. 998), which
has up to this section moved swiftly, with only slight digressions
typical of the Wife's character. Now, however, the story is put

on one side whilst the hag gives her reluctant husband a long and sententious sermon.

The humour we have noticed in this 'bedroom-scene' preceding the sermon is humour which the Wife of Bath intends us to share with her, although at times throughout her tale we have been laughing at her assumptions as well as with her jokes. Now, however, the tone of the tale changes: the Wife becomes serious in showing the reluctant knight persuaded by what to her are logical and morally admirable arguments, whilst the reader and Chaucer himself continue to regard the narration ironically. The knight, stung by the hag's taunting of his behaviour in bed, ill-naturedly and in desperation draws her attention to three things which upset him:

> Thou art so loothly, and so oold also,
> And therto comen of so lough a kynde,
> That litel wonder is thogh I walwe and wynde.
>
> (D. 1100–2)

It is surely obvious that the first two of these objections – that she is ugly and old – are the more serious, yet it is the third and least important (though not unimportant) objection which the hag enlarges on somewhat illogically for over one hundred lines. The point is reached only by grasping that Chaucer is aware of the illogicality of the argument whilst the Wife herself is perfectly serious in repeating ideas which have become, by the time she is telling them, commonplaces of Christian and other literature. It is true that some of the ideas on 'gentilesse' which the hag expresses are similar to some of Chaucer's own favourite themes, but the manner in which these ideas are expressed here surely suggests that they are not meant to be taken as seriously as some modern critics have done. Kemp Malone has sensibly summed up the way in which the other pilgrims would have reacted to the Wife's arguments as a whole (although his emphasis on the poetic qualities of the sermon would be different from mine):

The Wife of Bath's unorthodox extension of the principle of female sovereignty from love affairs to married life undoubtedly struck our forefathers as funny. They did not take it seriously, and the so-called debate on the subject which modern men of learning with extraordinary *naïveté* have read into the *Canterbury Tales* is not really there. The Clerk, in the second ending tacked on to his tale, pokes fun at the Wife of Bath's kind of matrimony but he makes no effort whatever to refute her views. To him and to all the other pilgrims these views are merely amusing and need no refutation. The pilgrims, if not the modern scholars, take the Wife for the comic character that Chaucer meant her to be.[8]

In the sermon the argument is intentionally questionable. Germaine Dempster has brought out the problem of lines D. 1159–62,[9] and although James Winny has made an interesting alteration to the Robinson text in his edition of the Wife of Bath's Prologue and Tale (Cambridge, 1965) to avoid this problem, it seems possible that the illogicality of these lines is as intentional as the inconsistency of the hag discoursing at length on the theme of 'gentilesse' when the knight has raised other more pressing objections which are dismissed peremptorily at the end of her speech. W. P. Albrecht effectively confirms this general reading of the sermon in agreeing with J. F. Roppolo on the ironic fact that the Wife cannot qualify under her own (and to her serious) definitions of 'gentilesse'. As Albrecht points out, the Wife's 'method of disputation must have been pretty transparent to several of the pilgrims',[10] and he goes on to support Roppolo's arguments for the useful function of the sermon within the Tale.

Even so, some qualifications to Roppolo's article (to which I referred at the beginning of this paper) need to be made, for although the 'gentilesse' sermon certainly has a structural value within the Tale it is surely not simply in the way in which he goes on to define it. Primarily Roppolo's argument centres around the change in the knight's character which takes place as a result of the force and eloquence of the hag's speech, and he even goes so far as to quote (p. 267) an earlier critic (R. K. Root, *The Poetry of Chaucer*) to the effect that 'we are held captive by the spell of [the Lady's] poetry, and at the conclusion of the speech are not surprised to find that the speaker is of wondrous beauty'. This seems to be patently ridiculous. The Wife of Bath herself is certainly intending us to read the sermon in this way, but there seems to be little that is critically admirable in the poetry of this section. It is not only that 'the Lady's argument contains nothing original in ideas and outlook',[11] but also that the poetry itself is commonplace and laboured. The knight is persuaded not by the spell of the poetry or the logic of the argument, but largely because the speech goes on for so long that he is willing to accept anything to stop the flow of talk. He is offered the chance of making a choice between having her either old, ugly, yet a good wife on the one hand, or young and attractive, though licentious, on the other. This choice is not the usual one in the other versions of the folk-tale, but it is typical of the Wife of Bath's values and a repetition of the hag's concluding argument in the sermon proper, when she briefly deals with the knight's fundamental complaints about her age and ugliness by saying that in that case he need have no fear of becoming a cuckold (otherwise implicitly assumed by the Wife to be a distinct probability). However, the knight does not make the choice, but tells her to do what she thinks best, in a comment which is filled with wearisome and heavy irony :

> 'My lady and my love, and wyf so deere,
> I put me in youre wise governance . . .'   (D. 1230–1)

An element of irony is surely present in the effusion of sentiment of 'my love', 'wyf so deere', and particularly in 'wise' (for the knight has seen through her arguments as scholastically weak) – an irony which Chaucer intends but which neither the Wife nor the hag (fortunately for her husband) themselves detect. The Wife suggests that the knight is giving in for what to her are the right reasons of the hag's persuasive arguments, but Chaucer himself leaves some comic doubt as to the real motivation. One result of the long sermon has been to swing the reader's sympathies behind the knight and his unpleasant predicament, but the sermon as a whole has an essentially dramatic function in the Tale and is not simply 'dragged in as a makeweight'.[12]

In conclusion we might note that the ironic handling of the Wife's character is continued in the last few lines of her tale, where her sentimentality is clearly apparent. By this time she is perfectly serious in suggesting that the knight now deserves the sexual prize he gains when the hag changes into a young, beautiful, and yet virtuous woman. It is in one sense a typical ending to a romantic love story which middle-aged women like the Wife admire. Her sentimental ending is rather funny, but she is not so overwhelmed by the sentimentality that it has drastically altered her real nature, for in the last lines (D. 1258 ff.) she gives a parting insight into the vigour of her character which her tale has so marvellously brought out:

> . . . and Jhesu Crist us sende
> Housbondes meeke, yonge, and fressh abedde,
> And grace t'overbyde hem that we wedde;
> And eek I praye Jhesu shorte hir lyves
> That wol nat be governed by hir wyves;
> And olde and angry nygardes of dispence,
> God sende hem soone verray pestilence!

S O U R C E : *Modern Language Review*, LXIV (1969)

NOTES

1. Notably S. Eisner, *A Tale of Wonder* (Wexford, 1957).

2. D. S. Brewer, *Chaucer* (London, 1961), p. 130.

3. 'The Converted Knight in Chaucer's Wife of Bath's Tale', *College English*, XII (1951) 263–9.

4. 'Chaucer's Nameless Knight', *Modern Language Review*, XLIX (1954) 1–4.

5. *Chaucer the Maker* (London, 1962) pp. 147–8. Even so fine a commentator as G. H. Gerould talks of 'the momentary and lovely glimpse of the dancing elf-queen' (*Chaucerian Essays*, Princeton, 1952, p. 79).

6. For a well-argued opposite view, see Kemp Malone's article, 'The Wife of Bath's Tale', *Modern Language Review*, LVII (1962) 481–91.

7. Gerould, p. 75.

8. Malone, pp. 489–90.

9. ' "Thy Gentilesse" in the Wife of Bath's Tale, D. 1159–62', *Modern Language Notes*, LVII (1942) 173–6.

10. 'The Sermon on "Gentilesse" ', *College English*, XII (1951) 459.

11. Winny, p. 26. But note that my interpretation of the Tale as a whole, and of the function of the 'gentilesse' sermon within it, is almost entirely opposed to that put forward in Mr. Winny's introduction.

12. Paull F. Baum, *Chaucer: A Critical Appreciation* (Durham, N.C., 1958) p. 133.

John Burrow

IRONY IN THE MERCHANT'S
TALE (1957)

The Merchant's Tale is usually classed as a 'fabliau tale', and
the classification has its point. But it has perhaps drawn attention away from those qualities which distinguish the Merchant's
Tale from the rest of Chaucer's 'fabliaux'. These are qualities
which it shares, not with the comic tales of the Miller or the
Summoner, but with the moral fable of the Pardoner – the per-
sistent irony, the seriousness which informs even the farcical
climax. This climax (the gulling of January in the 'pear-tree
episode') is no more simply comic than the death of the
Pardoner's rioters. It is much more closely realised than, for example, the dénouement of the Miller's Tale; and Chaucer, in
filling out the fabliau form in this way, makes something new.
The French fabliaux may be cruel, but they are also casual – one
gets just enough about, for example, the duped husband to make
the joke, and no more. The comic effect depends on the preservation of the skeletal bareness of the story. The reader is never
allowed to get near enough, as it were, to be seriously involved.
In contrast, the Merchant's Tale is full of 'close-ups':

> . . . Januarie hath faste in armes take
> His fresshe May, his paradys, his make.
> He lulleth hire, he kisseth hire ful ofte,
> With thikke brustles of his berd unsofte,
> Lyk to the skyn of houndfyssh, sharp as brere,
> For he was shave al newe in his manere.   (E. 1821–6)

The clarity of the observation is given a sharp point, here, by the
simile of the dogfish, and by the ironic comment in the last line.
The reader is forced to visualise the scene, as never in the French
fabliau, to grasp its human reality; and in the process the moral

issues, with which the French authors were not concerned (Bédier called them 'amoral'), come alive.

Unlike the other 'fabliau tales', but like the Pardoner's Tale, the story of January and May faces up to the moral issuses it raises. This involves a radical modification of the fabliau method. The treatment of January's dream life (his 'fantasye') recalls, not the carpenter or the miller, but the Pardoner's rioters with their dreams of wealth :

> This yongeste which that wente to the toun
> Ful ofte in herte he rolleth up and doun
> The beautee of thise floryns newe and brighte.
>
> (C. 837–9)

> Heigh fantasye and curious bisynesse
> Fro day to day gan in the soule impresse
> Of Januarie aboute his mariage.
> Many fair shap and many a fair visage
> Ther passeth thurgh his herte nyght by nyght.
>
> (E. 1577–81)

But it is the distinguishing characteristic of the Merchant's Tale that the ironic contrast between the dream and the reality, the self-centred and insecure 'heigh fantasye' of the old knight and the predictable course of his marriage, should be pointed insistently at every turn. In the Pardoner's Tale there is a strong general dramatic irony. The rioters pursue their own downfall; and they ignore the old man, as January ignores Justinus. But there is nothing like the accumulation of local irony which marks the Merchant's Tale.

Take, for example, the opening passage of the poem (E. 1245– 1398) where January, in what is really an internal monologue, persuades himself that he will find permanent 'ioye and blisse' in marriage with a young wife. The general irony of this is clear. The mistake would have been as obvious to a medieval reader as the rioters' mistake about the gold ('But mighte this gold be caried from this place . . . than were we in heigh felicitee'). But the point is made more heavily – January's dotage is much more ridiculous than anything in the Pardoner's Tale. He turns pro-

verbial and biblical lore inside out in a way that places him
decisively in the moral scheme of the poem – 'Old fissh and yong
flessh wolde I have ful fayn', 'Do alwey so as wommen wol
thee rede'. These lines, and lines like them, suggest the proverbs
of which they are distortions (elsewhere in Chaucer – 'Wom-
menes conseils been ful ofte colde' 'Men sholde wedden after hir
estaat, For youthe and elde is often at debaat'). One more
quotation will illustrate the tone of the poem's opening:

> Alle othere manere yiftes hardily
> As londes, rentes, pasture or commune,
> Or moebles, alle been yiftes of fortune,
> That passen as a shadwe upon a wal.
> But drede nat, if pleynly speke I shal,
> A wyf wol laste, and in thyn hous endure,
> Wel lenger than thee list, paraventure.   (E. 1312–18)

The last line makes a joke out of what is obviously a philosophical blunder. It is interpolated into the sequence of January's
thoughts to point the irony, like an aside in an Elizabethan
play. January is subjected to the most unblinking scrutiny
throughout the poem. His fantastic thoughts and desires, his
slack skin and his bristles, are all rendered in unsparing detail;
and every detail carries a point, strengthening the general with a
local irony:

> Adoun by olde Januarie she lay
> That sleep til that the coughe hath him awaked.
>   (E. 1956–7)

(This technique is familiar from the General Prologue, where
the poetry is all detail – of behaviour or dress or appearance – and
the ironies depend on the implications of the details). The insistent irony, and the answering choice of detail, expose the
characters of the poem in a brilliant light, which makes the Pardoner's Tale feel almost kindly by comparison.

Now, although Chaucer was by no means always 'gentle
Chaucer', he was not characteristically a destructive poet. His

irony, as in the portrait of the Prioress, is often so fleeting as to be genuinely ambiguous, at least to the modern reader; his tone is most often that of Theseus in the Knight's Tale – 'The god of love, a benedicite, How mighty and how greet a lord is he' – and can modulate easily, as in the same speech of Theseus, into a sympathetic generalization – 'A man moot be a fool, or yong or oold, I woot it by myself ful yore agon'. It is an irony which does justice to its victims; the destructive or critical impulse does not work unchecked. Of course, there is no *a priori* reason why the Merchant's Tale should not be an exception to this generalization; it might be argued that a ruthless almost hysterical story was called for at this point in the 'Marriage Group' from the disillusioned Merchant. But I want to suggest that the 'corrosive, destructive, even hopeless quality' which Mr. Patch, and other critics, found in this poem, and with which I have so far been concerned, is not the whole story; and that, if it were, the poem would not be as good as it is. The Merchant's Tale is not only a poem of clarity, critical observation, and disgust – a medieval *Madame Bovary*. There is an opposing impulse, an impulse to approach and understand, which appears in a tendency to *generalize*. This I consider to be a feature of all Chaucer's best narrative poetry.

Take one line from the description of January's marriage – 'tendre youthe hath wedded stouping age'. The point is a critical one again (it is the old fish and young flesh theme) but there is no mistaking the genuine lyrical note. There is generalization, but it is not the dry generalization of a proverb inside out. A generosity about the line contrasts sharply with the nagging irony we have been noting. The gentle contrast between 'stouping' and 'tendre' is not like the sharp and disgusting physical contrast between January's bristly chin and May's 'tendre face' in the description of the wedding night from which a passage has already been quoted. There is a generous lyrical note about the line which we find again in the introduction of Bacchus and Venus into the wedding festivities :

> Bacus the wyn hem skynketh al aboute,
> And Venus laugheth upon every wight,
> For Januarie was bicome hir knyght,

And wolde bothe assayen his corage
In libertee and eek in mariage;
And with hire fyrbrond in hire hand aboute
Daunceth biforn the bryde and all the route.

(E. 1722–8)

There is malice in the equating of liberty with marriage; but
hardly, it seems, any mock heroic effect in the introduction of
Bacchus and Venus. January's marriage takes on a festal dignity in the archaic 'skynketh', and the last buoyant couplet.
There is another finer couplet on this theme a little later:

So sore hath Venus hurt hym with hire brond
As that she bar it daunsing in hire hond.   (E. 1777–8)

(Here the 'daunsing' can refer either to Venus, or to the torch; it
effectively goes with both.) The effect of such lines as these is to
dignify the emotions involved by setting them in the general context of human feelings represented by the gods. It will be clear
from these examples that there is nothing thin or abstract about
the generalization. It is done concretely, and is felt as a sort of
lyrical expansiveness in the verse (an effect I do not find in the
Pardoner's Tale).

There is, further, a perceptible drift towards allegory in the
poem. The names January and May, Justinus and Placebo, suggest this. At one point there is a significant reference to what for
Chaucer was the allegory par excellence, the *Romance of the
Rose*:

He made a gardyn, walled al with stoon,
So fair a gardyn woot I nowher noon.
For, out of doute, I verraily suppose
That he that wroot the Romance of the Rose
Ne coude of it the beautee wel devyse . . .

(E. 2029–33)

The garden, which is here being introduced, plays an important part in the poem. As it serves to dignify and strengthen
January's feelings by generalizing them, and to counter the 'cor-

rosive' irony to which they are exposed, it may fittingly be considered here.

January's desire for a young wife is presented from the start as 'fantasye' – self deception (the word is a favourite of Chaucer's, occurring very frequently in *Troilus and Criseyde*). But it is associated equally, in a series of contexts at the beginning of the poem, with the image of the earthly paradise, the general fantasy of the great good place. 'Wedlock' January thinks 'is so esy and so clene, That in this world it is a paradys' . . . 'Wyf is mannes help and his confort, His paradys terrestre and his desport'. Then at the wedding 'Ianuarie hath faste in armes take His fresshe May, his paradys, his make'. Marriage is like the earthly paradise quite specifically in being at once 'esy' and 'clene' – delightful and morally irreproachable. Desire and duty are at one in marriage, as January points out to May on their wedding night – 'Blessed be the yok that we be inne, For in our actes we mowe do no sinne.'

It is true that January's 'heigh fantasye' is made to look ridiculous in the poem. When he worries lest he should have 'myn hevene in erthe here' and pay for it later, Justinus remarks:

> Dispeire yow noght, but have in youre memorie,
> Paraunter she may be youre purgatorie.
> She may be Goddes mene, and Goddes whippe,
> Thanne shal youre soule up to hevene skippe
> Swifter than dooth an arwe out of a bowe.
>
> (E. 1669–73)

But it is not only ridiculous. It draws strength from association with the image of the earthly paradise (or the garden of Genesis as is clear from E. 1325–32). January's 'fantasye' is broadened by these allusions to include a general human fantasy; it is not only the delusion of a besotted *senex amans*. Here again the generalizing lends dignity and significance to the action of the poem, contributing to the reader's sense of an intelligible and meaningful narrative progression.

It seems clear that in this progression January's garden in the second part of the poem takes over from the image of the 'paradys terrestre' in the first. It is in fact the paradys of his sexual fantasy realised; in the poem the garden has something approaching a symbolic status (as gardens often have in medieval literature). The opening of the description has already been quoted. It goes on :

> Ne Priapus ne myghte nat suffise,
> Though he be god of gardyns, for to telle
> The beautee of the gardyn and the welle
> That stood under a laurer alwey grene.   (E. 2034–7)

The *Romance of the Rose* has already been explicitly introduced into the description, and the well under the laurel is certainly meant to recall the well in the garden of the *Romance* which, in Chaucer's translation, lies 'under a tree, Which tree in Fraunce men cal a pyn'. The laurel must have been substituted for the pine to link the garden with January's erotic fantasies. It is meant to recall his earlier boast :

> Though I be hoor, I fare as dooth a tree
> That blosmeth er the fruyt ywoxen bee;
> And blosmy tree nys neither drye ne deed.
> I feele me nowhere hoor but on myn heed;
> Myn herte and alle my lymes been as grene
> As laurer thurgh the yeer is for to sene.   (E. 1461–6)

This suggests that Chaucer is considering more than the narrative necessities in organising the detail of the tale. There is a further suggestion of the sexual significance of the garden in the introduction of Priapus here. The repetition, through the opening description (E. 2029–37), of the words 'garden' and 'beauty' gives to the lines an emphatic, almost incantatory, ring, which disposes the reader to look for 'meanings', as if it were the garden of the *Parlement* or of Dante's *Purgatorio*. It is in this garden of love, for such it clearly seems to be, that January 'payes his wyf hir dette'. He guards it as jealously as if it were May herself, and walls it off, like the garden of Guillaume Lorris, with stone.

January goes blind, and the extravagance of his jealousy (it is 'outrageous') is noted in the best fabliau manner – although not without gestures of sympathy ('O Januarie, what myghte it thee availle, Thogh thou myghte se as fer as shippes saille?'). His fantasy, no longer associated with the solid and persuasive ideal image of the fertile garden of love, becomes almost imbecile ('He nolde suffre hir for to ryde or go, But if that he had hand on hire alwey'). But, with the opening of the final scene in the garden, the tone changes again :

> ... in a morwe unto this May seith he :
> 'Rys up, my wyf, my love, my lady free,
> The turtles voys is herd, my dowve sweete,
> The wynter is goon with all his reynes weete.
> Com forth now with thyne eyen columbyn,
> How fairer been thy brestes than is wyn.
> The gardyn is enclosed al aboute.
> Com forth my white spouse! . .   (E. 2137–44)

This very striking passage, as Skeat pointed out, is a mosaic of phrases from the *Song of Solomon*. It is beautifully timed. The strong impersonal lyric note re-establishes January's passion, bringing out the essential intelligibility of his behaviour, making sense of him again after the fabliau comedy of the preceding passage. And the garden, the symbolic home of his ideal of fertility and privacy, gains a further reference. 'The gardyn is enclosed al aboute' recalls, from the *Song of Solomon* : 'A garden enclosed is my sister, my spouse; a spring shut up, a fountain sealed'. Chaucer has turned this metaphor into a literal statement about January's walled garden, and it might seem that the resulting line would sit oddly in the middle of the passage, which in general preserves the elaborately metaphoric style of the biblical original. That it seems quite natural suggests how the literal garden of Chaucer's poem has itself gathered a kind of metaphorical significance.

This is not to deny that there is meant to be some kind of mock-heroic effect in the passage, although I think it is faint. The passage primarily works in the other direction, resisting the 'corrosive' irony. Chaucer certainly damps the Solomon passage down with his comment 'Swiche olde lewed wordes used he' (where 'lewed' seems to mean 'lecherous' rather than 'ignorant').

But the final effect is rather of pathos than of irony. As January speaks, Damyan slips in through the gate and hides behind a bush; and January, 'blynd as is a stoon', follows him in with May. He *is* presented as pathetic, absurd, and repulsive (there is more pathos in him as the poem progresses, though this never involves any sort of moral concession towards him on the author's part). But he is not only the object of ironic sympathy and contempt. Chaucer makes out of his sexual 'fantasye' something that the reader can feel is real and intelligible, by extending the poem's field of reference beyond the range of its narrative particularities, drawing on the common literary experience of his culture. The *Romance of the Rose* and the Bible were the obvious common points of reference (knowledge of the Italian poets was much more restricted), and these works are very much present in the Merchant's Tale.

This width of reference seems to me to be a general characteristic of Chaucer's best poetry. It is this which marks the Merchant's Tale off from the two other fabliau tales which are sometimes associated with it – the Friar's Tale and the Summoner's Tale. These poems have in common with the Merchant's Tale a quality of destructive wit (which appears at its best in the ironically observed speeches of the Friar to Thomas) and of farcical popular humour (which appears in the dénouements of the poems). The anecdotes are filled out with ironic detail. The Friar comes to see Thomas :

> . . . fro the bench he droof awey the cat,
> And leyde adoun his potente and his hat,
> And eek his scrippe, and sette hym softe adoun.

> (D. 1775–7)

The Friar's smooth impudence is superbly conveyed in the rhythm and even the rhyme of these lines. It is comedy – more obviously comedy than the close-up of January sitting up in bed which was quoted earlier. The first part of the Summoner's Tale is brilliantly successful. But if we compare the poem as a whole with the Merchant's Tale we may feel that it lacks solidity. The Friar is taken at his face value – the common satiric type of the corrupt cleric. The tone of the poem never modulates from the ironic and critical; the method is exclusively mimetic. It is 'poetry of the surface'. We find these qualities in the Merchant's Tale too. But January's behaviour is not only observed, it is explored (the key word, I have suggested, is 'fantasye'). It is traced back to a compelling sexual fantasy, which is linked, through the garden, with the fantasies of the Earthly Paradise, the *Song of Songs*, and the *Romance of the Rose*. There is a lyrical expansiveness ('tendre youthe hath wedded stouping age') in the poem, where the anecdote is being generalized in this way. The particularity of the Summoner's Tale is invigorating (at least in the earlier part); but in the end the poem does not add up to much. It remains an extended anecdote.

It seems obvious that the quality in the Merchant's Tale which is being described bears some relation to Allegory. The allegorical suggestions of the names January and May, Placebo and Justinus, are apparent enough. The reader of *Piers Plowman* will recognise in the system of cross-references which links January's garden with other gardens, and all these gardens with the theme of sexual fantasy, a familiar technique. It bears little relation to the strict allegorical method, which some critics detect in *Piers* – the method of four-level meaning deriving, ultimately, from biblical interpretation; but neither does most medieval allegory. Usually the technique is loose, flexible, and intermittent. The equations may for a time be very fixed and clear ('Petrus id est Christus'); but they may equally well amount to nothing more than a casual cross-reference. Only on a too rigid definition could the part played by the allegorical method in the Merchant's Tale be ignored. Its story is not in itself allegorical; neither is the story of the Eighteenth Passus of *Piers Plowman* (the story of the crucifixion and resurrection) with which, technically, the poem has something in common. In both, allegory is at work generalising and equating (Christ is Light is Piers; January is Age, his garden is Adam's and Solomon's and Lorris'). In both, allegorical figures can enter the story without anomaly (Mercy, Peace, Truth and Righteousness; Venus and Bacchus).

The point here is that this generalizing impulse (characteristic of allegory) exists side by side in Chaucer with the ironic or satiric impulse (characteristic of fabliau) which tends to isolate its object and particularize it. It is this dual impulse which makes the Merchant's Tale a saner and more balanced poem than the conventional account might suggest. It is unlike the Summoner's Tale in having a significance beyond its anecdotal content, in having a 'meaning'. The irony is controlled (and this is surely characteristic of Chaucer) by a recognition that January's case illustrates general human weakness – a suggestion that is rigidly excluded in the treatment of the Summoner's Friar. It is a knowledge of 'fantasye' which informs the poem and gives it its moral framework within which the irony works. This knowledge appears in the unobtrusively allegorical treatment of the story, notably of the garden. The poem owes as much to the allegory as to the fabliau, bringing to the anecdotal clarity of the latter a scope and significance which belong to the former tradition. This seems to be one of the secrets of Chaucer's best narrative poems. They grow in the mind without losing the precision of their outline.

S o u r c e : *Anglia*, LXXV (1957).

Robert B. Burlin

THE ART OF CHAUCER'S
FRANKLIN (1967)

Modern criticism of the *Canterbury Tales* has greatly sharpened
our image of many of the pilgrims, and clarified, though perhaps
not settled, the theoretical issue of the dramatic propriety of the
tale to its teller. In the specific instance of the Franklin, however, a
fundamental disagreement persists. The critical record contains
wildly divergent estimates. Early in this century, Robert K. Root,
thinking of the Franklin's autobiographical statements, compared him to a 'Toledo oil-magnate' bewailing 'the vicious ten-
dencies of the son whom he is lavishly maintaining at Yale or
Harvard'.[1] Yet the English critic, Raymond Preston, has recently
given him academic status : 'a comfortable don of an ancient
college, careful to be wise and not too serious, and telling his
story with mellow vinous satisfaction'.[2]

Perhaps the most significant attempt to reconcile 'The
Character and Performance of Chaucer's Franklin'[3] was made
by R. M. Lumiansky. Like Root, he gives us a socially minded
individual, by nature belonging to the 'everyday, practical
world', yet aspiring to the rarefied atmosphere of the 'gentils'.
Rebuffed by the Host, the Franklin offers meek apologies and
shameless flattery, yet is unable to abandon his preoccupation
with the idea of 'gentillesse'. In the Tale and particularly in the
character of Dorigen, Lumiansky sees the same clash of social
values : the sophisticated, aristocratic ideal of courtly love
against the practical bourgeois insistence upon a perfect, happy
marriage. Thus the character and performance of the Franklin
exhibit a consistent uncertainty of response to conflicting social
demands.

The opposing (and, I believe, 'orthodox') point of view has,
however, been restated by Roland Blenner-Hassett,[4] who paints a
formal portrait of the wise and dignified Franklin in legal garb –

a man of perfect self-possession consorting with a professional Lawyer for whom certainty is a prime requisite. This critic more or less identifies the Franklin with Chaucer himself, on the basis of similar technical background and professional experience, and the brusque treatment accorded both men by the Host. Finally, the 'semi-legal language' of the Franklin is said to invest his tale with an 'added seriousness' which makes it a 'fitting summation, artistically and intellectually, of the problems raised in the so-called Marriage Group of Tales'.[5]

Where some readers, then, have found conflicting motivations and a tale full of incongruities, others see dignity and high seriousness. Clearly, this radical disagreement over the Franklin points either to failure on Chaucer's part or to complex purposes which have not yet been fully articulated. There seems to be ample justification for reopening the entire case and exploring the second of these alternatives: the possibility of multiple intentions on the part of the poet. A firm distinction between the art of the Franklin and that of his creator will lead inevitably to thematic considerations of some consequence to a full understanding of Chaucer's poetry.

One major difficulty in assessing the Franklin's character is the obscurity of the portrait in the General Prologue. It is partly an obscurity imposed by the passage of time. Even the meaning of the term, 'franklin', has been in dispute. The *N.E.D.* had relegated that rank to a position in society 'next below the gentry', but G. H. Gerould[6] has substantially established that the franklin in Chaucer's day was of a sufficiently exalted position to be considered 'gentil'. Yet Lumiansky, wishing (as I do) to stress the Franklin's social aspirations, ignores Gerould's evidence and reverts to Kittredge's estimate:

Socially, he is not quite within the pale of the gentry, but he is the kind of man that may hope to found a family, the kind of man from whose ranks the English nobility has been constantly recruited.[7]

Some confusion arises from the slipperiness of the word 'gentry', which Kittredge seems to equate with the aristocracy. The modern English use, however, first appearing in the late sixteenth century,[8] designates the class immediately below the nobility, and it is here no doubt that Gerould would place the Franklin. Such a class depends not on title, but on the appearance of gentility, on an established position in society, the result of wealth and political ability over a number of generations; it would, therefore, be accessible to the bourgeois in a way that the nobility would not. The *Canterbury Tales* alone provides sufficient evidence that a 'gentry' class in this sense existed in the fourteenth century, and that they commanded considerable power and prestige.

The Franklin, though a man of ample means and political prestige, clearly does not belong to that order of society for which 'gentilesse', in its primary sense[9] at least, is assured by birth. Moreover, the perpetuation of those gifts which the Franklin abundantly possesses is by no means guaranteed. Political and social abilities are not hereditary, and wealth, unlike a title, can be consumed in a single generation. It is just such a prospect which the Franklin has painfully before him in the person of a young son who

> to vertu listeth nat entende;
> But for to pleye at dees, and to despende
> And lese al that he hath, is his usage.
> And he hath levere talken with a page
> Than to comune with any gentil wight
> Where he myghte lerne gentillesse aright.
>
> (F. 689–94)

The Franklin himself professes belief in a 'vertu' which exceeds in value all the material wealth he possesses. This 'gentillesse' is not simply social rank, but a nobility of manner which can be learned and imitated, so that, in all but title, the son of a franklin might become indistinguishable from the son of a knight.

But there is a telling betrayal in the Franklin's words to the Squire:

> I have a sone, and by the Trinitee,
> I hadde levere than twenty pound worth lond,
> Though it right now were fallen in myn hond,
> He were a man of swich discrecioun
> As that ye been!   (F. 682–6)

'Discrecioun' and 'gentillesse' are not, the Franklin realizes, qualities that can be bought, but he automatically and naturally thinks in such terms. He is a man used to buying what he wants. The precision and the immediacy with which he envisions the twenty pound worth of land falling at that moment into his hand expose him as one more at ease when exchange takes the tangible form of land or currency than with the exchange of ideas or mere words, where values are more difficult to ascertain. Yet it is just these intangibles which attract the man who is so exceedingly comfortable in other ways. The Franklin, who is a St. Julian of hospitality as well as a frequent and popular office holder, is, because of this fatal attraction, an unhappy father. The vigour and passion with which the Franklin lauds the young Squire and abuses his own son betray the uneasiness of his paternal relationship. But even as the father reveals his attempts to lead his son toward 'vertu' and 'gentillesse', he unconsciously stresses with equal force that he is leading him *from* sins of prodigality. The motives are clearly not distinguished in the Franklin's mind; the preservation of a tangible power and the acquisition of intangible but socially esteemed virtues contend for prominence. These words of the Franklin, then, support the description of one comfortably ranking with the 'landed gentry', but uncomfortably unsure of real gentility.

It is his exchange of words with the Host, however, which most strikingly confirms our notion of the Franklin's social insecurity. Precisely at the word 'gentillesse', the Host can bear no more and puts an end to the old man's confessions. Harry Bailly has heard a great deal about 'gentillesse' in the last tales, ever since the Wife dragged the issue into her story by its heels. It may well be that he has heard too much precious debate on the subject by members of the pilgrimage who are manifestly trying to compensate for want of good birth and good breeding. It is perhaps the Franklin's use of such terms that the Host finds particularly offensive; that, as Nevill Coghill suggests, he 'could see at a glance that there was a penny short in the shilling of the Franklin's gentility'.[10] In any case, the Host, using the familiar pronoun, treats him with unusual rudeness. The Franklin's social position seems not to permit him a rebuke; nor is he lofty enough to withdraw in a huff as the Monk does. He replies with a humble, elaborate submission which would certainly be far from 'the realities of social intercourse', as Kemp Malone implies,[11] were the Franklin truly to be considered of untouchable social respectability.

Perhaps the most serious objection to my estimate of the Franklin's social position is the portrait in the General Prologue. Scholars have almost unanimously found it an approving depiction of a white-bearded gentleman endowed with a sanguine and generous disposition and considerable prestige accruing from the high offices he has held. This view is difficult to refute. The Chaucerian attitude toward the representatives of the moneyed class is in general cold and impersonal. In the case of the professional men – the Merchant, the Lawyer, the Physician – there is, however, clear negative evidence of unscrupulous money-grubbing. In most of the other portraits there is a recognized code of behavior – the chivalric ideal, the monastic rule – against which the pilgrim is measured. But there is no indication of the Franklin's dishonesty, and no established ideal of conduct is alluded to, if indeed one was available.

Yet twenty-one of the thirty lines devoted to the Franklin in the General Prologue are given over to the elaboration of something like an ideal – the wholly worldly philosophy of Epicurus,

> That heeld opinioun that pleyn delit
> Was verray felicitee parfit.   (A. 337–8)

And the pilgrim Chaucer is at great pains to convince us that his new friend is the true and perfect representative of this 'opinioun'. Most scholars have allowed themselves to be convinced without perhaps carefully assessing what they were being convinced of, for the ideals of Epicurus are hardly of the sort which could be granted any serious validity in the theocentric world of the Middle Ages.[12] This is not to say that Chaucer might not have found something to admire in the sumptuous completeness of the Franklin's devotion, but it seems unlikely that he would have shared his narrator's enthusiasm for such unabashed materialism. It is only Chaucer the pilgrim who warmly embraces excellence of performance without questioning the virtue of the action itself.

This distinction is reinforced by the tone of the portrait. Every kind of verbal extravagance is lavished upon the man whose primary concern is the splendid display of unsurpassed wealth and taste. He is not merely an epicurean; he is the legitimate heir of the founder of the cult. The rhetorical superlatives heaped upon his gastronomic stores (A. 342–6) nicely complement the excessive vigilance of the Franklin's activities as host, and even the images playfully emphasize the absorption of the man in good food (A. 345, 358–9). Equally suggestive is the juxtaposition of details. The enumeration of the Franklin's high offices follows directly, without syntactical connection, upon the description of his 'table dormant'. Lumiansky has pointed out that an epicurean delight in pure pleasure is a rare trait in one whose 'important public offices' proclaim him a man 'of outstanding ability and industry'. He concludes that possibly 'good hard work is more important in Chaucer's Franklin than his love of food, drink and pleasure; if so, his lavish hospitality becomes in some respects play acting'.[13] Some such interpretation would help explain another curious juxtaposition – the companionship of the Franklin with the Sergeant of the Law. Such pairings in the General Prologue seem to reflect a kind of propriety, and the Sergeant is a worthy companion in terms of wealth and social prestige. But the worthiness of his portrait as a whole is unquestionably flawed by a recurrent element of false-seeming. It is not unlikely, then, that their association is meant to call attention to an element of incongruity in the Franklin's behavior, though hardly one of calculated deception as in the Lawyer's. In short, the evidence of the General Prologue may well be taken to support the image of an otherwise sober, capable man of practical affairs who is innocently infatuated with an aristocratic performance which he can imitate but not quite fully understand.

This estimate of the Franklin's character is immediately reinforced by the opening of the tale itself. The first thing the narrator tells us is that it is a Breton lay, a form which in his mind has an aristocratic pedigree :

> Thise olde *gentil* Britouns in hir dayes
> Of diverse aventures maden layes.   (F. 709–10)

He seems, further, to have 'deliberately emphasized the ancient air of his own Breton lay', as J. S. P. Tatlock long ago pointed out.[14] Not only do we have the pagan atmosphere of ancient deities and heathenish arts of magic, but also such conscious archaisms as 'Armorik' (729), 'Briteyne' (for England, 810), and the Latin forms of Arveragus and Aurelius. A study of the sources, however, indicates that, whereas the prologue and the descriptions of the geographical and topographical locale are elaborately designed to give the impression of a Breton tale and a Breton setting, the plot itself belongs to an Italian tradition and is perhaps directly indebted to Boccaccio.[15] The Breton veneer, then, seems to reflect a conscious procedure on the part of the poet.

A purpose behind this generic pretension is suggested by the literary status of the Breton lay at the time of the composition of the *Canterbury Tales*. Laura Hibbard Loomis, in an article on the Breton lays in English, has indicated that manuscript evidence implies that in the latter half of the fourteenth century 'the lays were not in vogue, that they were not being recopied by scribes, and were not, presumably, being discussed by contemporary literati'.[16] The literary genre, which is so evidently imposed upon the plot of the Franklin's Tale, may well have seemed as faded and outmoded to Chaucer's audience as the Arthurian romances of the Victorian poets to the public of Pound and Eliot. Mrs. Loomis speaks of the 'noble but old fashioned tastes of the whitebearded Franklin', but it may well be that Chaucer intended the choice of literary mode to represent a conscious attempt on the part of the Franklin to attract the attention and admiration of the aristocratic members of his audience with the most 'refined' sort of tale he could resurrect from his somewhat fossilized memory. He offers a tale which he considers in the best taste, but it is the taste of a previous generation. In emphasizing this generic choice, Chaucer may have been consciously adding to his portrait of a man slightly out of touch with the ways of the nobility, here making a conspicuous attempt to close the gap.

The imitation of noble ways is nowhere more apparent than in the Franklin's use of rhetoric. It is precisely the high manner of the telling that he admires in the performance of the young Squire and considers to be the true manifestation of his 'gentillesse'. He praises the youth for his 'wit', predicts that he will soon have no peer 'of eloquence', and wishes him continuance 'in vertu', that is, in these rhetorical accomplishments.[17] Furthermore, he asserts that the only way to 'lerne gentillesse aright' is 'to comune with any gentil wight' (F. 693–4), to attend to and then imitate the elegant discourse of courtly circles. The final compliment paid to the Squire by the Franklin is to do just that, to pattern his style in the prologue after that of the Squire, which he has evidently heard with delight and with profit.

One of the devices used repeatedly by the Squire is the formula of 'affected modesty'.[18] The pose of the plain, blunt man ('Thyng that I speke, it moot be bare and pleyn', 720) is appropriated by the Franklin to serve a dual purpose. It will pacify the Host and the other 'lewed' men who will take it seriously, but at the same time it will appeal to the 'gentils' who recognize it as a highly learned device. The Franklin, in fact, extravagantly calls attention to his learning in the very act of disclaiming it. He refers directly to 'Marcus Tullius Scithero', the great foster-parent of medieval rhetoric, and indirectly to Persius, 'that most rhetorical of Latin poets'.[19] And, in his witty play on three meanings of the word 'colours', he exhibits ostentatious proficiency in the rhetorical color, or figure of speech, called *traductio*.[20] Indeed, there is very little true modesty in the Franklin's professions, though it may be true that, as he says, his 'spirit feeleth noght of swich mateere' (727).

The flow of rhetoric by no means stops with the Franklin's prologue. Benjamin S. Harrison claims to have discovered 'at least 70 rhetorical forms which correspond to the Latin colors'.[21] Though many of these colors are common tricks of speech which pass unnoticed in everyday conversation, the medieval man of letters, intensively trained in rhetorical forms, would have been conscious of using them, whether he had sought after them, as the handbooks recommend, or not. Chaucer was able to avoid drawing attention to them in the low comic tales, where rhetorical colors were considered inappropriate. In the aristocratic tales, the abundance of rhetoric seems to be a part of the world of the poem, whether the theme be profoundly philosophic like the Knight's or superficially 'gentil' like the Squire's. The mannered style of the narration seems to be perfectly wedded to the mannered behavior of the characters, and both are natural projections of the rank and education of the narrator. Not so with the Franklin. He seems almost as uncomfortably conscious of the way in which he is telling his tale as he is of its meaning. Both consequently are forced upon our attention.

Many rhetorical passages obtrude because of their sheer bulk alone: the extensive *sententia* (F. 761–86), for example, which comes too late and too long to be merely a graceful way of opening the tale,[22] yet manages to interrupt just as the tale is getting under way; the formal descriptive pieces, of the garden (901–17), of the apparitions of the 'tregetour' (1139–51 and 1189–1208), of the 'colde, frosty seson of Decembre' (1245–55),[23] particularly notable for its elegant and irrelevant *circuito* in the figure of Janus, and for the anachronistic cries of 'Nowel' in this predominantly pagan setting; the detailed and highly technical recitation of astrological procedure (1273–93), which is prefaced by 'I ne kan no termes of astrologye' and is punctuated by grumblings against the very idea of such 'supersticious cursednesse'; and finally, most telling for sheer lengthiness, the string of twenty-two *exempla* in the forty-eight hour marathon complaint of Dorigen (1364–1456).

Transitions are often noticeably abrupt and, unlike those in the Knight's Tale, convey the impression of a narrator uneasy about the behavior of his noble characters and with the rhetorical requirements of his chosen genre.[24] One passage in particular calls for comment. It is the notorious example of *expolitio*[25] which follows the first interview between Dorigen and Aurelius:

> But sodeynly bigonne revel newe
> Til that the brighte sonne lost his hewe:
> For th'orisonte hath reft the sonne his lyght!
> This is as muche to seye as it was nyght!   (F. 1015–18)

Critics have chosen to interpret this matter-of-fact statement as Chaucer's satiric 'sly comment' on his own rhetoric. Manly[26] appropriately cites the inanity of the rhetorical handbooks on the matter of *periphrasis* or *circumlocutio*. Geoffroi de Vinsauf, for example, seems unable to distinguish between amplification for its own sake – mere bombast or dishonesty – and the use of such figures for their poetic extension of the 'plain sense' through implication and connotation.[27] But if there is an apparent naiveté or pedantic stupidity in these lines, then the fault must be that of the Franklin and his rhetorical pretensions. He either feels compelled to explain his figure in simple terms to those who are less informed than he; or he has launched himself on a bit of fancy, Italianate description and, not quite knowing where to go with it, decides to sink the whole matter.

However one chooses to reconstruct this little crisis in the Franklin's narrative, it has dramatic validity only if one accepts some such interpretation of the Franklin's character as I have been trying to suggest here; it would be quite impossible, for example, to attribute to him the amused detachment of the Nun's Priest. The way in which the Franklin feels called upon to tell his tale points to the same kind of person we found in the links and prologues – a man of considerable ability and virtue who is markedly over-reaching. His rhetorical practice indicates that he is a man for whom the art is not instinctive and easy. Nor does he seem to be sure of its essential value or purpose. The Franklin's success is considerable, but he is betrayed by the occasional clumsiness or excess, and by the intermittent grumblings of the practical man of good common sense and solid Christian virtues who feels that the whole business is perhaps a bit foolish and a bit undignified for one of his age and position.

The Franklin's greatest rhetorical blunder, for which Chaucer has taken all the blame and some faint praise, is the Complaint of Dorigen. Manly, elsewhere so sensitive to the satiric use of excessive rhetoric, felt that the tale, otherwise so 'finely told, is nearly spoiled by one hundred lines of rhetorical example'. 'What reader', he concludes, 'modern or medieval, would not have been more powerfully and sympathetically affected if Chaucer with the psychological insight displayed in *Troilus and Criseyde*, had caused his distressed and desperate heroine to express the real feelings appropriate to her character and situation?'[28]

It would indeed be difficult to contend that the Complaint is not a blemish upon a 'fine tale', if the tale were in fact as fine as the Franklin wished it to appear. Nor can the passage be written off as rhetorical parody, 'a *reductio ad absurdum* of the use of *exempla*' as Manly was later to propose.[29] As parody, this monstrous intrusion is more of a bore than an absurdity. Here, as in the similar excursions of the Wife of Bath's Prologue and Tale and in the debate of the cock and hen in the Nun's Priest's Tale, Chaucer has not only made his rhetorical parody subtly appropriate to the speaker, but has given it a saving comic grace in the immediate narrative context.

The character of Dorigen must occupy our attention before the dramatic right or wrong of her Complaint can be decided. Lumiansky argues that the device of the formal complaint, characteristic of the world of courtly love, as well as the 'noble choice of suicide rather than dishonour',[30] can be explained by the fact that Dorigen, the noble wife, enters the story somewhat incongruously as a courtly love heroine and retains something of that role throughout. James Sledd,[31] on the other hand, maintains that the Complaint is a 'deliberate bit of rhetorical extravagance, intended as an assurance that all shall yet go well' : as a heroine, Dorigen belongs to the realm of tragicomedy, where the outcome is potentially tragic, but is turned aside 'not to the ludicrous but to the pleasant'. The tone of the Complaint insures that the audience will remain sufficiently detached from the painful emotions of the character and avoids just such pathos as Manly once required. The tale, as Sledd sees it, is a 'tragicomedy with a moral – a serious but pleasant story of recognizably human people'.

But Sledd has the Franklin in better control of his rhetoric than I would allow. He interprets the obtrusive rhetoric, as well as the numerous intrusions into the tale of the Franklin *in propria persona*, as deliberate attempts on his part to allay the fears and disengage the emotions of his audience. If my interpretation of the character of the Franklin is correct, such rhetorical suavity is out of the question. Furthermore, the impression one gets from the Complaint is not that of a deliberate manipulation of the audience by the teller, but of a conspicuous lack of control on the part of the narrator as well as the actor.

My own understanding of the dramatic values of the Complaint has been aided immeasurably by Mrs. Dempster's picture of Chaucer at work on his copy of Jerome. Having looked hard

at the poet's use of his sources, she discovered with satisfaction
that he treated them 'with a degree of *negligence* and *rape,* not to
say boredom, of which we find very few other instances in his
works'.[32] Though we may differ with her conclusions, Mrs.
Dempster's study is of great value in determining the way in
which the Complaint was assembled and the degree of seriousness involved in the process. The choice of *exempla* begins with
appropriate selection and careful elaboration, but concludes in
a crescendo of hasty inconclusiveness and irrelevance. The first
seven *exempla* (F. 1368–1418) are treated in some detail and
are all virgins and wives who sacrificed life to maintain chastity.
They seem to have been drawn from memory or from Jerome
directly with deliberate concern for aptness to the particular situation. But after what professes to be a conclusion at lines 1419–25,
the *exempla* begin again, coming now with increasing rapidity
until with the concubine of Alcibiades (F. 1439–41), appropriateness is abandoned. The rest of the Complaint proceeds with ever
increasing brevity and decreasing relevance, until in the final
couplet no less than three heroines of antiquity are forced to find
accommodation. Of the magnificent impertinence of these
histories to Dorigen's problem, Mrs. Dempster remarks:
'Valeria's glory had consisted in refusing to remarry, Rhodo-
gune's, in killing her nurse, and Bilia's, in never remarking on the
smell of her husband's breath!' The study of sources has shown
that after composing what would have passed as a respectable
complaint, Chaucer deliberately returned to Jerome several
times. Adding one *exemplum* after another, he finally abandoned
all pretense to cogency and threw them all in, with a disregard
for relevance which must have amused him greatly. If this was
'negligence and rape', it was clearly undertaken with the purpose
of destroying any hope of pathos or serious concern on Dorigen's
behalf.

Even without reference to the sources, one can sense the humor
of the monologue. The air of dogged intensity in the opening line
(1367) is followed by the simple righteousness and enthusiasm
for authority of the first *exempla* (esp. 1377–8 and 1402–3).
Dorigen has to wrestle with the temptation to unpack the whole
bag of more than a thousand stories (1412–13); she allows herself one more, then determines to conclude (1422 ff.); but finds

herself betrayed by a rhyme into just one more, and the bag rips open. She rushes through the second half of the Complaint desperately attempting to pile up names until there is scarcely enough breath to get through the final couplet :

> The same thyng I seye of Bilyea,
> Of Rodogone, and eek Valeria.   (F. 1455–6)

One is quite convinced that Dorigen can go on in this way for two days without intermission, and it is equally evident that she has no intention of committing suicide. She is the sort of woman who loves to indulge her emotions and knows how to make the most of a melodramatic situation. What the Franklin had intended to be a noble parade of dignified authorities collapses into the garrulousness of an attractive, but hysterical, rather silly woman. Where Sledd has chosen to find a tragicomic situation produced by the Franklin, I prefer to see the Franklin's stiff tragedy developed simultaneously with Chaucer's high comedy.

Of course, such a characterization of Dorigen would be untenable, were it not that from the beginning, in spite of the best intentions of the Franklin, there is something awkward about her 'nobility'. The opening description of the courtship and the marriage 'trouthe' is too formalized – in the evocation of courtly love as well as in the rhetoric – to throw light on the characters. The casual metamorphosis of a courtly love knight and mistress into man and wife is, however, sufficient to put us on our guard. But once Arveragus sets off to war and Dorigen is left alone, we have a good opportunity to estimate this 'faireste' lady of such 'heigh kynrede'. She performs not with the stately tragic grace the Franklin had probably hoped to dramatize, but with a curious lack of propriety, with a somewhat mechanical excessiveness by which Chaucer has made of her an engaging heroine in a high comic mode. Again the Franklin's uncertainty about the manners of gentility and in the use of rhetoric has been put to work by the poet for his own complex artistic purposes :

> For his absence wepeth she and siketh,
> As doon thise noble wyves whan hem liketh.
> She moorneth, waketh, wayleth, fasteth, pleyneth . . .
>   (F. 817–19)

One cannot help but catch an unconscious suggestion on the part of the practical, sensible Franklin that this sort of behavior (whose worth he accepts only on faith) is the prerogative of an idle class, a useless but ornamental activity to be indulged at will by those who have nothing better to do. The sudden and rather stiff list of verbs in line 819 (rhetorically an *articulus*) acknowledges, however, that this kind of thing certainly does fill up one's time.

The monumental 'hevynesse' of Dorigen is industriously opposed by the host of friends who try to bring her back to society and good sense. But the task seems as difficult as removing the rocks from the Brittany coast. The juxtaposition of sensible social behaviour and Dorigen's conspicious display of grief makes her actions seem something less than truly dignified, somewhat too much in the proper manner, inappropriately stylized, and rather silly. The woodenness of her determination to play unflinchingly the role of a devoted noble wife convinces us of her simplicity, but it is not until we observe her treatment of the squire Aurelius that we fully appreciate the scope of her irrational, almost giddy femininity. At first there is dazed terror in her voice when she replies to his confession. She becomes conscious of his existence for the first time, just as the terrifying black rocks only took form for her when she saw them as a threat to her stubborn search for happiness.

> She gan to looke upon Aurelius:
> 'Is this youre wyl', quod she, 'and sey ye thus?
> Nevere erst', quod she, 'ne wiste I what ye mente.'
>
> (F. 979–81)

The shock and incredulity with which she begins, modulates to the fierce tenacity which she has previously demonstrated. She seems about to wish Aurelius to hell with the rocks, when she suddenly recollects herself in the garden world of play. Rashly she makes her promise, obsessed with all she sees that prevents her happiness. The 'trouthe' she plights, with the identical legalistic phrase she offered to Arveragus (F. 759), combines a slightly cruel revenge on the importunate Aurelius with her irrational *idée fixe*, those 'grisly rokkes blake'. The promise is not only self-contradictory; it is also somewhat haughty and malicious – professing to be motivated by pity ('Syn I you se so pitously complayne'), but pitiless in its intentional absurdity. Dorigen concludes with the moral indignation of a franklin :

> What deyntee sholde a man han in his lyf
> For to go love another mannes wyf,
> That hath hir body whan so that hym liketh?
>
> (F. 1003–5)

But our sympathy has turned to the badly treated squire who is left to face a 'sodeyn deth horrible', while Dorigen rejoins the mirth and company of her friends. The folly of her woe has driven him to raving, and we are fully prepared to enjoy the spectacle of this haughty woman writhing in turn through her *exempla*-ridden complaint. The values and sentiments which the Franklin had hoped to dramatize cannot be contained in his peculiarly ignoble *personae*. By such frequent reversals in our sympathy (from Dorigen to her well-meaning friends to the squire), we have been spared the Franklin's heavy tragic involvement and are preserved in a splendid comic detachment.

The invitation to detachment, dramatically extended in the figure of Dorigen, is equally apparent in the other major characters. Aurelius is a bundle of clichés, conventional notions and emotions, cold and distant echoes of the Knight's Tale and *Troilus*.[33] He loves, moans, suffers, pines, and wastes away in tactful silence, according to the rules, and never insults his lady by doing any of these things for a shorter period than two years. Our acquaintance with Arveragus is brief but impressively formal and stiff. His actions are noticeably only those of a proper knight, a conventional counterpart for the courtly heroine and wife : 'Servant in love, and lord in mariage' (F. 793). From the beginning his every action betrays a meticulous concern for two ideals which soon find themselves awkwardly in conflict: 'gentillesse' (754) in his personal, and 'degree' (752) in his social relationships. It is the second of these, his lofty consciousness of his position and rank in society, which determines him to abandon his wife and give equal time to his knightly duties. 'A

yer and moore' of 'blisful lyf' is judiciously balanced with 'a yer
or tweyne' (809) of service at arms in England, a duty which
he seems to embrace with equal pleasure, with 'al his lust' (812).
Obviously, this nice devotion to 'degree' is necessary to the plot;
Arveragus must be got out of the way. But the Franklin has
handled it so that the trip to England appears a bit too suddenly dutiful, too business-like in its attention to the prescribed
demands upon knighthood. Perhaps it is again the Franklin's
bewilderment over the strange ways of the nobility which leads
him to justify Arveragus' behavior with reference to a written
source: 'the book seith thus' (813). The narrator seems to feel
that the demands of knighthood would be as pressing as those
of commerce and as strictly regulated as those of the shire. In
fact, one is hardly surprised to find that, when next Dorigen is
in need of her lord and master, 'out of towne was goon Arveragus'
(1351), no doubt busy once again about the business of being a
knight.

The 'gentillesse' of Arveragus is equally automatic and consciously *comme il faut.* When Dorigen rehearses her shattering
tale, the husband not only replies without hesitation: 'Is ther
oght elles, Dorigen, but this?' (1469), but he does so with a
somewhat astounding display of 'glad chiere, in freendly wyse'
(1467). One begins to suspect that, like Shaw's Octavius, he
regards 'the world as a moral gymnasium built expressly to
strengthen [his] character in'.[34] His decision is immediate, un-
faltering, and mechanically 'gentil'. Not until he has pronounced his *sententia* upon 'trouthe', does he exhibit the
humanity of bitter tears, shattering the noble image with a command of secrecy (upon threat of death) and with his desire to
keep up appearances. His feelings are efficiently compartmental-
ized; his stiffly principled nobility and his real but less exalted
emotions never quite meet.[35] But the bravado of his 'gentillesse'
is more than its own reward; it releases a cascade of imitation
and promotes the *embarras de gentillesse* in which the tale
tumbles to a conclusion.

Thus, Dorigen, Aurelius, and Arveragus are all elegant but
artificial puppets pieced together from bits of faded romances,
from clichés of character and conventions of courtly behavior.
Behind them lurks a reality which is, however, not their own but

that of their narrator. It reveals a sensibility perhaps less refined and idly extravagant in emotion and ideas, but more practical, prejudiced in favor of common morality and the familiar virtues of Holy Church, and above all, more fundamentally human. It is this reality, the everpresent personality of the Franklin, which gives the lie to the posturing and the self-conscious nobility of his characters, who in turn owe their very existence to his own self-consciousness before the 'gentil' pilgrims of Chaucer's complexly creative *dramatis personae* in the *Canterbury Tales*.

I have examined the Franklin's narrative manner in considerable detail because I believe it not only important for its own sake but essential to an estimation of what the poem is really about. If the Franklin's Tale is in fact the work of two creators, of Chaucer and Chaucer's Franklin, then the thematic possibilities of the narrative are obviously multiplied. It was clear that in the handling of the rhetoric and character, the intentions of the teller were not those of the poet. The purposes of the two creators diverge, though they are often expressed in a single phrase or gesture.

The Franklin's intentions are not difficult to isolate. They are twofold and part of a drama of ideas in the sequence of tales initiated by the Wife of Bath. The Franklin begins his tale with an explicit exposition of his concept of the ideal marriage. In reply to the Wife's advocacy of female sovereignty and to the Clerk's demonstration of wifely submission to her wedded lord, the Franklin proposes a compromise of mutual obedience and equal mastery. Neither love nor liberty is compromised; each partner remains unconstrained in spite of the bonds of marriage. Furthermore, the initial success of the experiment, the 'blisse' and 'solas' (802) of Arveragus and Dorigen, is offered as an antidote to the grim cynicism of the Merchant's depiction of 'wepyng and waylyng, care and oother sorwe' (E. 1213) to be found in wedded life.

But as the story unfolds, a second, less explicit purpose reveals itself – a working definition of the noble ideal of 'gentillesse'. Here again, the Franklin takes his cue from the Wife of Bath, who devoted much of her tale to a digression on that 'verray

gentillesse' which comes not of birth but of God's grace alone
(D. 1162 ff.). To prolong the discussion of this theme, to which
the Franklin, as we have seen, is extraordinarily responsive, he
drags his characters through all the absurdities of his plot, from
the rash promise to the magical illusions, in order to establish a
dilemma which can only be resolved by the gracious operation of
'gentillesse', specifically in terms of its two most significant com-
ponents, 'trouthe' and 'fredom'. The drama of the tale is a
result of the two conflicting 'trouthes' of Dorigen, the vow of
fidelity to Arveragus and the promise to Aurelius. The necessity
of keeping one's plighted word, no matter what the circumstances, is one of the prime requisites of knighthood:

> Trouthe is the hyeste thyng that man may kepe.
>
> (F. 1479)

The acceptance of the requirements of 'trouthe' on the part of
Arveragus enables him to exercise the equally fundamental virtue
of 'fredom'. He generously sacrifices what is most precious to
him, his wife's purity, that she may be true to her word. Aurelius
and the 'Orliens' clerk follow suit in making what obviously seem
to the Franklin to be equally generous sacrifices, to demonstrate
that 'gentillesse' and 'fredom' are not the exclusive prerogatives
of knighthood. The structural weight given to the exposition of
these virtues is increased by the conclusion of the tale in a
demande d'amour:

> Which was the mooste fre, as thynketh yow?   (F. 1622)

The concern with an ideal marriage has been replaced by a
broader but no less idealistic theme.

That 'gentillesse', 'trouthe', and 'fredom' were in reality
serious, valid ideals for Chaucer's audience and for the poet himself is fully demonstrated by their prominence in the portrait of
the Knight in the General Prologue: 'Trouthe and honour, fredom and curteisie' (A. 46). But the Wife of Bath's Tale with its
ungainly digression and ill-mannered 'gentil' squire indicates
equally well that these terms could be comically misdirected by
the poet to inappropriate hands. Just as the Franklin's noble

actors are much nearer the real thing than the grotesque
imitation of the Wife, so, too, his handling of these abstractions
is more artful and profound. But nevertheless, the flaws in the
Franklin's narrative are to be reckoned with in a final estimation
of the poem's substance. They force us to consider that the ideals
which the tale treats so prominently are those of the Franklin
and not necessarily at this moment the poet's primary concern.
What is true in the case of the quixotic ideal of a marriage conceived in courtly love[36] must also hold for the loftier, more en-
compassing ideal of 'gentillesse', though it is at other times de-
monstrably Chaucerian.

Isolation of the Franklin's simple notion of what his tale is
about makes it immediately clear that his two themes are not
quite adequate to cover all the material in his narration. The
'prayers' of Dorigen and Aurelius, as they are elaborated by the
Franklin, are not structurally necessary to the plot. The removal
of the rocks is effected by magical illusion with no suggestion of
the assistance of a deity. The two prayers, identical in petition
but conflicting in motive, and the irony of their fulfillment seem
to belong to another narrative structure – one, for example, like
that of the Knight's Tale, which is similar to this in pattern, but
whose conclusion clearly focuses upon the intervention of the
gods and the philosophical issues raised by the precarious
relationship between humanity and divinity. The Franklin's Tale,
as far as its themes of marriage and 'gentillesse' are concerned,
could well have dispensed with such metaphysical implication.[37]

Dorigen's prayer, or first 'complaint' as it might better be
called, grows out of her excessive grief and defines the intensity
of her *idée fixe*, the black rocks. Her hysteria leads her to
absurdities which are clearly beyond the scope of the tale as the
Franklin envisions it. She challenges the very order of the Universe, the reasonableness of Creation; she turns the amorous
problem into a metaphysical issue. She invokes an unmistakably
Christian God and not the pagan pantheon of the rest of the
poem :

> Eterne God, that thurgh thy purveiaunce
> Ledest the world by certain governaunce, . . .
>
> (F. 865–6)

All things are reputed to have a purpose, but she can find nothing in the rocks except 'a foul confusion of werk' (F. 869–70). They are a source of grief to all the orders of Creation, destroying its fairest creature, man. She acknowledges that there is another way of looking at things :

> I woot wel clerkes wol seyn as hem leste,
> By argumentz, that al is for the beste,
> Though I ne kan the causes nat yknowe.
>
> (F. 885–7)

But in her wild protest she throws disputation of clerks to the winds and demands that the rocks be sunk into hell for her husband's sake. Her last words, 'thise rokkes sleen myn herte for the feere' (893), indicate, however, that her grief is basically self-centered and wilful.

This complaint, then, becomes more than just a wife's lament. It is a piece of metaphysical foolishness in the course of which the theological reply to such protests is clearly stated. The black rocks loom for Dorigen as symbols of all that in the human condition is adverse to human happiness. Such adversities, as the Church obviously has told her, can be overcome not by violent rebellion, but by faith in divine purveyance and a patient acceptance of the world as we find it. Our perception is humanly limited; only God can know final purpose.

For Aurelius, too, the rocks come to represent the sole obstacle to personal happiness, but his prayer is more devious. He avoids calling upon the chaste goddess of the moon directly to aid his lustful cause. Going over her head, he calls upon Apollo to lead her astray in an incestuous, cosmic intrigue which will draw the earth's waters above the rocks. The powers invoked in these two prayers are thus appropriate to both the nature of the cause and the justice of the complaint: Dorigen's love is sanctified and holy; Aurelius', adulterous and pagan. Dorigen inveighs against divine Providence; Aurelius, his personal amorous fate. But in each case the intense distaste for the black rocks is loosed by a dissatisfaction with things as they are and an inability to suffer patiently the trials of adversity.

An unconscious awareness of the metaphysical implications of these protests is evident in the fact that their conversation is punctuated with oaths invoking God in His office of Creator: 'by God that this world made' (967), 'by thilke God that yaf me soule and lyf' (983), 'by that Lord . . . . that maked me' (1000). We are made forcibly aware that the universal order is being inadvertently questioned and tested by this excitable wife and her pathetically amorous squire. It is now evident why we must remain detached from them as characters and why they are allowed to seem so stiffly comic and absurd. They have, in fact, muddled themselves into an ultimate foolishness of metaphysical dimension, which will be repented at leisure in the complex of events resulting from their prayers. They will be made to see the folly of their ways precisely by having the prayers granted; the dilemmas of grief and obligation which follow the prayers will far exceed those which preceded them.

Yet, though the implications of the story are to be taken seriously, never are the actions or characters invested with a tragic seriousness. They are mannered in a style of high comedy obliquely imposed on them by their overanxious narrator. The begrudging involvement of the Franklin with terms of astrology, Dorigen's run-away rhetoric in the grand Complaint, and the 'fredom' contest which places a wife's virtue on an equal footing with a thousand pounds – all contribute to the high comic tone of a tale which is set in motion by the self-indulgent folly of Dorigen and Aurelius, and reinforced by the book-governed chivalry of Arveragus. In his ingenious art, Chaucer has taken advantage of the limitations of his story-teller to add another dimension to his tale. The Franklin remains a perfectly valid and consistent dramatic creation, and his tale is appropriate to him in both theme and method, but Chaucer has made the poem do more than he permitted the Franklin to see.

The Franklin's myopia is nowhere more apparent than at the opening of the narrative where he indulges in an extended discourse on patience, the very virtue which will be the submerged theme of his tale. His ears still ringing with the debate of the Wife of Bath and the Clerk, the Franklin is only concerned with the narrow problem of patience in love, yet his words are equally appropriate to the larger virtue which his Dorigen so flagrantly neglects:

> Pacience is an heigh vertu, certeyn,
> For it venquysseth, as thise clerkes seyn,
> Thynges that rigour sholde nevere atteyne.
> For every word men may nat chide or pleyne.
> Lerneth to suffre, or elles, so moot I goon,
> Ye shul it lerne, wher so ye wole or noon.   (F. 773–8)

And so indeed Dorigen learns to suffer against her will, because she had unconsciously placed that will, her petty, immediate desires, against the will of God.

There is no surprise in finding this theme of patience in adversity in a poem of Chaucer's. The *locus classicus* is, of course, Boethius's *Consolation*, which Chaucer first translated, then allowed to filter into his serious works of philosophic romance. The theme is particularly crucial to the *Troilus*, and emerges again and again in the *Canterbury Tales*. Witness most notably the complaint of Arcite in the Knight's Tale :

> Allas, why pleynen folk so in commune
> On purveiaunce of God, or of Fortune,
> That yeveth hem ful ofte in many a gyse
> Wel bettre than they kan hemself devyse? (A. 1251–4)

One couplet especially is equally pertinent to the situation of the Franklin's Tale :

> We seken faste after felicitee,
> But we goon wrong ful often, trewely.   (A. 1266–7)

But it is the Clerk's Tale, in dramatic proximity to the Franklin's, which presents the most interesting parallel. Not only is the theme identical, but it, too, arises as an extension of the more limited concern of the tale itself. As in the case of Dorigen, Griselda's example is not to be confined to married life, but applied to human existence in general :

> For, sith a womman was so pacient
> Unto a mortal man, wel moore us oghte
> Receyven al in gree that God us sent; ...

> And for oure beste is al his governaunce.
> Lat us thanne lyve in vertuous suffraunce.
>
> (E. 1149–51; 1161–2)

If I am correct in my estimation of the Franklin's character and of the submerged theme of his tale, the connection between the two will be immediately apparent. The Franklin's excessive concern for 'gentillesse', for rank and position, is merely another kind of dissatisfaction with things as they are. Like Dorigen, he places personal well-being above a humble respect for the established order. But he is clearly not a vicious man, and accordingly the tone of the tale and the exposition of his limitations are good-humored and kind. The underlying theme of the tale, which recoils upon the teller, is not a deadly sin, as in the Merchant's and Pardoner's, but imperfect virtue. A stern moral purpose, which is never totally absent from the *Canterbury Tales*, forces us to admit that there is something foolish and misdirected in the actions of the Franklin and his heroine, but the comic method gracefully acknowledges that 'Pacience is an *heigh* vertu, certeyn'.

S O U R C E : *Neophilologus*, LI (1967); this reprint incorporates the author's revisions of the original text.

NOTES

1. *The Poetry of Chaucer* (Cambridge, 1906) p. 273.

2. *Chaucer* (London, 1952) p. 274.

3. *University of Toronto Quarterly*, XX (1951) 344–56, reproduced in his *Of Sondry Folk* (Austin, 1955) pp. 180–93.

4. 'Autobiographical Aspects of Chaucer's Franklin', *Speculum*, XXVIII (1953) 791–800.

5. Blenner-Hassett, p. 791.

6. 'The Social Status of Chaucer's Franklin', *P.L.M.A.*, XLI (1926) 262–79.

7. George L. Kittredge, 'Chaucer's Discussion of Marriage', *Modern Philology*, IX (1912) 458; above, p. 83.

8. *N.E.D.*, 'gentry', 2. In Chaucerian usage, the term seems to be synonymous with 'gentillesse' and refers to personal qualities,

polished manners, courtesy, and generosity, not to a social stratum. See esp. the Wife of Bath's Tale, III, 1152–7, where the two are clearly distinguished.

9. See *M.E.D.*, 'gentillesse', I (a).

10. *Geoffrey Chaucer* (London, 1956) p. 14. A similar interpretation was suggested by Lumiansky, p. 347, who would read line 695 : 'Straw for *youre* gentillesse'.

11. *Chapters on Chaucer* (Baltimore, 1951) p. 193.

12. Compare Gower, *Mirour de l'omme*, ed. Macaulay, ll. 9529 ff., quoted by D. W. Robertson Jr., *A Preface to Chaucer* (Princeton, 1962) p. 276, as a good summary of the fourteenth-century attitude toward Epicurus.

13. Lumiansky, p. 346.

14. *The Scene of the Franklin's Tale Visited*, Chaucer Society, Second Series, No. 51 (London, 1914) pp. 17–36.

15. See W. F. Bryan and Germaine Dempster, *Sources and Analogues to Chaucer's Canterbury Tales* (Chicago, 1941) pp. 377–97. Mrs. Dempster and J. S. P. Tatlock offer as a 'highly probable' source the story of Menedon in Boccaccio's *Filocolo*.

16. 'Chaucer and the Breton Lays of the Auchinleck MS', *Studies in Philology*, XXXVIII (1941) 14–33; see esp. pp. 16–17.

17. On this translation, see Robinson's note on l. 689. The value of the Squire's rhetorical accomplishments has recently been subjected to considerable scholarly analysis. See Gardner Stilwell, 'Chaucer in Tartary', *Review of English Studies*, XXIV (1948) 177–88; D. A. Pearsall, 'The Squire as Story-Teller', *University of Toronto Quarterly*, XXXIV (1964) 82–92; and Robert S. Haller, 'Chaucer's Squire's Tale and the Uses of Rhetoric', *Modern Philology*, LXII (1964–5) 285–95. All of these critics take the Squire's performance as dramatically appropriate to the youthful aristocrat whose command of rhetoric is superficial and ostentatiously exhibited as a requisite of his social status. Haller (p. 294) concludes his essay with an estimate of the Franklin which is similar to mine : 'The Squire is "gentil" by blood and presumably may outgrow his ideas of the meaning of his degree; but in the meantime he has fed the pretensions of a man whose only qualification for gentillesse is self-indulgence.'

18. See Eleanor Hammond, *English Verse between Chaucer and Surrey* (Durham, NC., 1927) p. 392, and Ernst Robert Curtius, *European Literature and the Latin Middle Ages*, trans. Willard R. Trask (Pantheon Books, 1953) p. 83. Among the modern critics taken in by this pose must be included the revered name of Kit-

tredge, *Chaucer and his Poetry*, p. 210: 'He is no cloistered rhetorician . . . Such a man lies under no suspicion of transcendental theorism nor vague heroics'.

19. J. M. Manly, *Chaucer and the Rhetoricians*, Warton Lecture on English Poetry XVII (Oxford, 1926) p. 5. The source of the allusion is the Prologue to the *Satires*, ll. 2–3:

> Neque in bicipiti somniasse Parnasso
> Memini, ut repente sic poeta prodirem

That this allusion would have been apparent to some of Chaucer's audience is suggested by the gloss in the MSS. El, Ad³, Hg-Ht, Ch, En³, Ps, Manly and Rickert, *The Text of the Canterbury Tales* (Chicago, 1940) III, p. 512, all fifteenth-century manuscripts, some of them probably quite early in the century.

20. Defined in the *Ad Herennium* IV, xiv: 'cum idem verbum ponitur modo in hac, modo in altera re'. See also E. Faral, *Les Arts Poétiques du XIIe et du XIIIe Siècle* (Paris, 1924) pp. 178, 332, 351, and p. 169 (paranomasia).

21. 'Rhetorical Inconsistency of Chaucer's Franklin', *Studies in Philology*, *XXXII* (1935) 55–61; see p. 56.

22. Such a procedure was recommended by the handbooks. See, for example, Geoffroi de Vinsauf, *Poetra Nova*, 11, 180 ff. (Faral, pp. 202–3), or Matthieu de Vendome, *Ars Versificatoria*, I, 16 (Faral, p. 113).

23. See Harrison's analysis, pp. 57–8.

24. See esp. ll. 814–15; 1085–6; 1554–6.

25. Defined in the *Ad Herennium* IV, xlii: 'cum in eodem loco manemus et aliud atque aliud dicere videmur'.

26. *Chaucer and the Rhetoricians*, p. 13.

27. The statement that the opening lines of the *Aeneid* mean nothing more than 'I will describe Aeneas', or that the invocation by Boethius beginning: 'O qui perpetua mundum ratione gubernas' is in fact an assertion 'quod nihil aliud est quam, "O Deus",' actually denies the poetic value of rhetorical colors. The passage in the Franklin's Tale, like the more evident appeal to rhetorical authority in the Nun's Priest's Tale (B. 3347–54), reflects the literalmindedness of the handbooks. The speaker implies that to say 'th'orisonte hath reft the sonne his lyght', 'nihil aliud est quam, "nox erat".' Eleanor Hammond, *Modern Language Notes*, XXVII (1912) 91–2, has pointed out that just such a deflationary phrase actually occurs in a prose passage of Fulgentius which follows eleven lines of flowery verse describing the coming of night.

28. Manly, p. 20.

29. *The Text of the Canterbury Tales* (Chicago, 1940) vol. II, p. 315.

30. Lumiansky, p. 354.

31. 'Dorigen's Complaint', *Modern Philology*, XLV (1947) 36–45; esp. pp. 42–4.

32. 'Chaucer at Work on the Complaint in the Franklin's Tale', *Modern Language Notes*, LII (1937) 22. Roberts A. Pratt, 'St. Jerome in Jankyn's Book of Wikked Wyves', *Criticism*, V (1963) 316–22, suggests that the Franklin intends Dorigen as a foil for the Wife of Bath and that the additional virtuous *exempla* in her complaint are a critique of the Wife's conduct.

33. J. L. Lowes, 'The Franklin Tale, the *Teeside*, and the *Filocolo*', *Modern Philology*, XV (1918) 689–782, has demonstrated that his portrait is composed of echoes of Boccaccio's *Teseide* and Chaucer's early translations of Boccaccio in the Knight's Tale, and even of Chaucer's own Squire in the General Prologue.

34. *Man and Superman* (Baltimore, Penguin Books, 1952) pp. 68–9.

35. For a similar evaluation of Arveragus, see D. W. Robertson Jr., *A Preface to Chaucer* (Princeton, 1962) pp. 470–2.

36. Gervase Mathew, 'Marriage and Amour Courtois in Late Fourteenth-Century England', *Essays presented to Charles Williams* (Oxford, 1947) pp. 128–35, considers the Franklin's view to be the common English position of the time; but see also Donald R. Howard, 'The Conclusion of the Marriage Group : Chaucer and the Human Condition', *Modern Philology* LVII (1959–60) 223–32.

37. On the philosophical implications of the Tale, see Edwin B. Benjamin, 'The Concept of Order in the Franklin's Tale', *Philological Quarterly*, XXXVIII (1959) 119–24, and Gerhard Joseph, The Franklin's Tale : Chaucer's Theodicy', *Chaucer Review*, I (1966) 20–32.

Ian Bishop

THE NARRATIVE ART OF THE PARDONER'S TALE (1967)

The Pardoner's Tale has often been praised for its dramatic irony, its concentration and the sense of awe that it engenders; it has more than once been described as one of the best short stories in English. The purpose of the present article is to re-examine some of the ways in which Chaucer achieves this result.[1] I do not propose to do this by comparing the tale with its analogues – that has already been done by Mrs. Germaine Dempster among others.[2] I shall rather compare some aspects of Chaucer's narrative technique in this tale with techniques that he employs in some of the most successful of his other short stories. But that is not my principal intent. My main purpose is to suggest that the concentration and the uncanny power of this tale are the result of three things in particular: a threefold economy, a double perspective and a unifying irony.

It is generally agreed that much of the tale's fascination is due to the figure of the 'old man and a povre' who directs the three rioters to the treasure. Yet there has been considerable disagreement about the identity and the significance of this character. In a recent article in *Medium Ævum*,[3] however, John M. Steadman has offered an explanation of his function which is based more firmly upon Chaucer's text than are most of the other interpretations. According to Steadman the old man is not a sinister or a supernatural figure: he is neither the Wandering Jew nor Death in disguise. Moreover, although one of his functions is to act as a *memento mori*, he is not a personification of Elde, one of the traditional messengers of Death. On the other hand, Professor Steadman will not follow W. J. B. Owen to the position of extreme naturalism and argue that he 'is an old man and nothing more'.[4] Whereas Owen maintains that the old man invents the story about Death being under the tree as a convenient means of getting rid of the drunkards who offer him violence,

Steadman argues that, like the hermit in some of the tale's analogues, the old man really has seen the treasure and, in his wisdom, has passed it by because he 'knows the causal relations between cupidity and death'.[5] Steadman regards the old man as a generalized 'notion of aged humanity' and aptly remarks that Chaucer's 'attempt to delineate the general through the particular brings him close to the frontiers of allegory, but he does not actually cross'.[6] The way in which this generalized figure hovers near the frontiers of naturalism and of other modes of presentation is one of the factors that produce the double perspective which I shall discuss later.

The present article is not concerned with the tale's prologue and epilogue or with the relationship between the tale and its teller; it is concerned almost exclusively with the story of 'thise riotoures thre' as it is narrated between C. 661 and 894. Nevertheless, before I proceed to an analysis of the tale proper, it is necessary to say something about the discourse on the sins of the tavern which separates the false start of the story at l. 463 from its true beginning at l. 661. What I have to say about this digression is so obvious that it would be hardly worth mentioning, were it not for the fact that it seems to have escaped the notice of several scholars who have written about this tale and who have offered some extravagant and cumbersome explanations of the presence of this passage.[7]

The digression is, of course, entirely relevant to the *sentence* of the *exemplum* which it interrupts.[8] Although Avarice is the radical sin that is illustrated in the tale, the three sins that are denounced in the digression – drunkenness, swearing and gambling – all contribute to the bringing about of the tale's catastrophe. If the rioters had not been drunk, they would not have set out upon their quest to 'sleen this false traytour Deeth' in the first place. If they had not been so profligate with their oaths, they might have taken more seriously their covenant of brotherhood and might have paid more attention to the solemn, admonitory imprecations of the old man. 'Hasardrye' is obviously related to Avarice, but it is perhaps worth remarking that the habitual desire of each of the revellers to play for the highest possible stakes causes him to plot against one or both of his 'brothers' and so is directly responsible for inducing the internecine catastrophe.

Once the tale proper has begun there is no further interruption: the action moves forward with a relentless logic to what, when it is reached, appears to be the inevitable conclusion – given the rioters' characters and the circumstances in which they find themselves. This rapid, irresistible progression is reinforced by Chaucer's economy in narrative technique. Not only is there an absence of digression, but an economy in three things principally: in characterization, in description and in narrative itself. I shall consider each of these three in turn.

One of Chaucer's happiest methods of adapting his sources was to pay particular attention to distinctive details of characterization. This can be seen even in such a brief narrative as the Prioress's Tale, where the pathos is considerably enhanced by the way in which the 'litel clergeon' is individualized, mainly through his conversation with his more mundane schoolfellow. In the Pardoner's Tale, however, individualization of character is kept to a minimum. The only character to be described in detail is the old man and, as we have already seen, he is a generalized figure, compounded of 'commonplaces' that were traditionally associated with old age. He is sharply contrasted with the 'riotoures thre', but they are themselves hardly individualized at all: any one of them could have played the part of any other. It might be argued that this is simply because they are presented as a trio of 'sworn brothers', who speak and act in concert – 'we thre been al ones' (l. 696) – until they come upon the gold. It might be pointed out in support of this argument that Aleyn and John, the co-operative pair of clerks in the Reeve's Tale, are far less easy to distinguish than are Nicholas and Absalom, the pair of rivals in the Miller's Tale, whose characters are so carefully contrasted.

The clerks in the Reeve's Tale, however, are distinguished at least by name; whereas in the Pardoner's Tale all the characters, whose voices we hear so clearly, remain anonymous. It is true that this is not the only tale in which the characters are anonymous: there is the Prioress's Tale, for example; but, as we have seen, the 'litel clergeon' in that tale is endowed with a distinct personality of his own. What is so striking about the Pardoner's Tale is the combination of anonymity and impersonality. There is other evidence which suggests that this is deliberate on

Chaucer's part. It is uncertain how much importance should be attached to the fact that names are given to the rioters' counterparts in some of the analogues. But it is surely undeniable that it would have been simpler and more convenient for Chaucer if he had referred to the various members of his trio by using personal names, instead of resorting to the slightly clumsy and obtrusively impersonal means of differentiation that we find in the tale : 'the proudeste of the three', 'the worste', 'the yongeste', 'the firste shrewe', 'that oon', 'that oother' . . . What seems to me to clinch the matter is the answer that the servant gives when one of the rioters bids him :

> 'Go bet . . . and axe redily
> What cors is this that passeth heer forby;
> *And looke that thou reporte his name weel.*'

(C. 667–9. Italics mine.)

But we no more learn the dead man's name than we learn the name of the servant himself – or, indeed, the names of the rioters, the taverner, the old man or the apothecary. The servant informs his master merely : 'He was, pardee, an old felawe of youres.' Three lines later, however, the intention behind all this contrived anonymity becomes clearer. The final line of the master's command has alerted us : we expect to hear a proper name; but the fulfilment of our expectations is delayed and transferred. Instead of hearing the name of the stricken man, we hear the name of his assailant : 'Ther cam a privee theef, men clepeth Deeth. . . .' This is the only proper name we hear – apart from the name of God – until we reach the final episode.[9]

It is perhaps not too fanciful to argue that Death is the only 'character' in the tale who is completely individualized and presented as a complex personality. We are shown several facets of his character : his capriciousness; the arbitrary way in which he strikes or refuses to strike; his stealth and elusiveness; the subtlety and irony of his way of working. We also encounter some of his 'espye[s]' and those who are truly 'of his assent' : *not* – as one of the rioters and some modern critics allege – the old man; but plague and heart-attack, and – more pertinently – Drunkenness, Swearing, Gambling and, above all, Avarice.

This 'character study' is communicated to the reader through the dialogue and by means of implication. The only character who is described in detail is the old man, as we have seen, and that description is conveyed mainly through dialogue. In several of his tales Chaucer 'amplifies' his matter by introducing his characters through more or less formal *effictiones*, but also by giving descriptions, either concentrated or dispersed, of the setting and background of the action. In the Pardoner's Tale, however, he is content with a bare minimum of stage properties, which are introduced to indicate a change of scene and to provide a concrete centre around which the characters can group themselves. The rioters meet the old man 'as they wolde han troden over a stile'. He tells them that, if they 'turne up this croked wey', they will find Death under an oak. Nothing is seen of the funeral *cortège* at the beginning of the tale; the clinking of the bell is merely heard 'off stage' – and, incidentally, is all the more alarming for being introduced in the very next couplet after the one in which we are told that the rioters were sitting in the tavern 'Longe erst er prime rong of any belle'. When Romeo wishes to buy 'a dram of poison', Shakespeare indulges in an extended description of the apothecary's shop, but we are vouchsafed no description whatever of the establishment that the youngest rioter visits for his more venomous purpose. On the other hand, Chaucer reports in detail the false arguments that the rioter used to persuade the apothecary to sell him the poison, and then, modulating into *oratio recta*, he tells us precisely what the apothecary said in reply :

> 'And thou shalt have
> A thyng that, also God my soule save,
> In al this world ther is no creature,
> That eten or dronken hath of this confiture
> Noght but the montance of a corn of whete,
> That he ne shal his lif anon forlete;
> Ye, sterve he shal, and that in lasse while
> Than thou wolt goon a paas nat but a mile,
> This poysoun is so strong and violent.' (C. 859–67)

Chaucer's reporting this conversation in full, while remaining silent about the setting, brings me to the third kind of economy that is noticeable in this tale : what can only be called 'economy of narrative'. It has often been remarked that much of the tale consists of dialogue and that this is mainly responsible for its dramatic quality. But it has another consequence too : the fact that we so seldom hear the narrator speaking *in propria persona* means that plain narrative, when it does occur, is all the more arresting and telling. Before the full effect of this economy can be properly examined, however, it is necessary to observe just how much information about character, motive and circumstance Chaucer manages to convey through almost completely un-annotated dialogue.

The very first exchange sets the pace for the whole tale and subtly introduces two of its most disquieting features. We hear the master's peremptory 'Go bet', but his servant does not obey. There is no need for the serving-boy to leave the tavern in order to satisfy the rioter's inquiry about the meaning of the lich-bell; he knows the answer already : 'It was me toold er ye cam heer two houres' (l. 671). The uneasy sensation of having been anticipated – whether by another character, by events, or by un-seen powers – increases as the tale proceeds. The other disturb-ing feature I have already touched upon : the rioter asks for the dead man's name, but the boy gives him instead the name of his sinister assailant. This is symptomatic of the essential movement of the plot : when the rioters expect to meet Death, they find the treasure; they find Death, 'hwenne [hie] weneþ to libben best'.

From the boy's speech it emerges that he conceives of death in the way that his mother had taught him to do, as a 'privee theef' armed with a spear, who strikes men unexpectedly and goes stealthily on his way. Being but a child,[10] he is not so sophisticated as to know about personification and allegory; he accepts as literally true what his mother had told him : ' "Thus taughte me my dame; I sey namoore." ' The taverner confirms what the boy has said about the activities of Death during the current epidemic of plague. He continues to speak of Death as if he were a real person, following the boy's remark; but he is, presumably, speaking figuratively, whereas the boy was not. Per-haps we are meant to think of him as humouring the boy – with an innkeeper's tact – by continuing to speak in his phrase; to have questioned his conception of Death would, after all, have meant flouting his mother's authority. For the rioters, who are thoroughly drunk by this time (l. 705), the distinction between literal and figurative meanings has become temporarily blurred. Having heard the boy speak of Death as if he were a real person, and then hearing the adult taverner do likewise, they are convinced that he is a palpable public enemy. So they form themselves into a company of 'sworn brothers', like knights errant engaged on a dedicated quest, and resolve to seek out 'this false traytour Deeth' and slay him. The resolution is made to the accompaniment of many great oaths.

When, in the next scene, they meet the old man, they continue to rend 'Cristes blessed body' by their indiscriminate use of oaths. The old man, by contrast, is a courteous figure. He invokes the name of God only three times, and each time the invocation is solemn and deliberate. His last words to the rioters consist of such an invocation :

> 'God save yow, that boghte agayn mankynde,
> And yow amende !' Thus seyde this olde man . . .

But the name of God has become so devalued in their mouths that it rings hollow in their ears. They are so impatient that they can hardly stay to hear the old man's words, let alone to heed them :

> '. . . And yow amende !' Thus seyde this olde man;
> And everich of thise riotoures *ran*
> Til he cam to that tree. . . .   (C. 767–9. Italics mine.)

Within the space of two lines of narrative they have been precipitated into the third scene and transported to the place where the catastrophe is to be played out. After only seven more lines of narrative dialogue is resumed.

The success of some of the best of Chaucer's shorter tales depends upon the way in which, during the final scene, events move towards their end with an astonishing rapidity and seeming inevitability. But the unimpeded flow of the action at the conclusion of these tales is often made possible only because the author has contrived to introduce into the earlier part of his narrative much of the information and most of the stage 'properties' that are required for the enactment of the *dénouement*. This kind of anticipation is well illustrated in the Reeve's Tale, where the fact that the miller has a 'piled skulle' is mentioned in the description of that formidable character with which the tale begins.[11] A few lines later Chaucer smuggles in, by means of a parenthesis, a reference to the existence of the baby *and its cradle* at the moment when his principal purpose is to impress upon his audience the fact that – apart from this insignificant infant – the miller's daughter was his only child.[12] The reader will be able to think of other examples without much difficulty. In the Pardoner's Tale Chaucer goes even further: all the technical details of the murders are conveyed to the reader in advance in the course of the dialogue between the two conspirators and in the account of the youngest rioter's visit to the village. So that when the moment for the catastrophe arrives, there is no need to describe the action in detail; the fate of the three 'sworn brothers' is a foregone conclusion. It follows with an irresistible logic: the rioters are despatched without ceremony in ten lines of summary narrative that are delivered with the coolness and detachment of a mathematician spelling out the *quod erat demonstrandum* at the end of a theorem. The single couplet of misplaced exultation, uttered by one of the homicides, stands out in ironical relief in the middle of this passage where the narrator's own voice has now become dominant:

> What nedeth it to sermone of it moore?
> For right as they hadde cast his deeth bifoore,
> Right so they han hym slayn, and that anon.
> And whan that this was doon, thus spak that oon:
> 'Now lat us sitte and drynke, and make us merie,
> And afterward we wol his body berie.'
> And with that word it happed hym, par cas,
> To take the botel ther the poyson was,
> And drank, and yaf his felawe drynke also,
> For which anon they storven bothe two.   (C. 879–88)

But the theorem has a corollary. Although the narrator refrains from giving a detailed description of the rioters' death, he does not allow us to forget the implications of the apothecary's words that I have already quoted. The apothecary had recommended his 'confiture' to his customer by emphasizing the speediness of its action : it would kill any living thing in less time than it would take you to cover a mile at an ordinary walking pace. From the point of view of the writhing victims, however, twenty minutes is a very long time. Chaucer does not describe their death agony in a series of 'close-ups' as Flaubert does when he recounts the death of Emma Bovary after she has taken poison. He prefers implication to description : he 'distances' the scene and looks at it with the eyes of a coroner reading a pathologist's report that refers him to a standard medical text-book :

> But certes, I suppose that Avycen
> Wroot nevere in no canon, ne in no fen,
> Mo wonder signes of empoisonyng
> Than hadde thise wrecches two er hir endyng (C. 889–92)

The educated contemporary of Chaucer would have recognized more readily than the modern reader just how much the narrator has deliberately left unsaid.

The peculiar strength of this tale derives not only from the kinds of economy and narrative skill that I have examined above, but also from the presence of a double perspective. Looked at in objective sobriety, all the events in the story can be accounted for rationally. We have already considered how the revellers came to set out on their mission to slay Death. The presence of the treasure under the tree may seem extraordinary, but there is no need to resort to supernatural explanations of how it came there. The old man is not portrayed 'naturalistically' : his characterization embodies too many of the commonplaces traditionally associated with aged humanity to satisfy the canons of *verismo* representation. But, as we have seen, it does not follow from this that he is, in fact, a supernatural being or an allegorical figure. Finally, the catastrophe can be explained in simple, psychological terms : the rioters bring their deaths upon themselves as the result of their habitual sins.

But we also see the action from another point of view. Much of the dialogue, of which the tale largely consists, is spoken by the revellers while they are drunk. Inebriation has an effect upon them not unlike that which sleep exerts upon the narrator of a mediæval 'dream allegory' : they are transported 'In auenture þer meruayleȝ meuen'; we receive through their drunken eyes a glimpse of the world of 'Fayerye'. In that world the frontier between the realm of the marvellous and the realm of everyday experience is opened, so that denizens of the one may mingle freely with inhabitants of the other. It is an eclectic world in which giants and dragons live side by side with gods and demi-gods from various pantheons. Its origins have some associations with the Kingdom of Death (the classical underworld is easily metamorphosed into the fairy kingdom of *Sir Orfeo*); yet it harbours not only the shades of the departed, but also shadowy abstractions, personifications and allegorical figures. Death himself may be encountered walking abroad in this world with many of the attributes of a human being. Conversely, it is always possible that any human being one encounters there may, in fact, be a denizen of the 'other realm', who has slipped across the frontier. When the rioters meet the strange figure 'al forwrapped save his face', who seems to be too old to belong rightfully to the land of the living, they are at once suspicious and one of them accuses him of being Death's 'espye' in league with him 'to sleen us yonge folk'. Because Chaucer's presentation of the old man hovers near the frontiers of allegory and personification, the rioter's allegations seem sufficiently plausible to make the reader wonder whether there may not be some substance to them. The fact that this nightmare world is nothing more than a drunken delusion does not diminish the disturbing effect that it has upon the atmosphere of the tale.

When the rioters find the treasure, they experience the sober certainty of waking bliss. The quest that they had embarked upon in their drunkenness is forgotten : the company of 'sworn brothers' is no longer inspired by heroic intentions of ridding the world of a dangerous public enemy. In their sobriety their main source of inspiration is their avarice. As a direct result of their avarice they are destroyed; in their last game of 'hasardrye', Death sweeps the board.

The two points of view from which the action is seen are brought into a single focus by means of an intertwining irony. The irony of the rioters' 'finding Death' only after they have ceased to look for him is not original with Chaucer's version of the tale; but he develops it in a way that would appear to be his own. We have seen how, in the earlier part of the tale, Chaucer builds up the personality of Death, even to the extent of ensuring that he is the only 'character' to be allowed a proper name. We have also noticed how, through the medium of the dialogue, he creates an atmosphere of mystery so that the reader has a sensation of being in the presence of uncanny 'principalities and powers', in spite of the fact that the objective view of the action insists that this is all part of a drunken misapprehension. The *dénouement* reveals that 'principalities and powers' are indeed present, but that Death is not the prime mover. In fact, death is seen in the event to be something quite negative; a thing without personality. We do not hear his hollow laughter at his moment of triumph. The spectre of Death vanishes from the rioters' minds as soon as they find the treasure, but one of them attributes their discovery of it to the benignity of another personified power, Fortune (l. 779). She is the deity in whom these 'hasardours' really believe, rather than the God Whose name they are continually taking in vain. Later the malignant aspect of Fortune, of which the rioters are oblivious, is suggested by the context in which the phrase 'par cas' occurs at l. 885. Meanwhile the narrator indicates in passing (at l. 844) that the real power behind the scenes is neither Fortune nor Death, but 'the feend our enemy' who is intent on trapping promising victims by means of their own sins. The rioters are as deluded in the world of sober calculation as they were in their drunken fantasy.

I remarked earlier that in the last game of 'hasardrye' that the revellers play among themselves, Death steps in and sweeps the board. But Chaucer makes no such explicit comment. It would have been as inappropriate in the context as would any explicit reference to the 'false traytour' or the 'privee theef' with his spear. Nevertheless the naturalistic, objective narrative does happen to show, with tacit irony, how each of the rioters is slain by nothing other than a 'privee theef'[13] and a 'false traytour' – his own 'sworn brother'. When the Pardoner proceeds to his peroration,[14] and points to the *sentence* of his *exemplum*, his theme is not the omnipotence of Death, but the sin of Homicide and the other sins whose 'deadly' consequences are illustrated in the tale.

A further twist that Chaucer gives to the spiral of irony shows that he realized potentialities in the fable that would have appealed to a Greek tragedian; yet, at the same time, he in no way diminishes its propriety within the Christian ethos of his own day. When the rioters are about to set out on their quest, he causes them to boast in their drunkenness: 'Deeth shal be deed'.[15] This piece of ὕβρις [hubris] will sound to anyone acquainted with the Scriptures like a blasphemously materialistic application of St. Paul's promise that 'Death shall be swallowed up in victory'.[16] It is therefore entirely fitting that when Νέμεσις [Nemesis] follows it should afford a disturbingly *literal* illustration of another Pauline text: 'the wages of sin is death'.[17]

S O U R C E : *Medium Ævum*, XXXVI (1967).

NOTES

1. The edition to which reference is made and from which all quotations are taken in the present article is F. N. Robinson, *The Works of Geoffrey Chaucer*, 2nd edn (Boston, 1957).

2. *Dramatic Irony in Chaucer* (1932; reprinted New York, 1959) pp. 72–9.

3. 'Old Age and *Contemptus Mundi* in The Pardoner's Tale', *Medium Ævum*, XXXIII (1964) 121–30.

4. 'The Old Man in The Pardoner's Tale', *Review of English Studies*, N.S. II (1951) 49–55.

5. Steadman, p. 127.

6. Steadman, p. 123.

7. For an example of such an explanation see the separate edition of the tale by Carleton Brown (Oxford, 1935) pp. xv–xx. Brown's arguments are discussed and rejected by G. G. Sedgewick, 'The Progress of Chaucer's Pardoner, 1880–1940', *Modern Language Quarterly*, I (1940) 431–58. But Sedgewick's own solution – that the Pardoner contrives to introduce references to as many sins as possible, whether relevant to the *exemplum* or not, in order to affect his audience's consciences – seems to me hardly more satisfactory.

Scholars who have considered the digression to be irrelevant have made much of the fact that the Pardoner resumes his narrative at l. 661 with the words : 'Thise riotoures thre of whiche I telle' – al-

though he has never mentioned them before. A better knowledge of
M.E. idiom might have diminished their allegations of inconsistency.
The demonstrative was not infrequently used in M.E. to introduce
a new subject or character and the simple present was often used,
as in O.E., to express futurity (see, for example, *C.T.*, A. 3278, or
Pearl, l. 524.). The line could therefore be rendered idiomatically
as follows : 'The story I am going to tell you concerns three revellers'.

8. This has indeed been acknowledged by a number of scholars.
But insufficient emphasis has been placed upon the fact that, according to the logic of Chaucer's version of the tale, the catastrophe
could hardly have taken place, if the rioters had not been subject to
all three of these sins, as well as to Avarice.

9. See below, p. 217.

10. The taverner refers to him as 'child' at l. 686. The fact that
he is referred to as 'this boy' at l. 670 is probably not an indication
of his age; the word is employed in its older sense of 'servant'. See
E. J. Dobson, 'The Etymology and Meaning of *Boy*', *Medium
Ævum*, IX (1940) 121–54.

11. *C.T.*, A. 3935. Cf. 4300–6.

12. A. 3969–72. Cf. 4211 ff.

13. See C. 788–92. They are thieves because the treasure was not
theirs in the first place and also because they plot to take it from
each other by force. Notice especially the use of 'slyly' (l. 792), 'ful
prively' (l. 797), 'subtilly' (l. 798) – a singularly ironical use of the
word – and ' "Shal it be conseil?" ' (l. 819).

14. ll. 895 ff.

15. l. 710

16. I Cor. 15 : 54. Cf. Hosea 13 : 14. Part of this verse is quoted
in *Piers Plowman*, B, xviii, 35, to describe the consequence of the
Crucifixion : 'O mors, ero mors tua !'

17. Rom. 6 : 23.

Paul G. Ruggiers

THE NUN'S PRIEST'S TALE (1965)

'Toute est pour enseignement' – *Roman de la Rose*

From many points of view the Nun's Priest's Tale may be considered a high-water mark of complex thematic statement in the *Canterbury Tales.* Even with its proliferation of exemplary materials (such as we note in the tales of the Pardoner and Franklin), it constitutes a complex of most that is happy in Chaucer's artistic and intellectual equipment: a grasp of form, a subtle ironical tone, cleverness without slavery in the literary allusions, the subjection of high seriousness to the needs of the form, a casual finesse with rhetorical conventions, a sharpening of the theme of marital dissension, a suiting of moral utterance to the narrator, and a delicate balance between the romantic and comic modes. It is, in short, *sui generis.*

Its meaning has to do, in one sense, with the way in which reason and instinct are embattled (a sentiment common to the fabliaux), but it places these firmly against the larger questions of love, the destinal order, and human responsibility, and casts a final vote in favor of self-control. If this shift of balance to the side of reason suggests survival through canniness, we have, I feel, a merely ironical tale. By adducing the more serious questions of a rational universe, Chaucer widens the theological ambience in which his agents live, and tests the familiar triad of love, crucial adventure, and virtue acquired which are the heart of romance.

Coming as it does after the limited range of the Monk, the tale evinces an intellectual complexity which is its characteristic tone; just how far removed we are from the mechanical world of Venus, or Fame, or Fortuna, or from a vague retributive Justice meting out good and ill through apparent caprice is demonstrated by the tale of a cock, hen and villain fox, all of whom have responsibility in a world they not only must interpret, but create for themselves. It is a world seen not from the point of view of tragedy, but of thought and laugh-provoking comedy. It is comedy that comes as a response to the plea of the serious-minded Knight, a man of moderate disposition, albeit a slayer of his foes and a mighty warrior in fifteen battles. The complexity Chaucer attributes to him is not merely a matter of having such a man cry out for gladsome tales. If we compare his character in detail with that of the lugubrious and doleful tale-teller the Monk, we discover new ironies inherent in their actions.[1] The purely physical details of the Monk's hulking figure, his fine horses, his taste for fine food and clothes, his overbearing assertion of service to God outside the monastic world afford a sharp contrast to the figure of the Knight with his meek and maidenly deportment, his restraint of tongue, his avoidance of the signs of wealth, his fruitful activity in defense of the faith. To attribute to the one a limited vision of the meaning of suffering and to the other a preference for tales with a happy ending is to point up in yet another way an expanding complexity of character in the pilgrimage community. Chaucer is, as it were, focusing his own attitudes upon the perplexities of tragedy and comedy in preparation for a new kind of tragicomic vision far beyond the Monk's limited range.

In the Monk's Tale, the concept of tragedy, although it does not entirely omit the role of the will, is more mechanical than human, the effect of character upon action being restricted mostly to the defect of 'mysgovernaunce' and to the 'unwar strook' dealt out by Fortune. We note in it an absence of character development and the tendency to see human suffering only as the result of a fall. The form itself prevents a thoughtful interest in the development of ethos in the agents, in their ability to argue themselves into or out of situations and in the important consideration of the degree of human responsibility which the agents may assume in this life. In all justice to the tales related by the Monk, we must consider that any long treatment of these tragedies would conceivably entail a great deal of thought upon precisely such matters; indeed their defect is their brevity as much as it is the incompleteness of the whole view regarding Fortune and man's lot which they imply.[2]

The interruption by the Knight calls for something more in

literature; if not a correction of the view of Fortune in its relations to the law of the Prime Mover such as he himself has already
presented in his tale of Palamon and Arcite, at least an amplification of a view of life which allows for quite another way of fictive
presentation :

> '. . . whan a man hath been in povre estaat,
> And clymbeth up and wexeth fortunat,
> And there abideth in prosperitee :
> Swich thyng is gladsom, as it thynketh me,
> And of swich thyng were goodly for to telle.'

$$(B.^2 3965\ 9)$$

To this the Host gives scolding assent. His point of view may
not be that of the Knight, a representative of quite another class
of society, but he does know that what he has heard has become
a heavy burden to the mind, if not an outright bore :

> 'For sikerly, nere clynkyng of youre belles,
> That on youre bridel hange on every syde,
> By hevene kyng, that for us alle dyde,
> I sholde er this han fallen doun for sleep,
> Althogh the slough had never been so deep.'

$$(B.^2\ 3984\text{--}8)$$

And so the Knight and Host are united in common intention
if not in comprehension of the issue at hand. Both have objected to
the performance of the Monk, the Knight we presume because
he objects to the statement of a not entirely sound view of life
(if we may judge him from the story he has told) and because
'litel hevynesse / Is right ynough to muche folk, I gesse'. The Host
objects because there is 'no desport ne game' in these tales, and
furthermore the reiterated theme has become monotonous. Both
views have their healthy side.

The Monk, however, had had his say and declines to relate a
tale of hunting; his natural discretion, which has held him back
from engaging in badinage with the Host, again urges upon him
the better course of keeping his private life to himself. We turn
instead to another religious, the 'sweete preest, this goodly man,
sir John', who is urged to tell us a happy, cheerful tale. His horse,

a jade 'bothe foul and lene', offers a contrast to the sleek berry-brown palfrey of the Monk, whom the Nun's Priest now supersedes. But as we read we see that the paucity and poverty of material goods in the Nun's Priest do not preclude a richness of natural gifts and a depth of cheerful goodness absent from the performance of the materially endowed, self-limiting Monk.

For reasons which we can only surmise, Chaucer has not given explicit details about the person and character of the Nun's Priest. In the Prologue of the Nun's Priest's Tale the Host describes his horse, and in the famous epilogue, regarded by some as a cancelled link, substantially repeats a line and a sentiment which we have already heard him apply to the Monk: 'Thou woldest han been a tredefowel aright' (B.² 3135). We can only conjecture that Chaucer has, by the shift of the line to the previous performance, exhausted one view of the ecclesiastical male and temporarily, at least, abandoned the matter of expanding upon the character of the Nun's Priest. On artistic grounds it seems suitable too to explore the matter of celibacy and marriage (the lives of Monk and Host) immediately following upon the 'Melibee', a natural enough movement from the admonitions of Dame Prudence in that tale to the bodily threats of Goodelief in the Monk's Prologue, and thence to the plight of matrimony in a world from which the best men have escaped. It would seem that Chaucer is by degrees opening the door on the many-faceted subject of marriage, so that when he has finished the Nun's Priest's Tale, there is little reason for him to revert to the matter of priestly celibacy inasmuch as it diverts attention from the subject of the tale itself and repeats elements now applied to the character of the Monk.

Since Chaucer himself has told us little about the character of the Nun's Priest (some deductions may be made from the tone and attitudes of the tale assigned him), critical opinion has perforce to be conjectural. One commentator describes him as 'a handsome, strong, rosy-cheeked youngster, with a sense of humor unequalled in the company', who can 'deftly satirize the personal characteristics and the literary style of his predecessor without for a moment arousing the suspicion of his dignified superior'.³ Another later writer suggests that he is 'Scrawny, humble, and timid, while at the same time highly intelligent, well-educated, shrewd and witty', and further that he is 'weak in body and fawning in manner'.[4] These are tantalizing surmises; in the end, each reader will feel that the personality of the Nun's Priest is best derived from an examination of the story Chaucer chose to assign him.

As we have said, the tale masterfully integrates many elements which we have seen or noted singly or in combinations in other tales. More important perhaps than these elements taken one by one or in combination is the creation of a frame or envelope in which to contain the moral and quasi-mythic structure. This outer frame presents to us those human agents necessary to provide for the reader some ideal of human behavior, some rule of continence and contentment. The old widow, with her little cottage and her careful economy by which she provides for herself and her two daughters, offers by such details as temperance of diet and exercise and a contented heart an image of temperate law, of self-restraint and self-control, of sobriety and reasonable discretion. It is the widow's yard that is the world, apparently safe and secure, for Chauntecleer and his wives; it is into this world that evil intrudes in the shape of the sly fox; it is this world that the widow wishes to restore Chauntecleer at the conclusion of his adventure, setting in motion the final boisterous attempt at rescue.[5]

But it is Chauntecleer's plight which holds our interest and for which the outer human frame exists. It is Chauntecleer's character and his virtues or absence of virtues, his self-assurance and braggadocio, his pride, his sensuality, his susceptibility to flattery, and his sly intelligence that engage our minds. The opening description of Chauntecleer, replete with instinctive passion and joy, follows immediately upon the associations of poverty and patient, passionless temperance. Style itself echoes the contrast as Chaucer begins to employ the language of the romantic mode, and what is austere or even pedestrian in the opening of the tale gives way to something courtly, perhaps, and descriptively elevated, with even a momentary flight into lyric: 'My lief is faren in londe!'

This may be considered the high style, in keeping with the poet's intention to parody the purely tragic view of the Monk and to supply a corrective through the device of comedy. Hence the necessity for enhancing the character of the cock so that he may appear to be regal, hence the fall from good fortune, hence the philosophical rumination about the relation of will to necessity, the elevated speeches, apostrophes and exclamations, the comparisons with figures of classical antiquity, and hence the errors in judgment and the final moral tag. The subjects and mannerisms of tragedy must be present, even in ironical contexts, seen in contrast to the subjects and mannerisms of comedy: the world of love and marriage, of domestic quarreling, of deception and jokes, of personal arrogance and instinctive passions, of personal vanity and wishing to be right at all costs, of wit and hairbreadth escape, of chases and rueful laughter. The result is, in its way, like the relation of the Franklin's Tale to the Merchant's Tale, a saner, more humane attitude than the one stated in the previous tale.

A large section of the tale is composed of the debate between Chauntecleer and his beautous paramour Pertelote on the subject of dreams. Their speeches reveal a great deal of their character; Pertelote's lines beginning 'Avoy! Fy on yow, hertelees!' with their repeated exclamations and questions are full of feminine excitability and concern. Her admonitions are purely domestic: 'For Goddes love, as taak som laxatyf.' Her wisdom is for the most part the wisdom of the home dispenser. Chaucer is clearly enjoying the game. Chauntecleer's long-winded answer, beginning with an elaborate politeness ('Madame, graunt mercy of youre loore.') is a rejoinder of some haughtiness of tone. More than a refutation answering the alleged authority of Cato, the long recital of superior authorities allows us to see Chauntecleer as one of Chaucer's more self-conscious orators, more thoughtful, more playful and sly, more pompous and self-assured. The cock is a narrator of no little skill, constructing his two initial *exempla* with great care as to form and tone and attention to detail. Indeed he is so careful a constructer of plot, with its inevitable conclusions, that the moral statement with which the first one closes tends to overshadow the principal concern with the credibility of dreams:

> 'O blisful God, that art so just and trewe,
> Lo, how that thou bewreyest mordre alway!

> Mordre wol out, that se we day by day.
> Mordre is so wlatsom and abhomynable
> To God, that is so just and resonable,
> That he ne wol nat suffre it heled be,
> Though it abyde a yeer, or two, or thre.
> Mordre wol out, this my conclusioun.'   (B.² 4240–7)

But the point is made, first through a reluctant believer in dreams, and then through an actual non-believer who is proved to be wrong. Thereafter Chauntecleer warms to his task, and in a rapid mélange of instances drawn from Biblical, literary, and historical sources, within a space of some 40 lines as compared with the 126 of the first two *exempla*, he rattles off six additional stories to refute his wife's authority. His conclusion is inevitable, a mixture of the tragic assertion with the most bathetic comic statement :

> 'Shortly I seye, as for conclusioun,
> That I shal han of this avisioun
> Adversitee; and I seye forthermoor,
> That I ne telle of laxatyves no stoor,
> For they been venymous, I woot it weel;
>   I hem diffye, I love hem never a deel!'   (B.² 4341–6)

And the action that follows upon this long debate, in which each agent has but one major speech, bears out this prediction. But before the action there intervenes his love speech to Pertelote containing its bold and unself-conscious *ludum*, a joke at the expense of his less tutored wife :

> '... *In principio*,
> *Mulier est hominis confusio*, –
> Madame, the sentence of this Latyn is,
> "Womman is mannes joye and al his blis."'
>   (B.² 4353–6)

Whether we cheer or blame him in this joke upon his wife-paramour, the speech is that of the passionate lover, embellished with sincere regard, expressing gratitude for God's grace, joy and comfort in her companionship, as well as that up-surging confidence that enables him to defy dreams and visions. They have had their quarrel or debate, but their relationship is a happy and natural one elevated by the poet through the language of love. The jest that Chaucer puts in his beak hints at that double-edged truth to which the Middle Ages were dedicated by tradition on the one hand and by human nature on the other: in the beginning Eve was the source of Adam's fall. And yet, Chaucer's humane and comic realism forbids the dour anti-feminist implications[6] and provides a counterpoise in that other truth, that other affirmation, *Amor vincit omnia*.

> 'For whan I feele a-nyght your softe syde,
> Al be it that I may nat on yow ryde,
> For that oure perche is maad so narwe, allas!
> I am so ful of joye and of solas,
> That I diffye bothe sweven and dreem.'   (B.[2] 4357–61)

We see Chauntecleer here in all his pride, hardly deigning to set his foot to the ground, royal as a prince in his hall, says Chaucer, summoning all his wives with a mere cluck.

Up to this point (l. 4376) the narrative has supplied us with a situation which is to be fulfilled in the remaining part of the tale, and with some intellectual attitudes that are to be tested. Chauntecleer's pride has been placed before us not only in the details of his dainty high stepping and his grim lion's look, but in the whole context of his long answer to Pertelote. Chaucer hereafter plays against each other instinct and rational control in much the same way that he assays willfulness and human responsibility in *Troilus and Criseyde*.

With the return to a purely narrative tone in lines 4377 ff., Chaucer seems to take a deep breath before providing the catastrophe foreseen by Chauntecleer in his dream. In the midst of the beauties of May, when Chauntecleer's heart is full of 'revel and solas', he is to discover that the latter end of joy is woe. The Nun's Priest now raises the whole question of destiny and man's freedom as the catastrophe impends, and the fox waits to fall upon the cock. It is a burst of rhetoric in a variety of

tones: the extravagant comic sublime ('O false mordrour . . . /
O newe Scariot, newe Genylon, . . . o Greek Synon, / That
broghtest Troye al outrely to sorwe! / O Chauntecleer . . .')
merges into a more arid statement of simple and conditional
necessity familiar to readers of the *Consolatio*, and finally into
the traditional indictment:

> Wommennes conseils been ful ofte colde;
> Wommannes conseil broghte us first to wo,
> And made Adam fro Paradys to go,
> Ther as he was ful myrie and wel at ese.   (B.² 4446–9)

In the mouth of the Nun's Priest, such a statement is a kind
of bold impertinence; in Chaucer's mouth it is not less so if we
bear in mind the tradition of oral presentation at court. And
yet it has a kind of arch humor about it. It can be carried off
by welding it fast to the narrative context:

> My tale is of a cok, as ye may heere,
> That tok his conseil of his wyf, with sorwe,
> To walken in the yerd upon that morwe
> That he hadde met that dreem that I yow tolde.
>
>   (B.² 4442–5)

And so the narrator escapes responsibility both for philosophical
explanation and for the indictment of women. Just how much
involvement we can impute to Chaucer himself, or how much
the poet has made the indictment of women a statement assess-
able only in terms of the priest's character – these are questions
that we solve only with a kind of presumption.

And yet there may be a level of artifice here, a trick of narrative in which the artist-writer stands behind his creations and
allows some of his own personal attitudes to be expressed
through one of his agents, a form of play in which we sometimes discern the remoter *ludum* beyond the situation in which
the agents are involved: Chauntecleer has had his intellectual
fun in deceiving his wife with a Latin tag; Chaucer has had the
Nun's Priest offer us, in Chauntecleer's translation of the Latin,

two definitions of love which threaten to cancel each other out: Adam fell through Eve's counsel and bequeathed to their children similar falls without number; yet in the relationship of Chauntecleer and his wife-paramour there is a certain careless and lovely sensuality, a springtime 'revel and solas', an overtone of one strong tradition that sees the love of woman as the means by which man perfects himself. It constitutes a perennially perplexing ambiguity which man's mind declines to resolve, even if it could.

We pass out of the romantic and sensual into the mutability theme, into a commentary upon the turn of fortune's wheel, with which we have been bludgeoned in the previous performance. The joke becomes more serious; the sarcasm, faintly antifeminist in the priestly attitude towards women's taste in literature, is kindly enough if it is Chaucer's own view; if it is the Priest's, there is a want of decorum in his speaking even in so veiled a fashion before the Prioress, the Nun, and even the Wife of Bath, who can make a moral point herself, with considerably less ambiguity. But in the familiar lines dealing with the opinions of worthy clerks on the problem of evil and the relation of God's foreknowledge to man's free will, the universal problem of the freedom of all men arises, and one feels that it is not the Priest's reluctance to provide a solution, but Chaucer's own disinclination that is expressed in the line, 'I wol nat han to do of swich mateere'. It seems strange that this priest should not know what he believes, when all the other clerical tales stand squarely upon the strong base of assertion. It seems less strange that Chaucer should do what writers have always done in the spirit of play: allowed their creations to toy with notions they themselves would decline.

But the context is comic and philosophical. The elevation of Chauntecleer's fortunes to a level we expect of the epic and tragic has the obvious effect of comic incongruity and disproportion. The narrator's special task is to accommodate the mysteries of the destinal order, dreams, Venus, nature, and the rest to a Divine Foreknowing which yet allows to man significant action and a saving self-knowledge. As the subsequent appearance of the fox makes clear, Chauntecleer's original assertion was correct, and Pertelote was wrong: he will indeed have adversity as a result of his dream. Seduced by the confidence which may be the fruit of love, and following his wife's advice so far as to 'fly down from the beams', Chauntecleer makes obvious the difference between believing with conviction and acting upon that conviction. No matter how bad the advice of Pertelote, Chauntecleer cannot be exempt from the trials and temptations of his temporal existence. Indeed, the trials and temptations are themselves the means by which the Christian comedy achieves its happy goal, the battlefield upon which the soldier's mettle is put to the test.

The test offered by the appearance of the fox is compounded of flattery and deceit which in some measure balances out Chauntecleer's own towards his wife. In both deceptions there is that curious intermingling of instinctive self-preservation with soothing, blandishing flattery. Both deceptions are successful, the fox's more obviously so inasmuch as Chauntecleer's bird nature itself conspires to supplement the fall : like his father's, and presumably every rooster's before him, Chauntecleer's endeavors to match his parent's singing necessitate the closing of the eyes. 'Ah ! beware of the betrayal through flattery', cries the Priest, and in an instant, Chauntecleer is caught by his natural enemy.

It is difficult to refrain from pointing up the skill of the rhetorical pattern of complaint beginning with line 4528, 'O destinee, that mayst nat been eschewed !' and passing shortly to 'O Venus, that art goddesse of plesaunce', then to 'O Gaufred, deere maister soverayn', and finally to the capping mock heroics of lamentation in 'O woful hennes, right so criden ye', the quadruple outburst drawing into fearful and wonderful juxtaposition comedy of situation with the inflated sublime of exclamatory closet tragedy. Whatever may be lacking in internal unifying factors is more than adequately compensated by the poetic effort to hold in delicate balance the humble matters of comedy with the elevated, the transporting, and the philosophical matters of tragedy.

The poem draws to its closing act in a burst of vividly detailed activity. All that has been restrained, controlled, elevated gives way in style and subject matter to the hectic demands of a chase. The serenity and moderated quietude of the poor widow's household is dissipated in a flash by the spirit of mobilized rescue spreading like wildfire to 'many another man', and to the dogs, and in further hectic sympathy, to the hogs, cows, ducks and geese, and a swarm of bees. Then in a sudden move out of the excitement of the chase, the Nun's Priest closes in upon his moral goal in the colloquial and familiar tones of admonition : 'Now, goode men, I prey yow herkneth alle' (l. 4592).

The reversal of Fortune by which Chauntecleer's native wit brings about his escape gives us some clue as to the relation of man's reasoned actions to the providential plan. The flattery by which he himself deceived his wife was superseded by that of the fox; now again, the laying on of flattery and praise for the sake of personal safety wins the cock his freedom; the fox's last attempt with unctuous and specious humility to win back his loss is deservedly unsuccessful, and Chauntecleer's answer to his enemy is a famous locus in Chaucerian moral statement :

> 'Thou shalt namoore, thurgh thy flaterye,
> Do me to synge and wynke with myn ye;
> For he that wynketh, whan he sholde see,
> Al wilfully, God lat him nevere thee !'
>   'Nay,' quod the fox, 'but God yeve hym meschaunce,
> That is so undiscreet of governaunce
> That jangleth whan he sholde holde his pees.'
>   Lo, swich it is for to be recchelees
> And necligent, and truste on flaterye.
>
>   .   .   .   .
>
> Taketh the moralite, goode men.   (B.² 4619–30)

Not only Chauntecleer, but the fox as well has come to a kind of wisdom that goes beyond the use of wit : both of them must observe a law of governance; both of them must come to rueful admissions of their failure to recognize the advantages of self-control. In the famous lines quoted above, both have learned through error.

The Nun's Priest's Tale thus raises the questions of human responsibility and destiny in the manner of tragedy or the moral romance but dismisses them, as a kind of impertinence, in favor of man's ability to learn from daily experience, in the manner of an ironic comedy. Its subject matter is a weighing of two sides of the ledger of man's serious and comic interests.

A host of questions is set in motion in contexts domestic and destinal. Insofar as the questions can be confronted, they challenge the facile view of tragedy set up by the Monk. The answers, insofar as they are given, are couched in the terms of ironic affirmation : man is responsible for errors in judgment; from the errors flows self-knowledge. And about chance, or love, or destiny, the least said the better.

One level of its meanings can be described by the word 'quizzical'.[7] They arise out of the complex picture of man seen as willful and self-loving, yet amiable and capable of loving others; created in the divine image but somehow all-too-human; responsible for his actions yet somehow controlled by forces beyond himself. To assert that man is free and at the same time that he is not is in effect to make us accept both assertions as true. To offer the view that love yields joy and then that it offers sorrow, or to hold in balance the philosophy of Boethius and Bradwardine with a world of laxatives and remedies for ague, is in essence to concentrate our gaze upon the disparities in the experience of fallen man and to confess to a certain helplessness in the human condition.

On another more accessible level of meaning we encounter the ironist's pronouncements to those who must pick their way through the obstacles of life : beware of flattery which destroys self-control, blinds us to what we should see, and loosens our tongues when we should be still. The lesson spoken at the close by cock and fox is securely anchored to the real world of expedience in which there are errors in judgment, flattery, negligence, lack of governance, and an uneasy acceptance of another. Whether the promulgator of those pedestrian truths is the inscrutable Sir John pronouncing so knowledgeably on life and love or Chaucer speaking through a mask, a sane hope pervades them : the hope for rational creatures accepting the appalling truth of their day-to-day responsibility within (it is devoutly wished) a rational universe.

The final plight of Chauntecleer demonstrates the relation of instinct to rational control, of thoughtless vanity to presence of mind, of foolish pride to a just humility. The 'happy' ending, with the rivals standing hand in hand, so to speak, reciting what wisdom they have achieved, reveals some truths in miniature, truths mundane and pedestrian, but truths nonetheless.[8]

SOURCE: *The Art of the Canterbury Tales* (Madison, 1965).

NOTES

1. See R. E. Kaske, 'The Knight's Interruption of the Monk's Tale', *Journal of English Literary History*, XXIV (1957) 249–63.

2. Still useful is Theodore Spencer, 'The Story of Ugolino in Dante and Chaucer', *Speculum*, IX (1934) 295–301.

3. Samuel B. Hemingway, 'Chaucer's Monk and Nun's Priest', *Modern Language Notes*, XXXI (1916) 479–83.

4. Robert M. Lumiansky, 'The Nun's Priest in the *Canterbury Tales*', *PMLA*, LXVIII (1953) 896–906.

5. Needless to say this interpretation is somewhat willful, an insistence that the opening section has pertinence to the whole tale. Paull F. Baum, *Chaucer: A Critical Appreciation* (Durham, N.C., 1958) p. 134, sees it as a false start. See Mortimer J. Donovan, 'The *Moralite* of the Nun's Priest's Sermon', *Journal of English and Germanic Philology*, LII (1953) 505, for the identification of the widow with the Church.

6. But see Arthur T. Broes, 'Chaucer's Disgruntled Cleric', *PMLA*, LXXVIII (1963) 156–62; Charles A. Owen Jr, 'The Crucial Passages in Five of the *Canterbury Tales* : A Study in Irony and Symbol', *Journal of English and Germanic Philology* LII (1953) 309; and J. Burke Severs, 'Chaucer's Originality in the Nun's Priest's Tale', *Studies in Philology*, XLIII (1946) 37.

7. Two articles have opened up a new avenue of inquiry into the function of the fable as a literary type : Stephen Manning, 'The Nun's Priest's Morality and the Medieval Attitude toward Fables', *Journal of English and Germanic Philology*, LIX (1960) 403–16; and R. T. Lenaghan, 'The Nun's Priest's Fable', *PMLA*, LXXVIII (1963) 300–7.

8. Charles Muscatine, *Chaucer and the French Tradition*, (University of California Press, 1957) p. 242, offers salutary warning : 'Unlike fable, the Nun's Priest's Tale does not so much make true and solemn assertions about life as it tests truth and tries out

solemnities. If you are not careful, it will try out your solemnity too;
it is here, doubtless, trying out mine. . . . The shifting style and
succession of topics never rest long enough to serve a single view or
a single doctrine or an unalterable judgment. . . . None of the targets
of the poem's parodies are demolished, or even really hit at the
center. There are senses in which the solemnities of courtly love,
science, marriage, authority, eloquence, tragedy, the Monk, and the
Tale of Melibee are funny, but the Nun's Priest's Tale does not
make us feel that they are always funny . . . it offers no conclusion
but that sublunary values are comically unstable. . . . In the Nun's
Priest's Tale, as altogether in the mature Chaucer, we are compelled to respect the conservative conclusion because the question
has been so superbly well confronted. . . . The Chaucerian mixed
style illuminates the tale's microcosmic contradictions, just as it
expresses, in large, the great capaciousness of Chaucer's humane
vision.'

D. W. Robertson Jr, *A Preface to Chaucer* (Princeton, 1962) p.
281, notes with insight that Chaucer's humor, 'which is based on
the confident acceptance of a Providential order underlying the
apparent irrationality of the world and its inhabitants, is sometimes
more profound and more persuasive than any "highly serious" discourse couched in the grand style can possibly be. True humor . . .
requires an intellectual approach which permits a sense of detachment, not the detachment of the egoist or of the self-styled
sophisticate, but the detachment of a man whose faith is un-
shaken by the shortcomings of society and whose love for his fellows
enables him to regard both their pettiness and his own with a certain
equanimity.'

Charles Muscatine

THE CANON'S YEOMAN'S TALE (1957)

The abruptness of the Canon's arrival among the pilgrims, his equally abrupt flight, and the breathless, vehement urgency of his Yeoman's subsequent discourse, have led most critics from the poem to the facts that may have inspired it. Tyrwhitt's conjecture – 'that some sudden resentment had determined Chaucer to interrupt the regular course of his work, in order to insert a Satire against the Alchemists' – has not been generally accepted. But scholarship still tends to class the poem as a 'current event'. If not autobiographical, it is journalistic, and something like biographical interest still lurks in the much debated question of Chaucer's attitude toward alchemy. Was Chaucer a credulous, medieval dupe, or an initiate into alchemical mysteries, or was he modern, a skeptic? Speculation on questions such as this has robbed the poem of the critical interest due it. The story is widely regarded as a good one, a good piece of realism, and not much more.[1] Let it be admitted that there is hardly another poem of Chaucer's that seems so compact of fact, so little ulterior in its design. Its surface argument is determinedly simple; it is a warning against alchemy. Its materials are so solid as to seem to defy further 'interpretation'. If there is a philosophical pattern to the *Canterbury Tales*, this seems to be its one unassimilable lump. I am emboldened to present the following rather hypothetical reading partly by the conviction that journalism is un-Chaucerian, partly by the virtual absence of previous literary criticism, and partly by the enigmatic nature of the poem itself. The reader will have to judge how much to allow in it for the peculiar preoccupations of our own age,[2] and how much for my own conviction that Chaucer's realism is ultimately symbolic.

The poem divides itself into three parts which do not quite coincide with the formal, textual divisions. The first part (the Prologue and *prima pars* of the text, i.e. G. 554–971) describes the arrival of the Canon and Yeoman, the Canon's flight and the Yeoman's revelation of their alchemical activities. Its style is dramatic : all of the *prima pars* is, indeed, dramatic monologue. The second part (*pars secunda* to G. 1387) is the Yeoman's tale proper, of another swindling canon-alchemist. The narrative here, though it contains some rhetorical formalism, is so highly dramatized with interjections and asides that it harmonizes closely with the tone of the first part. In the third part (G. 1388–1481)[3] the stance of the narrator changes. Whereas before he has been represented as unlearned, and his very proverbs are accredited to hearsay,[4] now his voice carries its own authority. He cites Arnaldus de Villanova and the rather mysterious 'Senior' without embarrassment, and ends with a sober, philosophical statement that deepens the context of the entire poem. We must recognize here – what we have seen in the *Roman de la Rose*, in the *Troilus*, and elsewhere – the convention of philosophical amplification. The characterization of the speaker is suspended in favor of comment on the wider meaning of his position :

> Thanne conclude I thus, sith that God of hevene
> Ne wil nat that the philosophres nevene
> How that a man shal come unto this stoon,
> I rede, as for the beste, lete it goon.
> For whoso maketh God his adversarie,
> As for to werken any thyng in contrarie
> Of his wil, certes, never shal he thryve,
> Thogh that he multiplie terme of his lyve.
> And there a poynt; for ended is my tale.   (G. 1472–80)

This philosophical postscript expresses the ruling attitude toward alchemy in the poem. In the light of it, the poem expresses neither credulity nor skepticism, but rather a distinction between false alchemy and true, between men's alchemy and God's. The body of the poem, the first two parts, is an exposure of the alchemy without God, of faith in earth. Its skepticism is that of the believer, not of the scientist, who sees in technology another secular religion, as seductive in its way as the religion of Love :

> This sotted preest, who was gladder than he?
> Was nevere brid gladder agayn the day,

Ne nyghtyngale, in the sesoun of May,
Was nevere noon that luste bet to synge;
Ne lady lustier in carolynge,
Or for to speke of love and wommanhede,
Ne knyght in armes to doon an hardy dede,
To stonden in grace of his lady deere,
Than hadde this preest this soory craft to leere.

(G. 1341–9)

The poem's dualism of attitude is conventional. It corresponds to the division of the science between the charlatans and puffers on the one hand, and the philosophers and mystics on the other.[5] Medieval alchemical texts from about the early thirteenth century discuss pro and con the doubts already raised concerning the possibility of transmutation, and the Christian alchemical tradition is full of both practical 'skepticism' and the thoroughly orthodox but hardly credulous notion that to God all things are possible.[6]

As with other philosophical poems of Chaucer, we are more interested in the poetry than in the conclusion. The poetry everywhere evokes a profound sense of the futility, the cursedness, of a soulless striving with matter. The trickery of alchemical swindlers, illustrated by the 'tale' proper, stands also for the nature of the science itself. The chantry priest is swindled by the alchemist in the second part just as the alchemist is swindled by the science in the first. That the victim is a priest and the alchemists also canons may be owing to current events, for all we know.[7] But the poetic effect is to suggest that their activity is a deep apostasy, a treason, a going over to the devil himself. They are Judases (G. 1003). The falseness of mere deceit is not enough to account for the Yeoman's passionate insistence on 'this chanons cursednesse', and the ubiquity of 'the foule feend' in the Yeoman's discourse.[8] The following rhetorical invocation to an undistinguished victim can be anticipated only by our seeing something infernal in 'this chanoun',

roote of al trecherie,
That everemoore delit hath and gladnesse –
Swiche feendly thoghtes in his herte impresse –

> How Cristes peple he may to meschief brynge.
> God kepe us from his false dissymulynge !
> Noght wiste this preest with whom that he delte,
> Ne of his harm comynge he no thyng felte.
> O sely preest ! o sely innocent !
> With coveitise anon thou shalt be blent !
> O gracelees, ful blynd is thy conceite,
> No thyng ne artow war of the deceite
> Which that this fox yshapen hath to thee !
> His wily wrenches thou ne mayst nat flee.   (G. 1069–81)

Religious overtones are suggested equally by the context. The poem follows the Second Nun's Tale. There is perhaps something more than coincidence in the contrast between St. Cecilia, unharmed in her bath of flames, conquering fire through faith, and the blackened, sweating believers in earth, whose fire blows up in their faces. Cecilia, in her retort to the pagan prefect, curiously anticipates the Yeoman's teaching :

> 'Ther lakketh no thyng to thyne outter eyen
> That thou n'art blynd, for thyng that we seen alle
> That it is stoon, that men may wel espyen,
> That ilke stoon a god thow wolt it calle.
> I rede thee, lat thyn hand upon it falle,
> And taste it wel, and stoon thou shalt it fynde,
> Syn that thou seest nat with thyne eyen blynde.'
>   (Second Nun's Tale, G. 498–504).

> Though ye prolle ay, ye shul it nevere fynde.
> Ye been as boold as is Bayard the blynde,
> That blondreth forth, and peril casteth noon.
> He is as boold to renne agayn a stoon
> As for to goon bisides in the weye.
> So faren ye that multiplie, I seye.
> If that youre eyen kan nat seen aright,
> Looke that youre mynde lakke noght his sight.
> For though ye looken never so brode and stare,
> Ye shul nothyng wynne on that chaffare.
>   (Canon's Yeoman's Tale, G. 1412–21)

The extremely naturalistic characterization of the Yeoman serves the conception of alchemy as a blind materialism. He is a simple, unlearned soul. His greatest gift is a dogged sense of the world of matter. There is not the faintest glimmer of spirituality or mysticism about him. Screened through this personality, everything is lost but the world of rocks and stones. Thus his idiom is ruggedly dramatic. His narrative can be trusted to describe the slightest motions in the physical world:

> But taketh heede now, sires, for Goddes love!
> He took his cole of which I spak above,
> And in his hand he baar it pryvely.
> And whiles the preest couched bisily
> The coles, as I tolde yow er this,
> This chanoun seyde, 'Freend, ye doon amys.
> This is nat couched as it oghte be;
> But soone I shal amenden it,' quod he.
> 'Now lat me medle therwith but a while,
> For of yow have I pitee, by Seint Gile!
> Ye been right hoot; I se wel how ye swete.
> Have heere a clooth, and wipe awey the wete.'
> And whiles that the preest wiped his face,
> This chanoun took his cole – with harde grace!–
> And leyde it above upon the myddeward
> Of the crosselet, and blew wel afterward,
> Til that the coles gonne faste brenne.
> 'Now yeve us drynke,' quod the chanoun thenne;
> 'As swithe al shal be wel, I undertake.
> Sitte we doun, and lat us myrie make.'
> And whan that this chanounes bechen cole
> Was brent, al the lemaille out of the hole
> Into the crosselet fil anon adoun;
> And so it moste nedes, by resoun,
> Syn it so evene aboven it couched was.
> But therof wiste the preest nothyng, alas!
> He demed alle the coles yliche good;
> For of that sleighte he nothyng understood.

(G. 1176–1203)

His commentary, on the other hand, is dully repetitive; it is analysis frustrated and strangled by a limited vision. Blear-eyed, he has come to see only, as his modern counterpart might put it, that alchemy 'don't work':

> 'We blondren evere and pouren in the fir,
>   And for al that we faille of oure desir,
> For evere we lakken oure conclusioun.'   (G. 670–2)

> For alle oure sleightes we kan nat conclude. (G. 773)

> Noght helpeth us, oure labour is in veyn.   (G. 777)

> For lost is al oure labour and travaille.   (G. 781)

> Al is in veyn, and parde! muchel moore.   (G. 843)

> This is to seyn, they faillen bothe two.   (G. 851)

> The pot tobreketh, and farewel, al is go!   (G. 907)

>   be it hoot or coold, I dar seye this,
> That we concluden everemoore amys.   (G. 956–7)

Beneath the Yeoman's unconscious simplicity, this insistent chorus voices a frustration beyond that of mere mechanical failure. It registers a failure of vision. It says that dealing with matter as matter has no end, that is, no teleology. Medieval philosophical alchemy was nourished on hylozoism, on the feeling that matter was instinct with life. The Yeoman's recitation, however, evokes an opposite feeling, of matter spiritless and contingent, of that primordial impurity, 'corrupt', floterynge', from which only God can raise man.[9] To expect an end, a 'conclusioun', to the cooking of this hopeless stuff is the real irony of the alchemist's failure.

The technical imagery of the poem is very powerful in evoking the feeling of matter as matter. The Yeoman's recitation is dramatically motivated; now that the Canon is gone he will tell all that he can. The ensuing list of materials and equipment answers to a tradition of inventory in the alchemical writings themselves, but, given certain changes of tone, it answers also to the literary convention of the *parade*, the list of wares or drugs vaunted in the *Herberie* and in the *mercator* scenes of the passion plays.[10] Chaucer read alchemy for the matter. The manner belongs more to the tradition of Rutebeuf. Nowhere else in Chaucer is there such a solid, unspiritual mass of 'realism', and nowhere is its artistic function less to be doubted :

> Ther is also ful many another thyng
> That is unto oure craft apertenyng.
> Though I by ordre hem nat reherce kan,
> By cause that I am a lewed man,
> Yet wol I telle hem as they come to mynde,
> Thogh I ne kan nat sette hem in hir kynde :
> As boole armonyak, verdegrees, boras,
> And sondry vessels maad of erthe and glas,
> Oure urynales and oure descensories,
> Violes, crosletz, and sublymatories,
> Cucurbites and alambikes eek,
> And othere swiche, deere ynough a leek.
> Nat nedeth it for to reherce hem alle, –
> Watres rubifiyng, and boles galle,
> Arsenyk, sal armonyak, and brymstoon ;
> And herbes koude I telle eek many oon,
> As egremoyne, valerian, and lunarie,
> And othere swiche, if that me liste tarie ;
> Oure lampes brennyng bothe nyght and day,
> To brynge aboute oure purpos, if we may ;
> Oure fourneys eek of calcinacioun,
> And of watres albificacioun ;
> Unslekked lym, chalk, and gleyre of an ey,
> Poudres diverse, asshes, donge, pisse, and cley,
> Cered pokkets, sal peter, vitriole,
> And diverse fires maad of wode and cole ;
> Sal tartre, alkaly, and sal preparat,
> And combust materes and coagulat ;
> Cley maad with hors or mannes heer, and oille
> Of tartre, alum glas, berme, wort, and argoille,
> Resalgar, and othre materes enbibyng,

> And eek of oure materes encorporyng,
> And of oure silver citrinacioun,
> Oure cementyng and fermentacioun,
> Oure yngottes, testes, and many mo.   (G. 784–818)

The Wife of Bath's Prologue, as we have seen, has a notable collection of concrete, material images. But compared to this, it is spiritual and airy. If art and not journalism is at work in the Canon's Yeoman's Tale, this chaos of matter, refuse, excrement, represents the universe of technology.

In the context of this kind of interpretation, the headlong entry of the Canon and Yeoman cannot be read as Chaucer's afterthought. It seems thoroughly, artistically, premeditated. These men are not introduced with the other pilgrims, because they are not within Christian society. They do not go on pilgrimages; they are not headed for Canterbury, or rather, for the City of God that it represents. Their entry is dramatically motivated, to be sure. They see the pilgrims leave town and must therefore gallop to catch up. But Chaucer's emphasis on the haste and the hot sweat, like the Yeoman's stridency of tone, seems to call for a more-than-dramatic explanation. It is very well for the sympathetic Chaucerian Narrator to find an earthy zest in it all: 'But it was joye for to seen hym swete!' (G. 579). We must ask, nevertheless, whether the hot gallop and the high temperature are not at the same time precisely characteristic of the Canon's way of life, the way of technology. The Canon doubtless intends to swindle the pilgrims, but this is only one stage in the greater pursuit:

> 'To muchel folk we doon illusioun,
> And borwe gold, be it a pound or two,
> Or ten, or twelve, or manye sommes mo,
> And make hem wenen, at the leeste weye,
> That of a pound we koude make tweye.
> Yet is it fals, but ay we han good hope
> It for to doon, and after it we grope.
> *But that science is so fer us biforn,*
> *We mowen nat, although we hadden it sworn,*
> *It overtake, it slit awey so faste.'*   (G. 673–82)

The Canon is described as carrying peculiarly little baggage. Dramatically, this is explainable by the traditional poverty of alchemists. Poetically, it says what the Yeoman in a brief moment of reflection says later on :

> I warne you wel, it is to seken evere.
> That futur temps hath maad men to dissevere,
> In trust thereof, from al that evere they hadde.
>
> (G. 874–6)

The pathetic gravity of these lines suggests that the 'al that evere they hadde' is more than money and clothing and a fresh complexion. It is also, perhaps, the spiritual tradition that a community of men takes with it along the way, and that gives purpose and direction to the journey. Marie Hamilton remarks that the Canon was apostate, or else 'guilty of that *instabilitas loci* forbidden to monastics'.[11] Surely his flight, while it is dramatically motivated by 'verray sorwe and shame' (G. 702), poetically symbolizes an apostasy from the human congregation, an instability of place in life. Like the canon of the Yeoman's story, he abides nowhere.

Chaucer could make fun of the complacent ignorance that despises knowledge. The carpenter of the Miller's Tale is a victim of this vice :

> 'I thoghte ay wel how that it sholde be !
> Men sholde nat knowe of Goddes pryvetee.
> Ye, blessed be alwey a lewed man
> That noght but oonly his bileve kan !'   (A. 3453–6)

The Canon's Yeoman's Tale deals with an ignorance that is less funny : that complacent faith in science that despises God. Dante's Hell has its place for those who 'wished to see too far ahead'.[12] Chaucer is no less conservative. In attitude the poem is as medieval as the Knight's Tale. The dogged refusal to admit the intractability of matter, one of the virtues to which we owe so much of our civilization, is here represented by a group of sooty figures sifting and picking for salvage in a pile of refuse. He who cheers them on is a fool. In the light of later history, indeed, the poem is reactionary. This kind of alchemy gave us chemistry. Yet there is still time to judge whether the poem has not a germ of wry prophecy in it, whether already in the fourteenth century an acute consciousness could not have caught the future of technology in a single line :

The pot tobreketh, and farewel, al is go !

SOURCE: *Chaucer and the French Tradition* (California, 1957).

NOTES

1. R. D. French, *A Chaucer Handbook*, 2nd edn (New York, 1947) pp. 327–32, gives a brief résumé of the scholarship, including the quotation from Tyrwhitt. See also Thomas R. Lounsbury, *Studies in Chaucer*, 3 vols. (New York, 1892), II, pp. 389–90, 500–2 (on Chaucer's skepticism); G. L. Kittredge, *Chaucer and His Poetry* (Cambridge, Mass., 1915) p. 17 ('contemporary anecdote'); S. Foster Damon, 'Chaucer and Alchemy', *PLMA*, XXXIX (1924) 782–8 (Chaucer 'a serious student of alchemy'); Paull F. Baum, 'The Canon's Yeoman's Tale', *Modern Language Notes*, XL (1925) 152–4. W. C. Curry, *Chaucer and the Medieval Sciences* (New York, 1926) pp. xix–xxi, issues a useful *caveat* against reading Chaucer's scientific attitudes in his artistic works. Chaucer's interest, he says, 'was evidently centered in the personality of the Canon's Yeoman . . .'.

2. Thus I follow J. Speirs, *Chaucer the Maker* (London, 1951) p. 197 : '. . . the misguided effort . . . exposes itself as a scientific specialist drive, uncontrolled by humane intelligence as to ends, such as we have grown familiar with as a phenomenon of our own day'; and R. Preston, *Chaucer* (London, 1952) p. 282 : 'The evils of competition and applied science, after six centuries, are more completely out of control . . . and of this progress Chaucer observed the beginnings.'

3. This division is recognized by Damon, p. 783, and Baum, pp. 152–3.

4. Canon's Yeoman's Tale, G. 748, 786–9, 819.

5. See J. Read, *The Alchemist in Life, Literature, and Art* (London, 1947) pp. 23–4.

6. See M. Berthelot, *La Chimie au moyen âge*, I (Paris, 1893) pp. 238–9, 281, 344–5; Arthur John Hopkins, *Alchemy, Child of Greek Philosophy* (New York, 1934) pp 213–15; and the illustrative materials printed by John Webster Spargo in W. F. Bryan and Germaine Dempster, *Sources and Analogues to Chaucer's Canterbury Tales* (Chicago, 1941) pp. 691–8.

7. See J. M. Manly, *Some New Light on Chaucer* (New York, 1926) p. 246.

8. Canon's Yeoman's Tale, G. 705, 861, 916–19, 984, 1158–9, 1302–3.

9. See, for example, the Parson's Tale, I. 333; *Boece* III, met. 9.

10. On the alchemical inventory see Berthelot, pp. 14–15; note that the alchemical texts and criticisms printed by Spargo in *Sources and Analogues* occasionally fall into rhetorical cataloguing of 'dirty things'. On the *parade* see P. Abrahams, 'The Mercator-Scenes in Mediaeval French Passion-Plays', *Medium Ævum*, III (1934) 112–23. To this tradition also belongs the Pardoner's preliminary sales talk (C. 347–88).

11. 'The Clerical Status of Chaucer's Alchemist', *Speculum*, XVI (1941) 107.

12. *Inferno*, XX, 38.

SELECT BIBLIOGRAPHY

Note. This bibliography contains no more than a brief personal selection of books and articles. Essays reprinted in this book, and books mentioned in the Introduction, are not listed here.

BIBLIOGRAPHY

D. D. Griffith, *Bibliography of Chaucer 1908–53* (Seattle, 1955), continued by W. R. Crawford, *Bibliography of Chaucer 1954–63* (Seattle, 1967). Comprehensive.

EDITIONS

F. N. Robinson, *The Works of Geoffrey Chaucer*, 2nd edn (Boston and London, 1957). Standard edition.

A. C. Cawley, *Geoffrey Chaucer: Canterbury Tales* (London, 1958). Robinson's text, with marginal and footnote translations.

BOOKS ON CHAUCER AND THE 'CANTERBURY TALES'

Muriel Bowden, *A Commentary on the General Prologue to the Canterbury Tales* (New York, 1948). Very full commentary, giving a wealth of background information.

T. W. Craik, *The Comic Tales of Chaucer* (London, 1964). Detailed analyses.

B. F. Huppé, *A Reading of the Canterbury Tales* (New York, 1964). Wide-ranging consideration of selected tales, emphasising religious aspects.

S. S. Hussey, *Chaucer: An Introduction* (London, 1971). Lively general introduction.

Beryl Rowland (ed.), *Companion to Chaucer Studies* (Toronto, 1968). Summary essays by experts on various topics, with useful bibliographies.

Trevor Whittock, *A Reading of the Canterbury Tales* (Cambridge, 1968). Stimulating examination of thematic patterning.

ARTICLES ON CHAUCER AND THE 'CANTERBURY TALES'

J. V. Cunningham, 'The Literary Form of the Prologue to the *Canterbury Tales*', *Modern Philology*, XLIX (1952). Finds the genesis of the form of the Prologue in the dream-vision tradition.

Dorothy Everett, 'Some Reflections on Chaucer's "Art Poetical"', *Proceedings of the British Academy*, XXXVI (1950); reprinted in her *Essays on Middle English Literature* (London, 1955). Classic Study of Chaucer's rhetoric.

R. A. Lanham, 'Game, Play, and High Seriousness in Chaucer's Poetry', *English Studies*, XLVIII (1967). Interesting consideration of Chaucer's poems and themes (especially love, war, rhetoric) as 'games'.

R. T. Lenaghan, 'The Nun's Priest's Fable', *PMLA*, LXXVIII (1963). Illuminates Chaucer's poem by examining medieval concepts of fable.

R. A. Pratt, 'The Development of the Wife of Bath', in *Studies in Medieval Literature in Honor of Professor Albert Croll Baugh*, ed. MacEdward Leach (Philadelphia, 1961). Examines the way in which Chaucer puts together and develops the character.

Janette Richardson, 'Hunter and Prey: Functional Imagery in the Friar's Tale', *English Miscellany*, XII (1961). Skilful examination of the way in which Chaucer 'manipulates a cluster of images'.

G. H. Russell, 'Chaucer: The Prioress's Tale', in *Medieval Literature and Civilisation: Studies in Memory of G. N. Garmonsway*, eds. D. A. Pearsall and R. A. Waldron (London, 1969). Argues well for the artistic success of the tale.

NOTES ON CONTRIBUTORS

Ian Bishop. Lecturer in English, University of Bristol. He is author of *Pearl in its Setting* (Oxford, 1968).

Robert B. Burlin. Professor of English, Bryn Mawr College. He is author of *The Old English Advent: A Typological Commentary* (Yale, 1968).

John Burrow. Fellow and Tutor in English, Jesus College, Oxford, and University Lecturer in English. He is author of *A Reading of Sir Gawain and the Green Knight* (London, 1965), *Geoffrey Chaucer: A Critical Anthology* (London, 1969), and *Ricardian Poetry* (London, 1971).

E. T. Donaldson. Professor in the Department of English and Comparative Literature, Columbia University. He is author of *Piers Plowman: The C-Text and Its Poet* (Yale, 1949), and *Speaking of Chaucer* (London, 1970). He has edited *Chaucer's Poetry* (New York, 1958).

William Frost. Professor of English, University of California. He is author of *Dryden and the Art of Translation* (Yale, 1955), and is an associate editor of the Twickenham edition of Pope's Homer (Yale, 1967).

Arthur W. Hoffman. Professor of English, Syracuse University. He is author of *John Dryden's Imagery* (Florida, 1962).

G. L. Kittredge. Formerly Professor of English, Harvard University, 1894–1936. He is author of *The Language of Chaucer's Troilus* (London, 1894), *Chaucer and His Poetry* (Cambridge, Mass., 1915), and *A Study of Gawain and the Green Knight* (Cambridge, Mass., 1916).

Charles Muscatine. Professor of English, University of California. He is author of *Chaucer and the French Tradition* (California, 1957), and *Poetry and Crisis in the Age of Chaucer* (Notre Dame, 1972).

PAUL G. RUGGIERS. Professor of English, University of Oklahoma. He is author of *Florence in the Time of Dante* (Oklahoma, 1964), and *The Art of the Canterbury Tales* (Madison, 1965).

TONY SLADE. Senior Lecturer in English, University of Adelaide. He is author of *D. H. Lawrence* (London, 1969).

INDEX